Praise
Caring Schoo

MW01155319

"Caring is fundamental for learning. Ask any child. This book explores caring as a 'quality of relationship' that points educators in the direction of professional involvement to enhance the school and learning experience. Through an exploration of caring as a leadership responsibility the authors not only make the case that caring is crucial to learning, but that every adult in a school makes a difference in the life of every child entrusted to that school."

James Berry
Executive Director, International Council of Professors of Educational Leadership (ICPEL)
Professor, Educational Leadership
Eastern Michigan University

"Smylie, Murphy, and Louis employ research-based examples to lucidly explain and translate what they mean by 'caring school leadership' and they encourage exploring reflection and redefining school structures to facilitate integrating caring into current practice. They call on leaders to embrace caring by providing a range of approaches that include relying on norms and values of communities served, storytelling, positive modeling, and culturally responsive approaches to do their work."

Mark Anthony Gooden
Christian A. John Endeavor Professor in Education Leadership
Teachers College, Columbia University

"*Caring School Leadership* is what has been missing from both leadership theory and practical leadership studies. Without addressing the questions posed in this book, leaders are left unable to answer a central question: 'Why are you an educational leader?' Beyond the rich and timely theoretical contributions, this work guides practicing school leaders in their journey of becoming caring and nurturing toward the communities they serve."

Muhammad Khalifa
Beck Chair of Ideas in Education, University of Minnesota
President, Culturally Responsive School Leadership Institute

"There are times when wisdom cannot be found in the academy but rest assured that you will find wisdom in this book, which presents a compelling model for caring school leadership. Smylie, Murphy, and Louis offer the most incisive, analytical, and yet practical approach to developing school leaders who are caring leaders. This is an excellent resource for faculty teaching aspiring and current school leaders—a must-read!"

Pedro Reyes
Ashbel Smith Professor of Education Leadership and Policy
University of Texas-Austin
Former President of the University of Texas-San Antonio

"There are many international contexts today where the 'push-me-pull-me' approach to schooling outweighs the wisdom of compassion. This timely book offers a much-welcomed counter-narrative to that trend. The book is bursting with ideas—not surprising given the track record of the authors. I would encourage school principals to gobble up the book's many insights into the practice of caring leadership. Caring leadership—as the authors argue so powerfully—is a dynamic ministry. It is also the kind of moral endeavor so needed in our troubled times."

Kathryn Riley
Professor of Urban Education
University College of London

"For anyone interested in the difficult and vital work of creating caring school communities, this is a deeply thoughtful, humane and highly practical book. Drawing on a large body of research and the stories and wisdom of practitioners, *Caring School Leadership* compellingly articulates what caring is, how it functions and why it is at the core of human flourishing in so many aspects of our academic, social, emotional and ethical lives. There are no checklists or 'one size fits all' approaches here. This book provides a vision of caring school leadership that is contextual, fluid, and contingent upon the most basic aspects of human interaction and relationships. It is a vital resource for school administrators interested in both interpersonal and systematic ways of create caring and inclusive communities. It makes me hopeful that many more young people can develop the motivation and skills needed to recognize our shared humanity, support and help others in ways that are true and meaningful, and develop the sustained, caring relationships at the heart of a wonderful life."

Richard Weissbourd
Senior Lecturer, Harvard Graduate School of Education and Kennedy School of Government
Faculty Director, Making Caring Common Project

"Finally, a book that gets at the heart and soul of school leadership. Smylie, Murphy, and Louis describe what caring leadership looks and feels like, and how leaders create trust, build relationships, and develop a culture of caring so that students can focus on academics. Our schools need leaders who lead from the heart."

Jacquelyn Wilson
Executive Director, National Policy Board for Educational Leadership (NPBEA)
Director, Delaware Academy of School Leadership
University of Delaware

"*Caring School Leadership* goes straight to the heart of what it takes to be a great and good leader in today's schools: caring. Smylie, Murphy, and Louis provide a compelling vision for care-centered schools and support this vision with instructive examples and practical guidance. Although meant for the education community, the book provides valuable lessons for anyone in a leadership position in today's complex and demanding world."

Michelle D. Young
Professor and Chair, Leadership, Foundations and Policy
Curry School of Education
University of Virginia

Caring School Leadership

*To
Rachel,
LC,
and
Dan*

Caring School Leadership

Mark A. Smylie,
Joseph F. Murphy, and
Karen Seashore Louis

FOR INFORMATION:

Corwin

A SAGE Companyy

2455 Teller Road

Thousand Oaks, California 91320

(800) 233-9936

www.corwin.com

SAGE Publications Ltd.

1 Oliver's Yard

55 City Road

London EC1Y 1SP

United Kingdom

SAGE Publications India Pvt. Ltd.

B 1/I 1 Mohan Cooperative Industrial Area

Mathura Road, New Delhi 110 044

India

SAGE Publications Asia-Pacific Pte. Ltd.

18 Cross Street #10-10/11/12

China Square Central

Singapore 048423

Publisher: Arnis Burvikovs

Development Editor: Desirée A. Bartlett

Senior Editorial Assistant: Eliza Erickson

Production Editor: Tori Mirsadjadi

Copy Editor: Jared Leighton

Typesetter: Hurix Digital

Proofreader: Victoria Reed-Castro

Indexer: Maria Sosnowski

Cover Designer: Janet Kiesel

Marketing Manager: Sharon Pendergast

Printed in the United States of America.

Library of Congress Cataloging-in-Publication Data

Names: Smylie, Mark A., author. | Murphy, Joseph, 1949- author. | Louis, Karen Seashore, author.

Title: Caring school leadership / Mark A. Smylie, Joseph F. Murphy, and Karen Seashore Louis.

Description: Thousand Oaks, California : Corwin, [2020] | Includes bibliographical references.

Identifiers: LCCN 2019045614 | ISBN 9781544320113 (paperback) | ISBN 9781544320120 (epub) | ISBN 9781544320137 (epub) | ISBN 9781544320144 (ebook)

Subjects: LCSH: Educational leadership—Psychological aspects. | Caring. | Moral education.

Classification: LCC LB2806 .S5853 2020 | DDC 371.2—dc23

LC record available at https://lccn.loc.gov/2019045614

This book is printed on acid-free paper.

SUSTAINABLE FORESTRY INITIATIVE | Certified Sourcing
www.sfiprogram.org
SFI-00756

20 21 22 23 24 10 9 8 7 6 5 4 3 2 1

Contents

Preface

This is a book about caring in school leadership. In the many years that the three of us have worked in the areas of leadership and school improvement, in academic and professional settings, we have come to believe that caring is essential to effective schooling. And we have come to believe that caring lies at the heart of good school leadership.

In recent years, we have witnessed a growing emphasis on academic expectations, curricular and instructional specification, and accountability as primary levers for improving schools and raising student achievement. This emphasis has narrowed the primary focus of education to academic achievement, test scores, and "college and career" readiness. It has displaced attention to students' social, emotional, and psychological development; their preparation to live in and foster democratic society; and their overall well-being. This emphasis on the academic side of schooling has not come with commensurate attention to sources of caring and support that would help students succeed. Moreover, as research has begun to show, nearly exclusive emphasis on press and accountability makes it more difficult for educators to develop caring, supportive relationships that promote students' success in school. Indeed, the challenges to developing strong and caring relationships in schools appear part of the general erosion of social bonds in schools, in the workplace, and in communities at large.

We know that both academic press and support are necessary for student success in school. We know that both are necessary for students' overall learning, development, and well-being. The educators with whom we speak know this, and many are working hard to provide students with the support they need to grow and succeed. We are beginning to see some reconsideration of accountability as a primary lever of school improvement. We see more attention to students' social and emotional development and to creating schools that are more caring and supportive of students. More generally, we see renewed recognition of the human side of schooling and school leadership.

Purpose and Audiences

The purpose of this book is to examine the principles and practices of what we call *caring school leadership*. We recognize the importance of caring in leadership, and we wish to encourage more of it. We argue that caring is not some abstract notion, nor is it necessarily an additional domain of leadership work. It is the matter, the manner, and the motivation of all aspects of school leadership, manifest in many ways.

We wrote this book for several audiences but primarily for aspiring and practicing school leaders. While we refer mostly to principals and their practice, we see this book as useful to assistant principals, deans, department chairs, and others, including teachers, who perform leadership work in schools. It is for individual school leaders, for programs that prepare school leaders and promote their ongoing professional development, and for professional associations that guide and nurture school leaders and their practice. It is also for teachers and parents who may be interested in caring in schools and how all members of a school community can work together to promote the caring and support of students.

We take as a given that principals, assistant principals, and other school leaders care deeply about students, their learning and development, their well-being, and their success in and beyond school. We say the same for teachers, parents, and caregivers—those nonparent adults who raise children (e.g., relatives, older siblings, etc.). And we take as a given that in their day-to-day work, school leaders want to be caring of students they serve. School leaders are drawn to the profession because they care about children and feel a calling to support them. Yet we know that caring about students and being caring of them are not necessarily synonymous. We know that for myriad reasons school leaders' actions and interactions do not always reflect attitude and desire.

We hope that this book will inform and guide acts of caring school leadership. We wish for it to reveal possibilities, inspire, and motivate and for it to shape expectations that school leaders hold for themselves and that others hold for them. By focusing on practice, we hope that this book might help bring these expectations to life.

Organization of the Book

This book is organized in six chapters. Chapter 1 explores the concept of caring as the heart of caring school leadership. Chapter 2 applies the concept of caring to school leadership, presenting a model that lays out three arenas of caring leadership practice. The next three chapters explore these arenas. Chapter 3 examines how principals can be caring in their relationships with students. Chapter 4 discusses how principals can work with teachers and students to cultivate their schools as caring communities. Chapter 5 considers what principals can do to foster caring for students beyond the school in families and in the broader community. Chapter 6 explores different ways that caring school leadership can be developed. It presents activities and experiences of leadership development and the characteristics and qualities that make them effective. This chapter and the book conclude with a look at self-care as a means of caring school leadership development.

"You Are Here"

We are not the first to write about caring in school leadership, although this book is among the first to focus particularly on its practice. We follow several others who have explored the meaning and importance of caring in schools and in school leadership, notably Lynn Beck, Catherine Marshall, Nel Noddings, Leonard Pellicer, Kathleen Sernak, and Thomas Sergiovanni. Much of this earlier work stresses the role of human relationships in leadership and the importance of a supportive school community for student success.

References to caring and to related constructs can be found in recent work on school cultures that promote student learning and academic success (Bryk, Sebring, Allensworth, Luppescu, & Easton, 2010; Kruse & Louis, 2009; Murphy & Torre, 2014). This work points to the importance of environments that are student centered and characterized by personalized relationships with teachers, physical and psychological safety, and support for academic learning. Such environments are populated with programs and practices that provide academic and social support relevant to students' learning and developmental needs. They are anchored in norms of trust, valuing and respect, accessibility, fairness, and, importantly, care.

We also locate caring leadership within the broader construct of *positive school leadership* (Murphy & Louis, 2018). Derived from positive psychology and positive organizational scholarship, positive school leadership rejects deficit models of human behavior and the tendency to focus on ways to correct problems and punish misbehavior rather than to promote growth. Instead, it proceeds from optimistic and asset-based views of human nature and potential. It emphasizes capacity and agency in persons and communities and the building up of persons and communities through empowerment and learning. Positive school leadership stresses the moral and ethical dimensions of leadership. It emphasizes equity, fairness, and justice. It underscores character and virtues in leadership. Positive school leadership requires leaders at all levels of the educational system to act in the best interests of others. It brings to the fore personalism, trust, and respect. Many of these qualities are present in caring school leadership.

Finally, this book can be situated within the professional practices embodied in the Professional Standards for Educational Leadership (PSEL) (National Policy Board for Educational Administration, 2015). PSEL sets as the priority of school leadership the academic success and the broader learning, development, and well-being of students. Leadership is directed not simply toward the success and well-being of students generally but specifically toward the success and well-being of *each* student. Reflecting core ideas of positive school leadership, PSEL incorporates a humanistic and relational perspective of leadership. PSEL recognizes that student success in school depends on both robust academics and strong systems of social support working in tandem. Caring is relevant to each of PSEL's ten standards. Accordingly, we hope that this book can serve as a resource to bring PSEL to life.

Our Sources

We derived the ideas in this book from a number of sources. Through teaching aspiring and practicing school leaders, working with practicing school leaders in schools and at workshops and conferences, consulting with school leaders' professional associations, and hearing students, we gained insights into the importance of caring in school leadership and into issues concerning caring in school leadership practice. We sought input and feedback from individual school leaders and teachers about the general idea for this book and about specific substantive aspects as we were developing it.

We reviewed scholarly and professional literatures on caring in education and educational leadership, and we searched for additional perspectives in literatures of related academic fields and disciplines, including philosophy, ethics, sociology, political science, and the organizational sciences. We also looked for insights and lessons in the scholarly and practice literatures of other human service professions that recognize the importance of individual caring, the cultivation of caring environments, and even caring in the public. These professions include health care and social-services administration, nursing and medicine, and the ministry. Several of these human service professions provided useful insights for our thinking about how to develop caring in school leadership.

Much of our work with these literatures can be found in our earlier academic writing (Louis, Murphy, & Smylie, 2016; Murphy, 2016a; Murphy & Louis, 2018; Smylie, Murphy, & Louis, 2016). These books and articles lay the conceptual, theoretical, and empirical foundation for this book on practice.

Selection of Practices

Throughout this book, we discuss specific practices as examples of caring school leadership. We selected practices for their fit within our model of caring school leadership. Each has a foundation in theory and research and can be found in publications of a professional association, a research and development group, or a professional and academic publishing house. While we are not able to present empirical validation of all these practices, we believe that their grounding in theory and research, their logic, and their consistency with our ideas about caring and caring school leadership make them worthy of consideration. Moreover, we do not present these practices as "must do" recommendations. We present them to illustrate general principles of caring leadership practice.

How to Use This Book

This book is unlike many other books about school leadership practice. Readers will not find in this book "to-do" lists or scripts. Readers will not find compilations of strategies that are universally effective. This book is an exposition of ideas, principles, and values, illustrated with examples of how to make school leadership practice more caring. We present caring school leadership as situational, dynamic, relational, and personal. There is no "one size fits all" for caring leadership. We eschew the notion of recipes, of telling readers specifically what to do. Instead, we present a framework, principles, and possibilities to inform and inspire.

We encourage you to take the principles and possibilities contained in this book and consider them in relation to your current practice and the practice to which you aspire. Use these principles and possibilities to challenge yourself. Try to reflect upon different practices presented herein, but keep in mind the big ideas that underlie them. Choose among and adapt them to your particular situation. Create and experiment with practices that are consistent with principles of caring school leadership and are appropriate for you and for others in your school and community.

Acknowledgments

This book is inspired by scores of practicing educators with whom we have worked in schools and in our classrooms. It is also inspired by the K–12 students who we see prosper in schools when they are both challenged and cared for.

When planning and writing this book, we spoke with many practicing and retired preK–12 principals and teachers to gather their ideas and to test our thinking. We also spoke with a number of scholars in the field of educational leadership and other human service professions. For the support and guidance they provided, we thank the following individuals: Jane Banaszak-Hall, James Bell, Ryan Cantrell, Anna Case-Winters, Rainey Dankel, Vince Durnan, Jon Eckert, Andrea Evans, Dwayne Evans, Stan Faust, Leah Fowler, Richard Frank, Kevin Gallick, Jaco Hamman, Mike Heidkamp, Chala Holland, Jan Holton, Beverly Hutton, Pete Kahn, Deborah Kapp, Avi Lessing, Frank Maggio, Marylen Marty-Gentile, Richard Mertz, Randy Moes, Pete Monaghan, Jennifer Olson, Karin Pietrini, Harriet Potoka, Renee Racette, Carol Schnabl Schweitzer, Don Sibly, Paula Stephens, Becki Streit, Chezare Warren, Joan White, Ingrid Wilson, Tracy Wilson, Amy Woodson, and Carol Young.

We are especially grateful to Lora Dever, Lauren Gage, William Hayes, and John Marshall for sharing their stories of caring school leadership with us and giving us permission to use them here. We thank Arnis Burvikovs, Desirée Bartlett, Eliza Erickson, Janet Kiesel, Jared Leighton, and the rest of the team at Corwin for their support and guidance from the beginning to the end of this project. And finally, we are grateful to our families for their love, their support, and their caring.

Publisher's Acknowledgments

Corwin gratefully acknowledges the contributions of the following individuals:

Shelly Allen
Field Supervisor, Clinical Instructor
Lamar University
Beaumont, TX

Elizabeth Alvarez
Chief of Schools
Chicago, IL

David Cash
Professor, Retired District Superintendent
Los Angeles, CA

Donna Fong
Clinical Instructor, Dept. of Educational Leadership
Lamar University
Beaumont, TX

Neil MacNeil
Principal
Ellenbrook, Australia

Jay Rose
Retired High School Principal
Westerville, OH

Kristine Servais
Retired Professor of Educational Leadership
Naperville, IL

Christian L. Zimmerman
Teacher and Assistant Dean, ELA
Fort Myers, FL

About the Authors

Mark A. Smylie is professor of education emeritus in the Department of Educational Policy Studies at the University of Illinois at Chicago and visiting professor in the Department of Leadership, Policy, and Organizations at Peabody College, Vanderbilt University. Before his work in higher education, Smylie was a high school social studies teacher. Smylie served as secretary-treasurer of the National Society for the Study of Education and as a director of the Consortium on Chicago School Research at the University of Chicago. Smylie has worked with schools, school districts, and school administrator and teacher professional associations through joint projects, collaborative advising, and professional-development activity. He has served on advisory boards of numerous regional and national professional and policy organizations concerned with education generally and leadership in particular. Smylie's research focuses on school organization, leadership, and change.

Joseph F. Murphy is the Frank W. Mayborn Chair in the Department of Leadership, Policy, and Organizations and associate dean at Peabody College of Education at Vanderbilt University. He has also been a faculty member at the University of Illinois at Urbana-Champaign and The Ohio State University, where he was William Ray Flesher Professor of Education. In the public schools, Murphy has served as an administrator at the school, district, and state levels, including an appointment as the executive assistant to the chief deputy superintendent of public instruction in California. He was the founding president of the Ohio Principals Leadership Academy. Murphy's work is in the area of school improvement, with special emphasis on leadership and policy.

 Karen Seashore Louis is Regents Professor and Robert H. Beck Chair of the Department of Organizational Leadership, Policy, and Development at the University of Minnesota. Her previous positions include Tufts University; Abt Associates, Inc.; Harvard University; and the University of Massachusetts–Boston. She has served in numerous administrative positions at the University of Minnesota, including director of the Center for Applied Research and Educational Improvement Department, chair of Educational Policy and Administration, and associate dean of the College of Education and Human Development. Louis's research investigates school improvement and effectiveness, leadership in school settings, and knowledge use in education. She enjoys collaborating with school administrators as they consider how their problems of practice become important questions that can be addressed with data.

Introduction: Four Stories of Caring School Leadership

We introduce the idea of caring school leadership with four stories written by practicing educators. These stories tell of real principals, teachers, students, and parents in actual school settings, and they are presented in the storyteller's voice. They capture vividly and concretely many key elements and practices of caring school leadership that we explore in the pages to come. These stories illustrate how principals can be caring in their interpersonal relationships with students, how they can cultivate their schools as caring communities, and how they can be caring in their work with teachers and parents. They point to the purposes of caring, key virtues and mindsets of caring, and important competencies that bring caring virtues and mindsets to life in school leaders' work.

These four stories come from an archive of true stories of caring in school leadership that we elicited from practicing and retired principals, assistant principals, teachers, and others with whom school leaders work. From this archive, we have assembled about 100 stories into a companion volume to this book, titled *Stories of Caring School Leadership*, also published by Corwin. We compiled this companion volume of stories to further illustrate, instruct, and inspire the practice of caring school leadership explored in this book. Like this book, the book of stories is designed for practicing and aspiring school leaders to read and reflect upon individually and in groups, for programs of school leader preparation and professional development, and for use with teachers and others to promote leadership development and improvement in schools. It contains tips for using the stories in each of these contexts.

Now, four stories will introduce the present book.

Ana

Ana had a *terrible* fear of separation from her parents that began when she was about one and a half. By preschool, she had made some progress, but leaving her mom, in particular, remained just as challenging as it was when she was a toddler. Ana would become extremely upset as they drove to school and would cry, scream, refuse to leave the car, throw herself down on the floor in the entry hall, and grab at her mom's legs and ankles to stop her from leaving. Ana *loved* school, but the moment of saying goodbye absolutely terrified her. It was not a rational fear, but young children often have irrational fears.

And those fears are just as big and real as any other. Ana is extremely bright and highly verbal and in need of some help.

I saw what was happening and how stressful it was on Ana's mom, her teachers, and Ana herself! We had tried some on-the-spot interventions but knew it was time for a plan. At some schools, staff might leave parents to figure out issues like this on their own, but we valued family and community. Ana's fears and her mom's struggles were ours, too. We had to support them.

We created a safe, soothing entry routine and designated some grown-ups on standby to help as necessary. We knew we had to have some flexibility and a few layers. Some days, a ride up in the elevator with my administrative assistant was enough to facilitate the transition. Other days, time in the soft spot—a rocking chair in a semiprivate corner, with stuffed animals and small and engaging toys—would do the trick. On more difficult days, we had a nook set up in a nearby storage closet. It might sound odd at first, but we decked out this little space like a bedroom for Ana and filled it with things that she loved: a giant teddy bear, some toys, a small chair, and soft blankets. It was a bit like a pillow fort, and it was just for Ana. This snug, secure, and private space allowed her to have her big feelings, to calm down, and then to rejoin the class. A team of three or four teachers took turns, using the same routine and language with Ana, quickly decreasing the time she needed in the nook before she could join the class.

We gave Ana a lot of positive affirmations. "We care so much about you, and we're so glad you are in school today. I'm here, and I'll just sit and do a little work while you take some time and let me know when you are ready to go. Why don't you set five minutes on the timer and see how you're feeling then?"

Sometimes, recognizing what a child needs and finding a way to provide it is all it takes. After a few weeks, most days, Ana transitioned without visiting the nook. And even when she used the nook, it was typically for less time than even the timer allowed. We gave Ana space to have her feelings and gave her support as she learned to *regulate* them. She can now enter class and have a successful day—loved, seen, and cared for.

—Told by a former preschool head

Giving and Taking the Chance

I stood at the graduation podium giving my speech. The moment was full of joy and pride in the year's graduating class. I had made a point that I would mention every senior by name in some special way, recalling fond memories, acknowledging growth, and sending well wishes for their future. I paused as I got to the next name in my speech. While I did not say it, this student had proven to have the greatest impact on my career up until that moment and still to this day.

My first encounter with her was in a hallway of the school, breaking up a fight she was in with another young lady. I knew her vaguely as one of the younger students, a student with a bit of an attitude, and, at that moment, the center of an uproar in the middle of the hallway. In those few minutes, I judged her, and I assumed that she would be a problem next year when she got to the class I taught as one of my duties at the school. I assumed that she was another unmotivated, hard-to-reach troublemaker. The worst part was that I hadn't realized the degree to which I had negatively judged her in one instance until she came to my class the following year. She entered my room, and in our early conversations, I told her that I remembered she was the girl who got into that fight the previous year and that I hoped she didn't plan on bringing any of "that" into my classroom. In those few words, I created a wall of judgment. I never gave the girl a chance. And I couldn't have been more wrong about her.

The kid who entered my class looked the same and sounded the same as the year before, but the fact that I was now her teacher gave me the chance to get to know her. Her answers to questions were insightful, and her work habits were impeccable. She was driven, and I was compelled to do my part to make up for the wrong I had done and for all who had prejudged her before me. That year was full of ups and downs. I watched her conquer family challenges, the loss of friends, and the burden of providing for her family. But she continued to persevere and kept college on the forefront of her mind. I encouraged her and saw the hard shell she presented to the world begin to disappear. She became like a niece to me, and classroom lessons became infused with life lessons about being your best self and not giving up despite growing up in difficult circumstances. She laughed, she cried, and she got angry, and I promised her that if she did her part, she would find her place in college. She trusted me enough to tell me her dreams of one day being successful for her family, and she shared her fears that she would never achieve her dreams. I challenged her even harder, expected even more, and supported her every step of the way.

As I stood at the podium on that graduation day, I paused and then spoke her name. I announced to the audience of students, family members, and friends that I simply wanted to apologize. I wanted to apologize for not seeing the amazing student that she was, and I thanked her for giving me the opportunity to be a part of her journey. I thanked her for being a constant reminder that the future is what you make of it and greatness comes in all types of packages. I closed by congratulating her on the full scholarship she had received to attend a selective East Coast college. My own biases had almost hindered me from committing to and expressing the level of care necessary to see this student through to the finish.

I was reminded how important it is to care for our students when I received the following Facebook message from this former student five years later:

> I just want to thank you for everything you have taught me and your seriousness when it came to being an educator. Many of the things you told me still stick with me today. Like "you might have to work 10x harder to get where some other people are at and you have to do what you have to do". Although I knew I was going to college,

I'm not sure if I would be where I am today without your influence. Thank you. P.S.: I will never forget the fact that you really thought I was a hood rat because of that fight. Lol!

—Told by a high school assistant principal

Seth

Meet Seth. Seth is the younger brother of Jack by one year, both adopted by two moms from Central America. I had the pleasure of teaching both boys, back to back. It wasn't easy being Jack's little brother. Jack was a rock star, excelling academically, athletically, and socially. Seth didn't have it as easy. Seth had a medical issue that caused tumors to grow in his little body, leaving his moms terrified and his brain having to work harder than anyone in my class—and perhaps in the school. Each week, Seth saw a speech and language pathologist, an occupational therapist, a speech therapist, and a math tutor. He struggled to speak clearly, write legibly, and finish any assignment with success. Amazingly, these hardships were not obvious when you met Seth. Seth was one of the happiest boys I ever taught. He said, "Good morning!" *with* eye contact every day as he entered the classroom, not the most common thing for a fourth-grader to do. He cared for his peers, as when he would rub their backs when they were sad and when he would come and tell me he was worried about his friends. He made people laugh. He participated in class discussions. Seth was someone every lower-school teacher wanted in their classroom. Seth was in the fourth grade, and next year, he would enter the middle school, and the big question that was on the table was whether Seth would continue to make it here.

Seth's moms knew that he struggled. It was undeniable. They were paying thousands of dollars on top of independent-school tuition just to get enough tutors and therapists to keep Seth's head above water. But Seth was part of our school community, and it terrified his moms that he might not be allowed to continue on at this school. They wanted him here. *We* wanted him here. But the most important question was what was best for Seth. When Julie, the head of the lower school, came to me in late October to schedule a "touch base" meeting with Seth's moms about his future, I knew it was going to be difficult. I knew the meeting was going to be frightening for Seth's moms.

The meeting was scheduled for after school. I was running around to get my fourth-graders into their cars and to get back up to the mailroom to grab the last of the coffee. As I swung open the door and dashed out of the mailroom, I almost slammed into Seth's mom, Robyn. "Hi!" I exclaimed. She barely looked at me as she quickly strode down the hall. "Can I get you some coffee?" I asked, trying to keep up with her. "No." She brushed me off and entered Julie's office with me trailing behind. This meeting was going to be worse than I thought.

I entered the office as Julie was offering a beverage to Mary, Seth's other mom. "Sure!" she said in a friendly reply. Robyn sat across from Mary, saying nothing and still fuming. Mary looked across the table at Robyn and gave her a look to tell her to pull it together. To say it was awkward is an understatement. I just looked at Julie. After some awkward chitchat, Julie took the lead.

"Let's just dive in," Julie began. "How are you feeling about how everything is going for Seth?" That's all it took for Robyn to explode. She sounded off about how everything is so easy for Jack and how that isn't fair for Seth. She said she doesn't know how to help Seth. She cursed. She was red faced. She was angry. She asked if I was the best teacher for Seth. That hit a nerve for me, and I became visibly upset by her question.

Mary stopped her and said fiercely, "Robyn, if you are going to act like this, leave!" It was the most raw parent emotion I have ever seen. Julie intervened. "Let's take a step back. Let's relax for a minute. We are here *for* Seth. So what do you want *for* Seth?" That's when the tears started flowing. Robyn sat quietly wiping her eyes as Mary stepped in. "We want Seth to be happy. We want Seth to learn and be whatever he wants to be. We are scared for Seth. We are scared he won't make it here." The room was quiet.

Julie said, "We are not at this table to kick Seth out of this school. Let me be very clear. The question is how can we best support Seth?" I could feel the anger and fear leave the room. Julie's tone calmed the moms. She wasn't the authority figure in the room but rather a comforter and mediator to help the moms process Seth's situation. Julie reminded us to think about how Seth was feeling about his experiences in school. Are his struggles overcoming his confidence? Does he love school? Julie insisted that we keep Seth's feelings at the forefront of our conversation. This seemed to provide comfort for the moms.

Julie guided the conversation along. Her voice was calm and reassuring. She was fully present, focusing all her attention on the moms. There was no computer on the table, nor were there folders of information about Seth. Julie took no notes. It was all about making the personal connection and laying the foundation for future conversations and decision making. As she was talking, Julie gave examples of Seth's experiences in school, about how she had gotten to know him by talking with him in the mornings when he was dropped off at school. She spoke about the things that made Seth happy. She was assuring the moms that Seth is known at school and that the school is being supportive and caring of him. There were no negatives spoken, only positives. Julie kept Seth at the center of the conversation. Julie spoke about how the moms could learn more about Seth's strengths and struggles. She asked the moms for their insight into Seth and his condition. She asked the moms for their advice about what resources might be most helpful for Seth at school. Along the way, Julie put to rest Robyn's concern about Seth being in my classroom, saying, "I would not want him anywhere else." That meant a lot to me, as I hope it did to the moms.

We all hugged at the end of the meeting. We didn't reach a decision about whether Seth would continue at the school next year. But Julie had established a connection with the moms that would make further conversations and the ability to make this decision less difficult. She was clear that we care about Seth, that we care about his well-being, and that we care about his moms and how they are navigating their support for Seth. She was communicating the school's values of caring, openness, and support. This was enough for a first conversation.

A week later, the moms returned to school with packets of information about Seth's condition and about resources they thought the school should know about. They began to trust and open up to Julie and to me. They engaged more fully with Julie as partners in Seth's schooling. And two years later, at the time this story was written, Seth was still at the school, ready to enter the seventh grade.

—Told by an independent elementary school teacher

No One Graduates Alone

I had recently been named director of curriculum and assessment (9–12) for a network of charter schools. Having started as K–3 or K–5 schools and adding one grade per year, the Charter Management Organization had experience managing elementary schools but not high schools. At the time I was hired to lead curriculum development for the new ninth-graders who would start in the fall, I was the only staff member in the entire company who had ever taught in a high school. We were inexperienced, and we knew it.

Rory, the principal of the new high school, had been preparing for the role for several years. Hired as director of instruction in the middle school, he had assumed the title of principal over the seventh and eighth grades the previous year to prepare him to add the ninth grade the following year. In our planning, we wanted to make sure that ninth-grade students felt different—that ninth grade would not just be another year of middle school. We planned an orientation program during which students—about half continuing from the eighth grade and half new to the charter school—would begin to experience high school for the first time. At the end of the two days, which included several fun, community-building activities, as well as introductions to the academic expectations of high school, Rory gathered the fifty incoming freshmen and all of the high school teachers in the biggest classroom in the school.

After giving out some awards from some of the team-building activities earlier in the day and making some general announcements, Rory got to the point of the meeting. He spoke:

> Let me get real with you for a minute. The last couple days we've had a lot of fun, and that's great. But there's more to high school than playing laser tag with your friends.
>
> In this part of the city, less than half of kids graduate from high school. I want you to imagine the stage at graduation four years from now. All of the chairs are set up. Your family is all in the audience.

We've got some balloons and decorations, and you're wearing your cap and gown. And you're the only one on the stage. Would you be really happy at that moment? You still will have accomplished your goal, but I'll promise you that you won't be as excited as if you were graduating with all of your friends. Look around the room. Let's make this promise to each other: No one graduates alone. We're going to commit ourselves to doing whatever it takes so that four years from now, everyone who is in this room will be on that stage.

And that's not just a commitment for you to make. Look around the room again. In this room are your teachers. They will do anything and everything they can to make sure that we achieve that goal. When you leave the room today, one of the teachers by the door is going to hand you a card like this [shows example]. On it are the personal cell phone numbers of each of your teachers. If you need help with your homework or studying for a test or if you just need to talk through something, you can call any of us, and we will be there for you. The teachers in this room are some of the most amazing people I have ever worked with. One teacher in this room—and I'm not going to name names and embarrass any-one—but one teacher stayed after school every day and sometimes came in on weekends last year to help a student who was behind in math get caught up. Another teacher in this room, when they found out that a student didn't have money for clothes, took that student shopping and spent their own money to make sure that the student had what they needed. That's the kind of people these teachers are, and you are incredibly lucky to be able to spend the next four years with them.

We know that there will be good days and bad days—we'll be there for both good and bad. If you're not getting to school in the morning or if you start falling behind, I'm going to stay on you, and your teachers will stay on you. And I hope your classmates will stay on you, and you will stay on them. . . .

Before this week, I gave your teachers an assignment. I told them this: Make me a lighthouse. [The school and charter network used the symbol of a lighthouse.] I didn't give them any directions and didn't tell them why. Mr. L's is in the back of the room there. [He pointed to a model made of balsa wood.] Miss K's is right here. [He held up a drawing of a lighthouse illuminating kids, turning the picture so that everyone could see. Those kids nearest the light-house have schoolbooks in hand, and those farthest away where the beam widens are wearing caps and gowns.] Since ancient times, the lighthouse has been a symbol of hope. When sailors would be out at sea, they could look out and see the beam from the lighthouse and know where the coast was, and the beam could help them avoid danger and get them home safely. Together, we are going to be a lighthouse for each other—to help keep each other on course, to rescue each other if we get too close to the rocks—and in four years, we will all be together on that stage at graduation, and no one will graduate alone.

In that talk, Rory not only expressed his care for the students but also helped to establish a culture and ethic of care for the school as a whole. A few of the teachers in the room had been at the school teaching middle school grades previously, but some were new. For them, this was enculturation and expectation setting by offering positive examples of "what we do here." For the students, it established a sense of belonging—being part of a group with a collective commitment—and communicated clearly that the adults in the building cared and would demonstrate care.

While some students transferred out of the school, 100 percent of the students who stayed all four years graduated. All were accepted to at least one college. Two have since returned to the school as teachers.

—Told by a high school curriculum director

CARING: THE HEART OF CARING SCHOOL LEADERSHIP

We begin our exploration of caring school leadership by examining the concept caring. We make a case for why we should care about caring in schools. Then, we turn to what we mean by caring. We examine key elements that make a person's actions and interactions caring. Following this discussion, we explore how caring works, that is, how it leads to particular outcomes for ones cared for and ones who are caring. As part of our analysis, we examine conditions that enable or constrain caring and its functions. At the end of this chapter, we explore briefly the problematic aspects of caring. We speak of caring with few references to school leadership. Our purpose in this chapter is to develop a general understanding of caring before we apply it to school leadership.

A Case for Caring in Schools

There are four important reasons to care about caring in schools and to work to promote it. First, caring is an intrinsic good, a key element of the human condition. Second, caring contributes significantly to students' learning, development, and success in school. Third, the alternatives to caring are unacceptable. And fourth, although caring is thought to be what schools are by definition, caring's presence cannot be assumed. There is evidence that caring is highly variable in schools today and that caring is made difficult by the ways in which schooling is organized and by the primary approaches to school improvement that we have pursued. Indeed, this problem of caring in schools is symptomatic of broader social trends and a long-term "crisis of caring" across human service professions.

Caring Is an Intrinsic Good

The first reason to care about caring is because it is an intrinsic good, a worthy human endeavor in its own right. It is elemental to the human condition, a foundation stone of being moral. Education philosopher Nel Noddings (2013) contends that

> Natural caring [is] the condition that we . . . perceive as "good." It is that condition toward which we long and strive, and it is our longing for caring—to be in that special relation—that provides the motivation for us to be moral. (p. 5)

In a similar vein, philosopher Milton Mayeroff (1971) argues that

> through the caring for others, by serving them through caring, a [person] lives the meaning of his [or her] own life. In the sense in which a [person] can ever be said to be at home in the world, he [or she] is at home not through dominating, or explaining, or appreciating, but through caring and being cared for. (pp. 2–3)

Such observations about caring can be found in literature and the arts, religion, and the human service professions. For example, in his 1957 play *Simply Heavenly*, through the voice of the character Jesse Simple, author Langston Hughes writes, "When peoples care for you and cry for you—and *love* you—they can straighten out your soul" (L. C. Sanders, 2004, p. 201). Emmanuel Levinas (1969), scholar of Jewish philosophy and theology, calls caring a moral imperative. Nursing theorist Patricia Benner and medical researcher Judith Wrubel (1989) speak of caring as "the most basic human way of being in the world" (p. 368). According to occupational sociologists Pamela Abbott and Liz Meerabeau (1998) and political philosopher Joan Tronto (1993), caring is particularly important in human service enterprises and political and social institutions that affect the lives of those who are vulnerable and in need.

Caring Is Crucial to Student Success

A second reason that we should care about caring is because it is crucial to the learning and development of children and youth and to their success in school. We agree with former school administrators Helen Regan and Gwen Brooks (1995), who write, "We understand care to be the essence of education" (p. 27). And we concur with Noddings (2005), who calls caring the "bedrock of all successful education" (p. 27).

Students tell us this as well. Research repeatedly emphasizes the importance students place on caring (Jeffrey, Auger, & Pepperell, 2013; Luttrell, 2013; Murphy, 2016b). Students see teachers' willingness to care and their ability to bond with students as essential ingredients of a positive school climate and an effective classroom environment (Howard, 2001). Among the things students say they like most about school is when adults, particularly teachers, care about them and work hard to help them learn (Poplin & Weeres, 1992). Among the things they like least are feeling invisible, unsupported, and uncared for.

Students see caring as a crucial dimension of their relationships with teachers, in their perceptions of the quality of instruction they receive, and in how much they care about their own education. They see caring as key to their success in school. Students say that when they feel cared for, they are more likely to engage in school and work harder academically. They say they are less likely to behave in ways that might jeopardize their success. Conversely, students say that when they do not feel cared for, they do not invest much time and energy. These perspectives are clearly summarized in the common sentiment of highly successful African American and Latino young men, graduates of New York City high schools, naming the primary source of their success: "Teachers really care" (Harper & Associates, 2014, p. 21).

There is abundant additional evidence that caring benefits children and youth in and out of school (Murphy & Torre, 2014). These benefits derive from the positive nature of relationships with adults and peers. They also derive from the academic and social supports and resources that can be provided through these relationships. Caring relationships and commensurate support seem particularly powerful for students placed at risk, a subject we will explore in Chapter 2.

Research has linked caring relationships with adults and peers to healthy brain development and functioning (Cozolino, 2014). This relationship is especially strong during infancy and early childhood, when the brain is most rapidly developing. Early interactions build neural networks and establish biological "set points" that can last a lifetime. Because the brain remains malleable and experience dependent, caring relationships can shape the brain and its functioning throughout childhood, into adolescence, and across the lifespan.

Caring and nurturing relationships contribute to brain development and to cognitive and social-emotional functioning in several ways (Hawley, 2000; Newman, Sivaratnam, & Komiti, 2015). They provide positive emotional and cognitive stimulation that biochemically promotes healthy brain development and function. They provide safety, comfort, and pleasure that mediate stress, threat, and trauma, which further shapes the brain in healthy ways. Finally, in caring and nurturing relationships, adults (and peers) can provide repeated experiences of emotional responses and behaviors that become sources of social learning, which also contributes to brain development and function.

In school, experiences of caring lead to a number of positive psychological states, including self-concept, self-esteem, and self-efficacy. They also include feelings of psychological safety, hope, and persistence. Research indicates that caring by adults in schools can help develop children's capacity for resilience when they experience stress and mitigate some of the direct negative effects of trauma (Allensworth et al., 2018). Experiencing caring leads to social-emotional development and prosocial behaviors, such as cooperation, communication, empathy, and responsibility. These, in turn, enable academic learning and performance (Farrington et al., 2012; Reese, Jensen, & Ramirez, 2014).

Caring in schools also promotes students' sense of connection and belonging, trust in others, and social integration (Crosnoe, 2011; Jennings & Greenberg, 2009). Caring can lead to student interest and engagement in school and in classroom activities (Cherng, 2017; Roorda, Koomen, Spilt, & Oort, 2011). It also can result in improved motivation and effort, as well as persistence and retention (Kotok, Ikoma, & Bodovski, 2016; Rutledge, Cohen-Vogel, Osborne-Lampkin, & Roberts, 2015). These effects have been found from elementary grades through high school.

Students also experience academic success from caring and the social and academic supports that come from it. When their relationships with teachers and peers feel caring, students' academic achievement can increase (Roorda et al., 2011). The effects of caring on achievement are best understood in relation to academic challenge—high expectations, rigorous pedagogy, intellectual demand, and accountability. It is the mutually reinforcing combination of what Hallinger and Murphy (1985) long ago called *pastoral care* and support with *academic press* that makes the greatest positive difference (see Bryk, Sebring, Allensworth, Luppescu, & Easton, 2010). Indeed, academic challenge without sufficient caring and support from teachers and fellow students can lower performance.

Caring student–teacher relationships are also related to students' expectations for success in school and aspirations for postsecondary education (Cherng, 2017). Indeed, there is evidence that supportive, caring relationships have an indirect positive effect on college enrollment (Demi, Coleman-Jensen, & Snyder, 2010).

A final benefit is that caring can beget caring (Luthans & Youssef, 2007; May, Chan, Hodges, & Avolio, 2003). Children and youth who experience caring from adults and peers are more likely to act in caring ways themselves. Experiences of caring can model and teach caring (Noddings, 2013). Caring can neurologically and behaviorally promote caring among those experiencing it, biasing those cared for toward *tend-and-befriend* behavior—contributing to safe and protective school environments—and away from disassociation or *fight-or-flight* behavior (Newman et al., 2015). This can be seen in neuroscience research on infant and child development. And it can be seen in neuroscience research examining adults who serve as caregivers. Adults' ability to be caring is influenced positively by their own earlier and contemporary experiences of caring relationships. Experiencing caring (or lack of caring) as a child can have long-term consequences.

The Alternatives Are Unacceptable

We also should care about caring because the alternatives are unacceptable. Lack of caring or harmful uncaring can impede positive learning and development. Neuroscience research indicates that lack of caring and support can negatively affect the development of cognitive capabilities and of caring social behavior (Perry, 2002). It can negatively affect children's ability to regulate stress and form attachments with others (Newman et al., 2015). High-level stress and trauma that might otherwise be mediated by caring can be particularly damaging. The more *adverse childhood experiences* or *toxic stresses* a child has, the greater the chances of long-term physical and behavioral health issues that can even affect mortality (Felitti et al., 1998). Chronic stress and trauma can affect brain development and influence children's capacity to focus attention, recall information, exercise planning and self-control, and get along with others (Bailey, Stickle, Brion-Meisels, & Jones, 2019). These effects, in turn, can have negative consequences for children's lifelong learning, behavior, and health (National Scientific Council on the Developing Child, 2005/2014). As we suggested earlier, even persistent low-level stresses can bias the brain toward hyperarousal and dissociative fight-or-flight behavior rather than the tend-and-befriend behavior associated with caring. Even as social and emotional development can suffer, so too can intellectual and language development.

Lack of caring relationships in schools can negatively affect students. It can lead to feelings of isolation and detachment (Kotok et al., 2016). Students who perceive their teachers as not caring say they do not pay as much attention in class and lack concern about classroom rules. In their review of research, McGrath and Van Bergen (2015) found that the effects of negative student–teacher relationships are extensive, including antisocial behavior, peer rejection, negative attitudes toward school, adjustment difficulties, lower attendance, and poorer academic engagement. Others have made similar findings (Cherng, 2017; Jennings & Greenberg, 2009; Roorda et al., 2011). Not surprisingly, lack of caring is also associated with lower achievement gains (Jennings & Greenberg, 2009; Roorda et al., 2011). Students are more likely to drop out of school and hold lower expectations for their educational attainment when they do not see their schools as caring (Kotok et al., 2016).

On the other hand, when students at risk of experiencing negative relationships with adults in school experience a positive relationship, particularly valuable benefits can accrue. McGrath and Van Bergen (2015) tell us that these benefits include reducing student aggression, promoting positive peer relationships, improving students' attitudes toward school (particularly for students who perceive school to be a hostile and unsafe place), and facilitating social, behavioral, emotional, and academic adjustment. A negative student–teacher relationship history can shape students' and teachers' expectations negatively. But as McGrath and Van Bergen (2015) observe, where positive relationships form despite such expectations, the impact may be particularly positive and powerful.

Caring Should Not Be Assumed

A fourth reason to care about caring in schools is that we cannot assume that caring is a present and unproblematic quality of schooling. There is a paradoxical notion that caring is present and strong in schools because caring is what schools are supposed to do. This is an *assumption of caring*, an idealized sense of what health and social-care expert Ann Brechin (1998a) calls *spontaneously occurring* caring (p. 2). When we ask educators whether they and others in their schools care about their students, they respond with a unanimous and resounding "Yes!" Yet, when we ask whether caring receives the same attention as academic instruction and assessment, whether their schools enact strategies to bring caring to life, and whether their schools have evidence that individual students feel cared for, very few respond affirmatively or without equivocation.

Educators often see caring when students do not (Murphy, 2016b). This point is made clearly by Poplin and Weeres (1992), whose research finds that teachers generally perceive themselves to be very caring people who go into teaching to serve children and youth. Yet teachers are shocked when they learn the extent to which students feel that adults in their schools are not caring for them. The principal of the high school featured in the 2018 docuseries *America to Me* speaks eloquently and sincerely of how much he cares about the students in his school, especially, as an African American, how much he cares about the educational opportunities afforded to African American students. Yet this principal is disconnected from his students. Late in the docuseries, when he realizes that he needs to have greater presence among them, students react to him with ambivalence, wondering who he is and questioning what he is doing.

This assumption of caring is further illustrated in research conducted by the Making Caring Common Project at Harvard University (Weissbourd & Jones, 2014a). Data collected from ten thousand middle and high school students and a sample of teachers and parents in thirty-three school districts revealed that most teachers and parents say that caring and developing caring children is a top educational priority. They rank caring as more important than children's individual achievement and personal happiness. According to students, however, teachers' and parents' daily actions and the messages they send about individual achievement and personal happiness drown out messages about caring for others. In this contradictory-message environment, the assumption of caring is not borne out.

The fact is that caring is highly variable in schools today, particularly for students of color, students of low socioeconomic backgrounds, low-performing students, and students placed at risk (McGrath & Van Bergen, 2015). A national study found that of nearly 150,000 sixth- through twelfth-grade students surveyed, only 29 percent indicated that their schools provided a caring, encouraging environment (Benson, 2006). Another study focusing on racially and ethnically diverse high school students found that barely a majority reported that their teachers cared about them as both persons and learners (Cherng, 2017). Further, this study observes that not all teachers have positive personal relationships with students of color and children of immigrants. Some students reported no interactions with faculty and staff or discriminatory experiences. Indeed, de Royston and her colleagues (2017) observe that positive teacher–student relationships are not the norm for African American males.

Other research has reported similar findings. One study of middle-grade students in Chicago found that only 24 percent reported high levels of school social support for learning that reflects caring, whereas 26 percent reported low levels of such support (Lee & Smith, 1999). African American and Latino students were less likely than white students to report high levels of support. A more recent survey of Chicago students revealed that 14 to 19 percent reported that their teachers did not provide personalized academic support in ways that would suggest caring (Consortium on Chicago School Research, 2012).

Ironically, the way in which schools are organized makes caring problematic. Bureaucratic structures and hierarchical relationships, lack of resources, inconsistencies among programs and policies, and the stresses and strains these conditions impose restrict space and create obstacles to meaningful, caring relationships in schools (Green, 2014). The size of schools and classrooms, the way that time is allocated, the focus of teaching on transmission, the selection of content, and the singular emphasis on academic achievement together make caring difficult (Noddings, 2005). According to Murphy (2016b), rule-based hierarchy, a guiding principle around which we have organized schools for more than a century, is not designed to foster care. Indeed, Murphy observes, such hierarchy impedes caring in human service organizations generally and schools in particular. According to Poplin and Weeres (1992), when they feel pressed to cover the curriculum and to meet bureaucratic demands, and when they are asked to do too many activities unrelated to students, teachers say that there is little time left in the day to build relationships with students.

Moreover, the approaches we have taken recently to improve schools, notably regimes of curricular specification, testing, and accountability, have made it all the more difficult to develop supportive, caring relationships among adults and students. Even as reforms have focused on improving the instructional core, we have emphasized accountability and largely ignored developing the social, emotional, and academic supports that also are necessary for students to succeed (Rutledge et al., 2015). The corrosive effects of high-stakes testing and accountability-based reforms on teacher and student attitudes and emotions have been documented for some time (e.g., Smith, 1991). Recent research suggests that these reforms continue to make teachers' efforts to develop caring relationships with students complicated and challenging (Jeffrey et al., 2013; Wellman, 2007).

Educators with whom we speak tell us the same thing. They say that pushing and pulling students to success through specifying curricula and routinizing instruction, increasing the frequency and scope of testing, and focusing on high-stakes accountability impose substantial challenges for teachers in developing meaningful relationships with students and colleagues. Also complicating matters is the growing emphasis on data, dashboards, and metrics that can, even as they may disaggregate information by groups and favor depersonalization and objectification, pull educators further away from meaningful personal relationships. Educators with whom we speak point to an unhealthy shift in balance away from nurture, support, and community orientation in the classroom toward individualistic performance, accomplishment, and success. Said one elementary school teacher with whom we spoke during the writing of this book, "All this testing takes away time to develop good relationships with the kids." According to a middle school teacher with whom we spoke, "Relationships? Yea, well. . . . We've got to work on that."

The variability of caring in schools and the factors that make its presence difficult mirror strains and tensions in other human service professions. More than thirty years ago, psychologist Seymour Sarason (1985) noted a historical shift in medicine, psychology, psychiatry, and education toward more scientifically based, technical approaches to practice. With this shift came a de-emphasis on the human, relational side, on caring and compassion. Maintaining that the rise of technical approaches to practice have done much to advance these professions, Sarason argued that lack of attention to caring and compassion has harmed them. Historian Susan Reverby (1987) has also observed the emergence of a powerful dilemma in contemporary American nursing—how to fulfill the professional norm and duty to care in a society that refuses to value caring. And sociologist Susan Phillips (1994) has observed that caring in the helping professions has lost ground to "efforts to simplify, codify, categorize, control, explain, and diagnose" (p. 2).

Finally, the problems of caring in schools are symptomatic of broader social trends. To some observers, we are experiencing a long-term societal crisis of caring. Political philosopher Joan Tronto (1993) argues that "care has little status in our society" (p. 122). She contends that "care is devalued and those who do caring work are devalued" (p. 265). Children's advocate Diana Rauner (2000) contends that the idea of caring has been "made irrelevant to the public sphere," that "care no longer has a voice in discussions of how we act as workers, or what we expect of our peers or leaders" (p. 130). Phillips (1994) makes a similar argument that

> personhood and caring have been eclipsed by the depersonalizing procedures of justice distribution, technological problem-solving, and the techniques and relations of the marketplace. . . . Our culture has omitted a significant dimension of human being from consideration and attention. (p. 2)

Political scientist Robert Putnam has documented long-term trends in the breakdown of community, the weakening of social bonds, and the rise of individualism in American society. In his groundbreaking book, *Bowling Alone*,

Putnum (2000) argues that by virtually every conceivable measure—community organizational life, engagement in public affairs, community volunteerism, informal sociability, and social trust—social relationships and resources have "eroded steadily and sometimes dramatically over the past two generations" (p. 287). His data show that the weakening of civic and social connections has made us less healthy, less wealthy, and less wise. The erosion of relational bonds within families and communities weakens systems of social support and caring for children and youth. More recently, psychology and education scholars Naomi Way, Carol Gilligan, Pedro Noguera, and Alisha Ali (2018) documented similar trends, lamenting a worsening societal "crisis of connection."

What Do We Mean by Caring?

So far, we have used the word *caring* generally to represent qualities of relationships and of actions and interactions that exhibit concern, provide support, nurture, meet students' needs, and promote their success and well-being. Within these broad parameters, we have glossed over differences across literatures with which we are working. As we move toward our central subject of caring school leadership, it is important that we be more specific about what we mean by caring.

A Basic Definition

Writers in philosophy, ethics, and various human service professions make important distinctions between *caring*, our particular interest, and concepts of *care* and *caregiving*. *Care* is an action provided on behalf of another (Benner & Gordon, 1996; Noddings, 2013)—a nurse turning a bedridden patient, a doctor setting a child's broken arm in a hospital emergency room, or a pastor making a house call to a bereaved congregant. It is easy to think about the many acts performed by teachers and principals that constitute care for students in schools: providing academic assistance and emotional support, holding high expectations, and promoting prosocial behavior. Associated with particular vocations, such acts are considered professional care or caregiving (P. Abbott & Meerabeau, 1998).

Acts of care are clearly very important to address a person's needs and concerns. However, caring involves more. *Caring* is not only what one does but also *why* and *how* one does it (Benner, 1994; Mayeroff, 1971; Noddings, 2005). One can imagine a nurse turning a patient, a doctor setting a broken arm, a pastor making a house call, a teacher challenging students academically, or a principal disciplining students each done in caring or uncaring ways. Caring involves the matter, manner, and motivation of care, as well as its competent provision. It is a particular way of being in relationship with others. Caring involves observing and assessing, identifying with, and responding to the situations, needs, interests, joys, and concerns of others. It involves expressing particular virtues such as compassion, empathy, and respect. Caring does not rest on contractual obligation, power of authority, coercion, or expectation of return. It is grounded in and driven by motivation toward the betterment of others.

Caring holds the prospect for mutuality, in that persons in caring relationships may be, at different times and in various ways, both the ones caring and the ones cared for (Noddings, 2013). Mutuality need not be symmetrical and indeed is often asymmetrical, as in student–principal and student–teacher relationships. But the notion of mutuality provides for the possibility that caring can be two-way, that it can extend in multiple directions among individuals and groups. Caring can take on a covenantal quality that acknowledges asymmetry but also recognizes reciprocal responsibility of persons caring for one another (DePree, 2004; Sergiovanni, 1992).

Caring is not simply caring about—that is, having concern or sentiment for—someone or something. It is important to care about students and their success. However, it is another thing to be caring of them. Caring includes but goes beyond feelings of concern and sentiment to actions and interactions—practices—of being in relationship with others and achieving particular aims on their behalves (Benner & Gordon, 1996). However, caring is not defined by a specific set of actions, interactions, or activities. Indeed, caring cannot be defined by a particular set of activities that are necessarily different from those in which one regularly engages (Noddings, 2013). Caring is not necessarily another responsibility that adds to one's job description and workload. All actions and interactions, all activities, can be viewed through a lens of caring. Caring may be reflected in proactive initiative, in direct support, in being with, even in doing and saying nothing (Benner, 1994). Again, caring, as we define it, is a quality of a relationship—the matter, manner, and motivation of personal and professional action and interaction.

There is another important aspect of caring. Caring is perceptual, subjective, and imbued with personal meaning (Noddings, 2013; Tarlow, 1996). It is not simply what the person caring—the teacher or principal—intends or does. It involves the extent to which the person cared for—the student—considers that intention and action to be caring. In the extreme interpretation, caring is not genuinely caring unless it is experienced as such by the one cared for. In this sense, the effects of caring are dependent, in large part, on the ways in which intention and action are interpreted. This personal subjective aspect of caring helps to explain the effects of caring more fully. It helps to explain how teachers and principals can claim to care and be caring of students, but students can say, at the same time, that teachers and principals do not care or are not particularly caring and respond accordingly.

Elements of Caring

In our reading of various literatures, we find three elements that together make actions and interactions caring: (1) aims, (2) positive virtues and mindsets, and (3) competencies. These elements form a related system of antecedents to caring. Each element may have personal and professional dimensions. The enactment of these elements in caring action and interaction may be promoted or impeded by a system of contexts, which we will explore shortly.

Aims

Caring is neither aimless nor agnostic in purpose. For actions and interactions to be caring, they must focus on achieving particular aims. Caring can be a worthwhile endeavor in itself, promoting fulfillment of the human condition (Greenleaf, 2002; Vanier, 1998). It seeks to promote the functioning, success, and general well-being of others, as individuals and as groups (Liedtka, 1996; Tronto, 1993). Caring addresses particular needs of others and promotes their interests and projects (Mayeroff, 1971). Caring aims to help others grow and flourish in their own right. Caring is sometimes framed as a response to pain, suffering, and trouble (Dutton, Worhne, Frost, & Lilius, 2006). But it can also be proactive and an affirmative expression of joy and celebration.

In human service professions, the aims of caring are shaped by professional orientations and domains of work that distinguish one profession from another and that distinguish the professional from the personal. In nursing, for example, the aims of caring are not only to treat illness and promote health but also to promote hope and comfort and to protect and enhance patient integrity and dignity (Gadow, 1985; Watson, 2008). In disability services, caring aims to promote functioning and general well-being but also empowerment and autonomy (Morris, 1993; Swain & French, 1998). In ministry, caring seeks to respond to suffering and need and to affirm and celebrate joys. It seeks to promote general well-being but particularly spiritual growth and well-being in a person's relationship with God and with other human beings (Gerkin, 1997; McClure, 2014). It also seeks to develop communal or congregational caring. In education, we consider the general aims of schooling to provide for students' safety and nurturance; support their learning, development, independence, self-reliance, prosocial relationships, and ability to function in and contribute to community; promote academic success and general well-being; and prepare students for work, further education, and citizenship (Murphy & Torre, 2014).

Caring can aim to address particular needs, problems, and concerns of individuals or groups. It can aim to achieve tangible and instrumental benefits, the manner in which they are provided being as important as the benefits themselves. By tangible and instrumental benefits, we refer to what we characterized earlier as care: particular services and provisions. Caring can aim to promote certain experiential benefits—social, psychological, emotional, and behavioral—that accrue from being in caring relationships and feeling cared for. Finally, caring can aim to promote further caring.

Positive Virtues and Mindsets

A second element of caring consists of positive virtues and mindsets that are brought to the pursuit of the aims of caring (Mayer, Aquino, Greenbaum, &

Kuenzl, 2012; Parris & Peachy, 2013). These *virtues* include compassion, empathy, patience, sympathy, and kindness. They include fairness and justice, authenticity, humility, and vulnerability. They also include prudence, transparency, honesty, trustworthiness, and respect for others and their integrity. As caring involves perceptions and interpretations, virtues can be variously meaningful with different people at different times and in different situations. These positive virtues may be held personally and may also form a system of professional norms and values with which people identify. In nursing and medicine, this system derives from occupational traditions, institutions, and professional codes (Watson, 2008). In ministry, it derives from theological principles and faith traditions (Dykstra, 2005; Gerkin, 1997).

Four positive *mindsets* are particularly important to this second element of caring. The first is attentiveness to others. If caring is to address others' needs and interests, one must be attentive to understand, deeply and genuinely, who persons are and what their needs, concerns, interests, projects, and situations might be. Another mindset is motivational orientation. If caring truly means acting on behalf of others, one must be motivated accordingly, and this orientation cannot be diminished by attention to one's own needs and self-interests. Importantly, as Noddings (1996) argues, attentiveness and motivational orientation "need not lead to permissiveness nor an abdication of responsibility for conduct and achievement" (p. 22). "Rather," she continues, each "maintains and enhances the relatedness that is fundamental to human reality."

Personal and professional identities are also mindsets important to caring (see, e.g., Barley, 1989; Willetts & Clarke, 2014). How persons see themselves as human beings, as caring or uncaring, as capable or incapable of caring, is likely to affect their efforts to be caring. Likewise, how persons see themselves in a professional role, what they perceive the norms of the profession to require of them, and what they perceive as others' expectations for them in their role may influence caring. One's personal and professional identities may shape perceptions of others' personal and professional identities and their sense of caring (A. Abbott, 1988; Showers, 2015). For example, if a principal's professional identity is deeply entwined with her position in the administrative hierarchy, she may view teachers and students as subordinates, which can affect how she thinks about a principal's caring and, in turn, teachers' and students' caring.

Another mindset is playfulness. This mindset reminds us that caring is not a dour enterprise (Hamman, 2014b; Koppel, 2008). Albeit difficult and taxing at times, it can be joyful and fulfilling. Hamman (2014b) considers playfulness "a way of knowing and a way of seeing and engaging the world" (p. 47). It manifests creativity, inventive thinking, flexibility, and adaptability. Playfulness can reveal the world through others' eyes, a view that can be essential to understanding others, their situations, and ways to be caring of them.

Competencies

In addition to aims and virtues and mindsets, to be caring requires competency. According to Benner and Gordon (1996), caring professional practice "is always bound up in knowing and doing" (p. 50). As we noted earlier, one important area of knowing is the authentic understanding of others and their needs, problems, joys, concerns, and conditions. If educators have inaccurate understanding of who students are and what they want and need in relation to care, they may make well-meaning attempts to be caring but ultimately miss the mark as to what is caring and helpful in the eyes of students (Jeffrey et al., 2013; Murphy, 2017). Developing such understanding is related to one's ability to inquire, listen and hear, observe and see, assess and understand, and learn about others (Autry, 1991; Greenleaf, 2002). Also important is understanding persons' and groups' races, classes, genders, sexual orientations, languages, cultures, religious beliefs, and relevant contexts. As feminist education scholar Audrey Thompson (1998) argues, because "the possibility of adequate responsiveness to others depends upon our being able to understand their situations in ways that do not simply reduce them to projections of our . . . assumptions, . . . [school] administrators need to understand the full picture of the worlds in which their students move" (pp. 543, 541). For example, while it is critical to understand an African American tenth grader for who he is as an individual learner and person, he cannot be fully understood without also seeing his experiences as an African American male, with all the historical, contemporary, and personal contexts entailed, as well as an adolescent in a particular phase of human development (Van Dierendonck & Patterson, 2015).

A second area of competency concerns understanding the relative effectiveness of strategies to address the needs and concerns of others and to promote their interests (Benner & Gordon, 1996). This includes knowledge and skills to enact these strategies successfully. Effort and sincerity are important and may be appreciated, but particular actions and interactions may not be perceived as caring or very helpful if they are uninformed, misguided, inadequate, or inept. Caring requires knowledge and skill to develop or select, adapt, and enact practices that pursue the aims of caring, that bring virtues of caring to life, and that align with the understanding of others, their situations, and their joys, needs, and concerns. Caring further requires the ability to wrestle with ethical and practical dilemmas posed by different and competing needs and considerations.

A third area of competency concerns knowledge of self and the ability to develop and deepen one's capacity for caring. This area receives substantial attention in human service professions, such as medicine, nursing, and the ministry (Hamman, 2014a; Turkel & Ray, 2004; Watson, 2008). Knowledge of self involves understanding one's orientations and inclinations, strengths and limitations, and predispositions and prejudices. Recognizing the sources of one's fears and joys may be crucial in thinking and acting in a caring manner.

A fourth area of competency consists of knowledge and skills for developing caring among others and creating organizational contexts conducive to caring (Boyatzis, Smith, & Blaize, 2006; Fuqua & Newman, 2002). This area includes understanding how to think about caring as a property of classroom and school organization, not only as a quality of interpersonal relationships. It includes knowledge and skill related to professional learning and development and organizational change. It encompasses knowledge and skill to create supportive structures and processes, to design work and social arrangements, and to develop organizational cultures imbued with the virtues and mindsets of caring (Deshpande, 1996; Gossling & van Liedekerke, 2014).

Social-Emotional Intelligence

An area of competency that is particularly important to caring and caring school leadership is social-emotional intelligence. Because of its importance, we give it special attention here and again in later chapters. Social-emotional intelligence is usually defined as the ability to perceive, understand, and regulate emotions in oneself and others (George, 2000). It is linked in social-psychological research to the quality and stability of social relationships. Social-emotional intelligence can be particularly influential in relationships when coupled with cognitive intelligence. Social-emotional intelligence can help individuals navigate and adapt to the social environment. It can set the emotional tone for interpersonal encounters both positively and negatively. Social-emotional intelligence can guide thinking and motivate action, set expectations for encounters, and convey information about people's thoughts and intentions. It can facilitate communication and help coordinate encounters, influence one's focus of attention and decision making, and help manage conflict. Particularly important are abilities to discern the emotions of others and to understand and regulate one's own emotions. These associations emerge in research on social relationships of children and adults, and relationships both inside and outside the work setting (Lopes, Salovey, Côté, & Beers, 2005).

Social-emotional intelligence has been associated with leadership effectiveness. As Bernard Bass (2002), a noted scholar of organizational leadership, explains, social-emotional intelligence is particularly important because of its contribution to a leader's ability to inspire and build relationships with followers. Social-emotional intelligence has been associated with a positive approach to leadership (Murphy & Louis, 2018). It is strongly associated with a leader's ability to understand and shape others' emotions. It has been associated with leaders' appraisal and expression of emotion, including the use of emotion to enhance cognitive processes and decision making (George, 2000). Moreover, social-emotional intelligence has been linked to forming and shaping the quality of leader–follower relationships and exchanges (Jordan & Troth, 2011) and to employees' perceptions of supervisor and executive leader performance and effectiveness (Kerr, Garvin, Heaton, & Boyle, 2006; Rosete & Ciarrochi, 2005).

While the literature on educational leadership has not explicitly connected social-emotional intelligence and caring, such an association seems reasonable. In their book, *Primal Leadership*, Goleman, Boyatzis, and McKee (2013) define emotional intelligence (what we have referred to until this point as social-emotional intelligence) as "how leaders handle themselves and their relationships" (p. 6). They, along with many other scholars (e.g., George, 2000; Riggio & Reichard, 2008; Salovey & Mayer, 1990), place social and emotional intelligence at the center of effective leadership. Arguing that great leadership works through emotions, they contend that no matter what leaders do, their success depends on *how* they do it. Even if they get all else right, if leaders fail to drive the emotions of others in a productive direction, "nothing they do will work as well as it could or should" (p. 3). In this regard, the emotional work of leadership is both the first and most important act of leadership. This perspective is supported by studies that demonstrate a strong relationship between emotional or socioemotional intelligence and transformational leadership (e.g., Bass, 2002; Harms & Credé, 2010; Kerr et al., 2006). Moreover, educators Maurice Elias, Harriet Arnold, and Cynthia Steiger Hussey (2003) contend that *EQ*—emotional intelligence—complements IQ, which is intelligence of a cognitive nature. They write, "If IQ represents the intellectual raw material . . . EQ is the set of social-emotional skills that enables intellect to turn into action and accomplishment. . . . Without EQ, IQ consists more of potential than actuality" (pp. 4–5).

Goleman and his colleagues (2013) describe four domains of competencies that compose leaders' emotional intelligence. The first domain is self-awareness. Self-awareness includes how leaders are attuned to their feelings and how those feelings affect them and their job performance. It also includes how leaders are attuned to their guiding values, see big and small pictures in complex situations, and intuit the best courses of action. Self-awareness involves leaders' ability for accurate self-assessment, knowledge of their own strengths and limitations, and understanding where they need to improve and how to engage the means for improvement. Self-awareness can lead to humble self-confidence. In knowing their abilities, feelings, values, and limitations, leaders can work toward positive strengths with a sense of presence and self-assurance.

A second domain of emotional intelligence is self-management. Self-management involves self-control and the ability to regulate emotions and impulses and channel them in useful ways. Self-management also involves positive transparency, an "authentic openness" to others about one's feelings, beliefs, and actions. This allows leaders to act with integrity, to openly admit mistakes, and to confront unethical behavior in others. Self-management also involves adaptability, an orientation toward improvement in oneself and in others, and a sense of efficacy that promotes initiative. Self-management further includes optimism. Optimistic leaders see others positively and expect the best of them. They see possibilities where others may see threats or setbacks.

A third domain of emotional intelligence is social awareness. One important aspect of social awareness is being attuned to the emotional signals of others. Another is empathy. Socially aware leaders listen attentively and grasp others' perspectives. An important aspect of social awareness is organizational awareness, that is, the ability to be socially and politically astute and read key power and interpersonal relationships accurately. A final aspect of social awareness is what Goleman and his colleagues call *service competence*. This is the ability to foster an emotional climate in an organization so that people working directly with customers or clients keep those relationships on the right track. Leaders with strong service competence monitor customer or client satisfaction to ensure they are getting what they need. They make themselves available to customers and clients as needed.

The fourth domain of emotional intelligence is relationship management. Relationship management involves the competency to inspire others, to guide and motivate them with a compelling vision, and to model that vision in one's own actions. It involves the ability to influence others, to be engaging and persuasive, and to build support among them. Relationship management involves the ability to develop others, to show a genuine interest in people leaders are helping, and to understand their needs, goals, strengths, and weaknesses. These competencies include the ability to manage conflict effectively—to surface conflict, to understand and acknowledge the feelings and views of all sides, and to find a shared ideal that everyone can endorse. Finally, relationship management involves the ability to promote teamwork, collegiality, and collaboration. It involves the ability to model respect, helpfulness, and cooperation; to draw others into active commitment to collective effort; and to build spirit and identity.

As we will see later, important elements of emotional intelligence, as outlined by Goleman and others, are embodied in caring school leadership. They overlap in significant ways with the aims and the values and mindsets of caring school leadership. They can be seen in the inventory of competencies that make leadership caring.

How Does Caring Work?

Having laid out a definition of caring and discussed its elements, we now examine how caring works to achieve the outcomes we discussed earlier in the chapter. First, we examine how caring functions for the ones cared for, particularly children and youth. We will make the important point that the outcomes of caring should be understood systemically, that is, as a totality of caring relationships that a person may experience. Then, we examine how caring functions for the ones caring. Next, we consider conditions that may enable or constrain caring and how it functions. We conclude with a look at the pitfalls of caring and potential negative outcomes.

For the Ones Cared For

At the beginning of this chapter, we discussed a number of positive outcomes associated with caring. In the literatures we reviewed, three explanations are given for how and why caring may contribute to these outcomes. One explanation focuses on the psychological mechanisms triggered by caring (Cozolino, 2014). These mechanisms are described by two general theories. The first, *attachment theory*, suggests that positive social relationships—in this case, caring relationships—promote feelings of safety, security, and comfort through the mediation of threat and stress (Newman et al., 2015). These emotional states are considered necessary preconditions for exploration, managing threat and stress, facing uncertainty, risk taking, and engagement in learning. Through modeling and social learning, caring attachments are thought to build a foundation for future social and emotional interactions. The second theory, *self-determination theory*, posits that for persons—children and youth in our case—to become motivated, three basic psychological needs must be fulfilled. These are needs for relatedness, competency, and autonomy. Adults can satisfy these needs through caring, providing clear rules and expectations, and giving children freedom to make their own choices. This theory holds that if these needs are met, children will be more confident and motivated to engage in learning activities. Consequently, they will learn more and achieve at a higher level.

A second explanation comes from what we might call logic models of caring. These models are built inductively, largely on evidence concerning relationships among particular elements bound together. One logic model of caring in schools and classrooms (Murphy, 2016b) argues that the care and social support received by students are related to four "intermediate" outcomes and two "end" outcomes. Caring and support are thought to promote student affiliation in schools and classrooms. Affiliation refers to students' sense of belonging and social integration. Caring and support are also thought to promote students' sense of competency and self, notably, academic self-concept, self-efficacy, and other positive psychological states. In addition, they promote student motivation to learn and academic engagement. Through these intermediate outcomes, care and support promote social and academic learning. The evidentiary and logical connections among these elements constitute the "big" argument that caring social relationships "power up" certain psychological states of students, which deepen engagement, which, in turn, fuels social and academic outcomes, leading to the conclusion that "without care, learning cannot occur" (Murphy, 2016b, p. 262).

A third explanation is that of instrumental benefits. As caring may prompt actions that provide tangible support and bring resources to bear on the needs, interests, and concerns of others, benefits may accrue. For example, out of caring by a teacher or a principal, a child may receive eyeglasses that help them see better in class, become more engaged in learning activities, and be more successful academically. Out of caring, a principal may initiate an instructional program to reduce bullying among students. Such support, resources, and services that come via caring can be consequential in and of themselves, without considering social-psychological benefits of caring.

Of course, these several explanations can be taken together and provide a robust understanding of how caring works. Psychological theories of attachment and self-determination help us understand how and why particular elements of logic models relate to each other. They help explain what it is about the caring nature of student–adult relationships that promotes students' sense of self, motivation, and engagement, among other things. The prospect of tangible and instrumental benefit fills in the picture.

The literatures we reviewed make the important point that caring and how it functions is best understood systemically, in terms of the totality of caring that persons may experience across social settings, including family and friendship networks, schools, churches, and other institutions (Luttrell, 2013). We must also consider outcomes in terms of the history of caring relationships and caring experiences. For children and youth, relational systems can be extensive. Recently, Marshall (2017) mapped the range of people who might influence a student's life. Between kindergarten and twelfth grade, a student may be taught by as many as one hundred teachers. This does not include others in school who may be in relationship with students—administrators, professional and nonprofessional staff, and student peers. Beyond the school is the family and the home environment; friends and neighbors, both peer and adult; leaders and participants in non-school-based programs, lessons, and sports; and persons associated with various community institutions, including religious congregations, social-service agencies, and community organizations. There are social media, the Internet, and television with and through which both positive and negative relationships can form. As Marshall (2017) contends, a crucial challenge of school leadership is creating *synergy*, helping to make these potential influences on students' lives add up to more than the sum of their parts (p. 45). We adopt a similar perspective and will show in Chapter 2 how different arenas of caring school leadership practice can strengthen and coordinate this broader system of caring relationships within and beyond the school.

Such systems of relationships are dynamic, and their elements likely influence each other. For example, while the close relationships they have with family, teachers, and close peers may affect students most, more distant relationships with other adults in their extended families, schools and communities and with other peers will also affect them. The characteristics and conditions of schools and families may shape students' close social relationships. The characteristics and conditions of communities and broader institutional contexts may influence schools and families and relationships within them. It is important to consider that elements of a system of relationships may be differentially strong and weak or absent for different students. Caring may be particularly strong for some students in family and community but weak or absent in school (M. G. Sanders, 2001)—and vice versa.

The strength of caring in some relationships may compensate for weakness in others. Again, it is the totality of caring that is important (Gomez & Eng, 2007; Noddings, 2013).

For the Ones Caring

Caring can have important benefits for the ones caring (Brechin, 1998b; Caldwell & Dixon, 2010). It can lead to joy and personal and professional satisfaction and fulfillment (Caldwell & Dixon, 2010; van Dierendonck & Patterson, 2015). It can also increase self-esteem, motivation, agency, persistence, and overall mental health (Cozolino, 2014; Savage & Bailey, 2004). These positive outcomes for the ones caring can, in turn, enhance the prospects of caring for the ones cared for.

Research on professional caregivers indicates that being caring and giving care can increase social and emotional closeness with those being cared for (Savage & Bailey, 2004). Neuroscience research on mother–child relationships shows the positive neurological and biochemical impact of caring contact on attachment bonds, strengthening and deepening them (Cozolino, 2014). The experience of caring for the one caring can beget more caring as it satisfies a sense of personal and professional calling (Noddings, 2013). However altruistic and selfless the one caring might be, the benefits of caring may be enhanced when the one cared for recognizes caring and responds in a positive way. Such recognition and response can enhance the esteem, motivation, and persistence of the one caring, which may enhance the intensity and quality of caring (Noddings, 2013; Tarlow, 1996). And this may increase the prospects for further and greater caring, creating a virtuous *cycle of caring*.

A number of factors in schools can complicate caring recognition and response. We previously mentioned asymmetry in relationships among adults and students in school. In addition, children and youth may have varying ability to acknowledge and respond to caring. Caring for students who are not otherwise familiar with caring may pose different challenges and opportunities for schools than caring for students who are familiar with caring (Cyr, Euser, Bakermans-Kranenburg, & van Ijzendoorn, 2010; Murphy & Torre, 2014). Further complicating may be the "scale" of caring in schools, say for a teacher and a classroom or for a principal and a school. Also complicating may be role-based, generational, racial, and other "distances" between the ones caring and the ones cared for, say the caring of a principal and that caring as experienced by an individual student.

Enabling Conditions and Constraints

Contexts can affect caring. Earlier, we wrote of three related contexts that are important to the function of caring—the interpersonal, the organizational, and the extraorganizational. We take a brief look now at how these contexts can enable or impede caring.

Noddings (2013) argues that caring occurs in and through social relationships that are enacted in *interpersonal context*. Most conducive to caring are interpersonal contexts that are enduring; that are personally deep, open, honest, and revealing; that are characterized by trust; and that are continuous. By continuous, Noddings means that attention is given both to the present and how the present relates to the past and the future. Such continuity creates opportunities for those in a relationship to know and understand each other and to deepen the motivational orientation to act on behalf of one another. Accordingly, in interpersonal contexts that are shorter in duration, are more shallow, are lacking in transparency and honesty, grow from mistrust, or fail to acknowledge the past or consider the future, caring is less likely to form and grow.

Organizational contexts can also enable caring. Particularly relevant to caring in schools are structures that create opportunities for students, teachers, principals, and other staff to interact and learn about each other; to develop long-term, deep, and trusting relationships; and to engage in caring action and interaction (Louis, Murphy, & Smylie, 2016). These structures include the ordering of programs, goals, roles, responsibilities, and relationships. They include the organization of time and work, as well as programmatic and informal systems of social and academic support and press, particularly performance expectations and means of accountability. They also include incentives and rewards that can direct attention and action toward caring (Murphy & Torre, 2014).

In addition to structural elements, school organizational climate and culture can enable or impede caring (Murphy & Torre, 2014). The climate of a school reflects the perceptions that students, teachers, and administrators have of each other, of their relationships, and of the school as a place for caring and learning. Particularly important to caring and other supportive behavior is how students and adults perceive the ethical climate of the school, that is, how they perceive one another as ethical (Arnaud & Schminke, 2012). Research in settings other than schools has shown ethical climate to be associated with attitudes and behaviors of caring, such as commitment to others and their success (Simha & Cullen, 2012). A school's organizational culture—that is, its system of orientations, taken-for-granted assumptions, and values, as well as the symbols, rituals, and routines by which they are communicated—can set expectations for caring and establish a foundation for mutual accountability in caring (Schein, 2010). Both climate and culture can be strong or weak, their content clear or ambiguous. Both can emphasize, be ambivalent about, or be antithetical toward caring.

Other aspects of organizational context may be important for caring in schools. One is governance and politics. Power and authority relationships and processes of school decision making create conditions that can support or impede caring (Slater & Boyd, 1999). Particularly relevant are how a school balances collective interests and individual interests and how it might engage in competitive and adversarial (win–lose) or consensual and constructive (win–win) politics (Blase, 1991). Also relevant is how a school may rely on consolidated or expansive distribution of power and influence (Bryk et al., 2010). The nature of micropolitics in schools—that is, how people exercise power outside formal structures and governance processes—can also influence whether and how caring is perceived and pursued.

Beyond the school are *extraorganizational contexts* that can affect systems of caring relationships. These outside-of-school contexts include families, communities, and broad policy and social-historical-cultural institutional environments. Earlier in this chapter, we referred to elements of the current policy environment that make caring in schools difficult. We can also consider other aspects of education policy, such as school codes and regulations that govern relationships between educators and students and relationships among educators themselves. We mentioned briefly social, historical, and cultural trends concerning the meanings and value of care and caring. We also considered the influence of particular social norms and values. Notable are those norms and values that emphasize the individual, such as independence, self-sufficiency, competition, and individual success, responsibility, and accountability, in juxtaposition with those that emphasize community, such as interdependence, cooperation, and collective responsibility and accountability.

A useful way to think about family and community contexts is the extent to which they provide *social capital* conducive to caring (Benson, 2006; Putnam, 2015). We think of social capital as resources for caring that reside in the presence and particular qualities of social relationships. In families, these resources can include the strength of love, attachment, and familial values. They can include understanding of children and their development, as well as their needs, interests, and situations. They also can include values and competencies of parenting. Parents' and caregivers' own experiences of caring may influence their capacity and approach to caring for their children. So too may the presence of supports and stresses on parents, caregivers, and families, including but not limited to financial and employment situations; educational, mental, and physical health issues; housing and food stability; networks of friends and extended family members; and community resources that constitute a broader system of social and emotional resources.

In communities, resources for caring include community values and orientations toward families and toward children and youth and their development. They also include social-emotional support from peers and from nonparent adults, such as relatives, family friends, and neighbors. Last but not least are the prospects for caring and support that come through community organizations and services. These include civic organizations, recreational and youth development programs, health care and social-support services, religious congregations, businesses, and local government. Economic and political forces, crime and violence, and population instability can mitigate the impact of these community resources.

Cautionary Notes: Problems and Pitfalls of Caring

Caring does not always function in a straightforward or positive manner, even when it is enacted with the best intentions. Boundaries must be negotiated. Relationships need to be monitored and managed. It is difficult to strike the appropriate point between professional underattachment and caring too little and overattachment and caring too much (Kroth & Keeler, 2009). According to Murphy (2016a), caring can cause embarrassment and make persons feel vulnerable. If not careful, caring can evoke a sense of obligation and reciprocity that is inappropriate or impossible to fulfill. Caring can reinforce asymmetries in power relationships. And caring can lead to objectification—people can be seen as inanimate problems to solve and relationships can become contrived. Caring is fraught with hazard, and missteps can occur.

Acting on particular virtues can create dilemmas as one virtue may bump up against another. Every dilemma presents choices to be managed. Education researcher Ernestine Enomoto (1997) illustrates this point when examining the dilemmas endemic to student attendance and truancy. School leaders must consider "the rules" and weigh actions that try to balance collective fairness and justice with an understanding of and concern for individual students and their problems, needs, and situations. The dilemma is this: To address a problem of truancy in a manner that is equally fair and just for all, principals may fail to support and address the unique and often heartbreaking needs of individual students. Likewise, to address the problem of truancy considering only the individual student's unique situation may violate an ethic of fairness that is defined in the setting as equal treatment of all.

Some virtues that drive caring can present benefits and unexpected problems at the same time. Empathy, the ability to share the feelings of others, is one such virtue. According to psychologist Paul Bloom (2018), empathy can be a positive force on how we act and interact with others by making it possible to resonate with their positive and negative feelings. Research has found that teacher empathy, coupled with warmth and encouragement of learning, is strongly associated with positive affective, behavioral, and cognitive student outcomes (Roorda et al., 2011). At the same time, Bloom argues, empathy can be superficial and biased. It can pose a cognitive trap by which presumptions and predilections can be reinforced to the detriment of another person. Empathy is usually aroused through vivid, concrete instances of individuals or small numbers of persons. It is less often aroused when large numbers of people are concerned, even though their needs and problems may be similar to those of individual cases. When large numbers of persons are concerned, empathy may not be a strong enough impetus for caring.

According to neuroscientists Tania Singer and Olga Klimecki (2014), empathy can lead the one caring in conflicting directions. Through empathy, we feel happy when we vicariously share the joys of others. We feel pain when we share the suffering of others. Shared happiness can be pleasant, but shared feelings of pain and suffering can be difficult, sometimes leading to stress and distress, which then can lead to negative feelings, withdrawal, antisocial behavior, and burnout. These negative outcomes can be problematic for human service professionals who address acute and persistent human need, making it difficult to be engaged and be caring. To guard against this prospect, Singer and Klimecki, as well as Bloom (2018), argue for linking empathy with compassion, another virtue underlying caring. Compassion consists of feelings of warmth, concern and care for another, and motivation to improve the other's well-being. Compassion directs empathic thinking in positive directions and helps avoid empathy's pitfalls and problems.

These examples only begin to reveal the complexities of caring and how it functions. They can, however, help us understand how caring can lead to unintended and potentially harmful consequences (Lilius et al., 2008; Swain & French, 1998). As mentioned earlier, caring can be extremely demanding and it can be psychologically, emotionally, and physically stressful (Frost, 2003). For persons in human service professions, caring and caregiving may lead to low life satisfaction and negative affect (Savage & Bailey, 2004) or stress, worry and depression, poor physical health, and burnout (Kroth & Keeler, 2009). Caring can result in *compassion fatigue*, the emotional overload that occurs when one gets overinvolved emotionally, overextends oneself, and feels overwhelmed by the emotional demands imposed by others (Boyatzis et al., 2006; Kinnick, Krugman, & Cameron, 1996). These problems are common concerns in professions that require constant work on behalf of others, where need is acute, and where environments are not conducive to caring (Brechin, 1998b). When associated with historically female-gendered professions, such as teaching, caring often becomes socially, organizationally, and politically marginalized work, placing undue burden on women (Finch, 1984; S. Gordon, 1996).

Finally, caring can spawn unintended harmful consequences for the ones cared for (Peterson, 1994; Swain & French, 1998). Caring relationships can develop inappropriate dependencies, codependencies, and transference. They can result in unwarranted control, subjugation, and infringement of privacy, autonomy, and rights. In the worst instance, the interpersonal closeness of caring can create opportunities for abuse and victimization. Without careful attention, without mindfulness and self-regulation, and without the monitoring and watchful support of others, the risk of negative consequences can emerge.

Questions for Reflection and Discussion

1. In what ways does the case for caring play out in your school? Can you think of examples of how your school may not be as caring as generally assumed? Can you think of examples of "headwinds" in your school and community that make caring difficult?

(Continued)

(Continued)

2. Can you think of how the actions and interactions that you consider caring reflect the three key elements of caring: aims, virtues and mindsets, and competencies? Can you give examples of your actions and interactions that, while emerging from caring intentions, "miss the mark" because of the absence of any of these three elements?

3. How do the organizational conditions of your school support and impede the development of caring relationships with students? How might the attitudes and expectations of parents and the policies of your school district support or impede the development of these relationships?

4. Think of three ways in which actions and interactions intended to be caring can go awry. Looking back to the key elements of caring— aims, virtues and mindsets, and competencies—think about how these examples of missteps and mistakes might be avoided.

A MODEL OF CARING SCHOOL LEADERSHIP

In this chapter, we apply our discussion of caring in Chapter 1 to school leadership. First, we define what we mean by *caring school leadership*. Then, we present a model that arrays foundational elements of caring school leadership with three arenas of its practice and outcomes for students. Then, we discuss several considerations for the practice of caring school leadership. We conclude by examining how caring school leadership is important to promoting educational equity and opportunity in today's schools.

Defining Caring School Leadership

We define caring school leadership as leadership that is itself caring, as we have described caring in Chapter 1. Caring school leadership proceeds from the aims of caring, positive virtues and mindsets related to caring, and competencies for the expression of caring in actions and interactions. Its practice may vary depending on the people involved, the organizational context of a school, and the dynamics of environments surrounding a school. Caring is not a specific domain of leadership, nor is it a discrete set of leadership strategies. It is a quality or property of leadership generally.

School leaders certainly care deeply and passionately *about* many things—children's learning, development, and success in school being paramount (Pellicer, 2008). Caring about children and their success is good but insufficient. We can care strongly about important things but act in ways that do not measure up. School leaders must go farther and be caring in their actions and interactions regarding that which they care about.

As a quality of relationship, as a quality of action and interaction, caring can infuse almost everything that a school leader says and does. Caring can cross the span of school leadership work. It applies to monitoring the halls between classes, working with a teacher and a student who seem locked in conflict, and organizing a routine staff meeting. Any aspect of leadership work can be caring, noncaring, or even uncaring. What matters is that a school leader brings the aims, virtues, and mindsets to life through competent action and interaction. As organization and management scholars Peter Frost, Jane Dutton, Monica Worline, and Annette Wilson (2000) remind us, care and compassion are not antithetical to or outside of normal work: "They are a natural and living representation of people's humanity in the workplace" (p. 25).

The relational aspects of leadership lie at the center of caring school leadership. Studies of how principals spend their time show that much of their work involves talk and interaction through interpersonal relationships that they form with teachers, students, and parents (e.g., Gronn, 1983; Spillane & Hunt, 2010). Yet, caring leadership is not confined to direct, daily interpersonal work. It can be infused in developing and promoting a school's mission, vision, and core values. It can be integrated into developing expectations for teaching and student learning. We can imagine caring at the heart of developing and implementing academic programs, of instructional leadership, of providing services for particular groups of students, and of allocating resources to support teaching and learning. We can imagine caring in academic demand and support, in testing and accountability, in student discipline, and in administrative decision making. We can imagine caring in designing and implementing programs of outreach to families and the school's community. And we can see caring school leaders' efforts to promote caring among others, to develop caring as a quality of the school as a community itself, and to encourage caring in the broader environment in which students learn and grow.

The aims and positive virtues and mindsets of caring often draw leaders toward practices that serve, empower, and enable others and that are compassionate, accepting, healing, and forgiving (Caldwell & Dixon, 2010; Dutton, Worhne, Frost, & Lilius, 2006). Caring leadership can elevate student and teacher participation in decision making, for example, from a method of task completion and problem solving to a way of working that reflects an understanding of and respect for others; addresses others' needs, interests, and concerns; and promotes others' success and well-being. Through caring school leadership, participation can become a practice that holds prospect for developing and promoting caring among others.

A Model

Following our discussion of caring in Chapter 1, we present a model of caring school leadership in Figure 2.1. This model contains three major components: (1) foundational elements for caring leadership, (2) arenas of caring school leadership practice, and (3) student outcomes. Reflecting our exploration

Figure 2.1 • A Model of Caring School Leadership

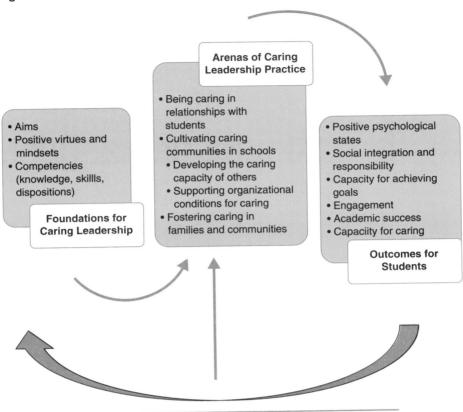

Arenas of Caring Leadership Practice

- Being caring in relationships with students
- Cultivating caring communities in schools
- Developing the caring capacity of others
- Supporting organizational conditions for caring
- Fostering caring in families and communities

Foundations for Caring Leadership

- Aims
- Positive virtues and mindsets
- Competencies (knowledge, skillls, dispositions)

Outcomes for Students

- Positive psychological states
- Social integration and responsibility
- Capacity for achieving goals
- Engagement
- Academic success
- Capaciity for caring

Source: Adapted from Smylie, Murphy, and Louis (2016).

of how caring functions, our model traces with arrows relationships among these components and how each relates to others.

Our model focuses particularly on principals, although we believe that it can apply with adaptation to any person—administrator or teacher—who may engage in leadership work in a school or a subunit of a school, including assistant principals, department chairs, and teacher leaders. We believe that it can also apply to administrative leaders at the district and subdistrict levels. We do not focus on every aspect of school leadership or how the totality of school leadership work might be performed in caring manner. Rather, we focus on three key arenas of practice particularly associated with caring for students. We focus on students because their learning and development, their academic success, and their overall well-being are the primary responsibility of school leadership.

In chapters to come, we briefly discuss caring leadership with regard to teachers and staff members and with regard to parents, caregivers, and families. We consider such caring with regard to developing broader systems of caring for students. For example, we discuss principal caring of teachers in the context of helping teachers be caring of students. And we discuss principal caring of parents in the context of helping them become engaged in school and be more caring and supportive of their children at home. Accordingly, the model does not depict how caring school leadership relates directly to the care and support of teachers, parents, and families (though they are very important in their own right). However, we believe that the principles and practices of caring that the model embodies apply.

Foundations for Caring Leadership

The model shows caring school leadership proceeding from three foundational elements: (1) the aims of caring, (2) positive virtues and mindsets, and (3) competencies of caring. What follows is a review of our discussion of each element from Chapter 1:

- Caring aims to promote the functioning, success, and general well-being of others, including addressing particular needs of others and promoting their interests and projects. It aims to help others grow and develop in their own right. Caring can seek to provide particular tangible and instrumental supports, help, and services to others, and aim to promote further caring.

- Positive virtues include compassion, empathy, kindness, fairness and justice, authenticity, humility, honesty, patience and gentleness, trustworthiness, and respect, among others. Positive mindsets include attentiveness to others and motivational orientation toward others' success and well-being. Personal and professional identities related to caring and playfulness are also among the mindsets related to caring action and interaction.

- Competencies for caring include a wide range of knowledge and skills related to, among other things, being caring in interpersonal relationships, knowing oneself and others authentically, communicating, and developing, selecting, and enacting strategies to achieve the aims of caring.

Our model indicates that the presence and strength of these elements will enable and shape the character and impact of caring leadership practice.

Arenas of Practice

At the center of our model lie three arenas of practice particularly associated with caring for students. The first arena involves school leader caring in interpersonal relationships with students, which we argue is a foundation for the other arenas of caring leadership practice. The second arena, cultivating schools as caring communities for students, involves developing the capacity and context for caring within the school. It involves developing caring learning environments in classrooms, and in student–teacher and student–peer relationships. And it involves developing organizational conditions that support the development and enactment of caring throughout the school. The third arena of caring school leadership practice focuses on fostering caring for students beyond the school, first with regard to families and then with regard to the community at large. Bridging the gaps between schools and families and communities is a crucial part of school leaders' work for which many leaders feel ill-prepared (Auerbach, 2010). It is work to which most principals devote little time. Nevertheless, school leaders can play an important role in developing the broader systems of caring that students experience and that contribute to their growth, success, and well-being.

In the lived work of school leaders, these arenas of practice are often intertwined, but our model does not presume that they are. In other words, a school leader may be particularly attentive to interpersonal caring with students but not to developing the school as a caring community—or vice versa. A leader may be strong in working outside the school with civic leaders and community organizations on behalf of students and their families but weak in interpersonal caring of students and developing caring within the school. Our model also allows for the possibility of one arena of caring school leadership practice compensating for another. For example, in one large vocational high school with which we worked, the principal could not have formed deep caring interpersonal relationships with more than a fraction of the nearly nine hundred students in the building. But he promoted caring throughout the school by modeling caring behavior in the lunchroom, making drop-in visits to classrooms, and frequenting public areas around the school. With several teacher leaders, he initiated a program in which families of new students were visited at home by a staff member during the summer before the first day of school. Teachers paid close attention and understood the principal's expectations for them to be caring in their relationships with students.

We would expect principals to act in caring ways and provide caring support to students with whom they are able to form trusting interpersonal relationships. At the same time, to ensure that every student receives caring support, principals can promote teacher and staff caring so that each student experiences caring relationships with a number of adults in the school. In this arena of practice and in fostering caring in families and in community, principals need not take on all the work themselves. It is not necessarily a workload issue. Principals will be much more effective if they develop the capacity of others, work in partnership with others, and guide and support others to "step up" and be better at caring.

Student Outcomes

The right side of our model shows the student outcomes that we expect from caring school leadership. Among the many outcomes we discussed in Chapter 1, the model lists several important to students, represented in categories: positive psychological states, social integration and responsibility, capacity for achieving goals, engagement, academic success, and capacity for caring. The model indicates that the stronger the practice of caring school leadership—that is, the stronger the caring in school leaders' relationships with students, the more successful the efforts to cultivate schools as caring communities, and the more effective school leaders are in fostering caring beyond the school in families and community—the more likely caring's benefits to students will accrue. We recall that students benefit most when the totality of caring they experience is strong and positive.

Dynamic Nature of Caring School Leadership

The major parts of the model are laid out in linear order, indicating with "one-way arrows" that the foundational elements of caring shape caring leadership practice, which, in turn, promotes student outcomes. The model indicates with "feedback arrows" that student outcomes can shape the nature of caring leadership practice and the antecedent elements of caring. For example, students' responses to positive experiences of caring leadership will motivate leaders to continue those practices. Similarly, when students ignore or resist particular actions or interactions intended as caring, attentive leaders may seek more information, reflect, and alter what they are doing. By closely attending to students' responses, school leaders may recognize the need to develop new knowledge and skills or may need to work harder and smarter to manage dilemmas that arise, for instance, when acting upon particular virtues. Moreover, the model's components are more interactive and mutually influential than the one-way arrows suggest. While it does not depict them, our model recognizes the importance of dynamic and interrelated interpersonal, organizational, and extraorganizational contexts that may enable or impede caring. Indeed, the importance of these contexts and the importance of developing and managing them is emphasized by our focus on the three arenas of caring leadership practice.

Finally, we recognize that there may be important differences between the model's application to a caring leader's relationship with an individual student and its application to a leader's relationship with a whole student body, with adults in the school, or with families and communities. We also recognize there may be differences between the caring of an individual school leader and the caring that emanates from a school's culture. The latter may hold additional meaning and exert greater influence than the sum of individual interpersonal caring relationships therein. Also, a view of general personal caring—the sort of caring in which we may engage as one human being with another—is not necessarily the same as professional or work-related caring. Certainly, personal caring is important in how adults and children act and interact in schools. But as we discussed in Chapter 1 and will discuss further subsequently, professional identities, norms, and competencies add value to caring school leadership, as well as set boundaries of its practice.

Considerations for the Practice of Caring Leadership

As we move from our model to examine the three arenas of caring leadership practice, we explore several important considerations. The first concerns how the practice of caring school leadership is framed and guided by the profession of school leadership. The second concerns for whom and for what school leaders should be caring. And the third concerns understanding caring school leadership as principled practice.

Framed by the Profession

Earlier, we made a distinction between personal caring as part of being human and caring as part of one's professional role and practice. The profession of school leadership defines the purpose, foci, and scope of caring school leadership work and pairs it with the substance of professional knowledge, orientations, and skills. The profession also defines critical boundaries that distinguish personal from professional caring and that distinguish caring school leadership from caring work in other human service professions.

The profession of ministry provides a useful analogy for school leadership and school leader caring. The work of imams, rabbis, priests, pastors, and other members of the clergy is defined by and carried out within different theological orientations and faith traditions, as well as by norms, role definitions, processes, and procedures of religious organization and polity. To varying degrees across faith traditions, much of ministerial work involves leadership in which pastoral care may play a significant role (Carroll, 2006; Willimon, 2002). A primary focus of ministry is on spiritual development and the cultivation and enactment of faith among individuals within a congregation and in the world. While it is often shared among clergy and congregants, ministry also includes congregational leadership.

The meaning of pastoral care hinges on the word *pastoral*, which defines its professional focus for caring (Clebsch & Jaekle, 1994). What is pastoral in the professional sense of the word involves an understanding and application of theology and faith traditions to individuals' and families' secular and spiritual conditions, joys, needs, and concerns. A professional meaning of pastoral sets boundaries for ministerial action and interaction within a religious tradition. For example, most religious traditions distinguish between providing spiritual guidance and making specific medical recommendations. Pastoral care often involves individual and family counseling, but professional boundaries remind clergy that they are not clinical therapists, that engaging in clinical therapy is beyond a minister's professional role and competence, and that crossing such boundaries may risk negative consequences for the persons cared for and for the minister.

Similarly, the value and parameters of caring school leadership can be charted by professional norms and expectations, as well as by role descriptions, rules, and procedures that define school leaders' work. School leadership focuses primarily on organizational leadership and management of schools to promote the learning, development, and well-being of students. As articulated in the Professional Standards for Educational Leaders (PSEL, npbea.org), the profession assigns school leaders responsibility for developing, advocating, and enacting a shared mission, vison, and set of core values of high-quality education for a school, acting ethically and according to professional norms, and striving for equity of educational opportunity and for culturally responsive practices. School leaders are to support intellectually rigorous and coherent systems of curriculum, instruction, and assessment and cultivate an inclusive, caring, and supportive school community. Moreover, school leaders are to develop the professional capacity and practice of school personnel and foster a professional community of teachers and staff, and they are to engage families and the community in meaningful, reciprocal, and mutually beneficial ways. Finally, school leaders are to manage school operations and resources and act as agents of continuous improvement. Each of these responsibilities is directed toward promoting each student's academic success and well-being.

PSEL articulates particular professional norms to guide the work of school leaders. These norms apply to leaders' personal conduct, relationships with others, decision making, stewardship of the school's resources, indeed all aspects of school leadership. School leaders should act according to the professional norms of integrity, fairness, transparency, trust, collaboration, perseverance, learning, and continuous improvement. They are to place children at the center of education and accept responsibility for each student's academic success and well-being. School leaders are to safeguard and promote the values of democracy, individual freedom and responsibility, equity, social justice, community, and diversity. They are to lead with interpersonal and communication skill, social-emotional intelligence and insight, and understanding of all students' and staff members' backgrounds and cultures. And school leaders are to provide moral direction for the school and promote ethical and professional behavior among faculty and staff.

These expressions of professional norms and responsibilities establish a framework within which caring school leadership neatly fits in the abstract and within which specific practices are enacted. They establish boundaries that focus the practice of caring school leadership, that direct it toward caring outcomes, and that keep it from straying into areas that provide little benefit or may pose harm.

The Subjects of Caring

Considering caring school leadership as professional work raises important questions about the subjects of caring, that is, for whom and for what should school leaders be caring. As an expression of professional norms and responsibilities, PSEL is clear that in all areas of their work, school leaders should care for and be caring of students, their academic success, and their overall well-being. This overarching expectation needs a bit of unpacking. Again, the profession of ministry provides a useful comparison.

Ministerial work focuses on caring for individuals, families, and groups and also on cultivating congregations as caring faith communities (DeMarinis, 1993; McClure, 2014). This includes developing the capacity of congregational members and lay leaders for caring. It can also involve *public ministry*, that is, ministry beyond the congregation, in, of, and for the public (McClure,

2014). Public ministry involves caring for and working to promote change in the broader community and in the social, political, and economic contexts that affect congregational members, others in the community, and particularly those who represent "the least of these": the poor and oppressed. It can also involve caring for the institution of the church, for its principles and precepts, and for the faith writ large.

Likewise, caring school leadership can have concurrent concern for individuals and groups, including students and student bodies, as well as teachers and professional staff. It centers on the school as an organization and how that organization supports a caring community for students, teachers, and staff. Caring school leadership can concern others outside of school who affect students' lives in school and in general. Most immediately, this includes caring for families and helping families be caring of students. Beyond caring for individuals and groups and for the school as an organization, caring school leadership can involve caring for the institution of schooling and for education in democratic society. Following the concept of public ministry, we can think of the professional work of caring school leadership as involving *public school leadership*, that is, school leadership in, of, and for the public. This extends school leader caring outside of the schoolhouse and beyond families to caring work in communities, advocacy on behalf of children and families, promoting conditions that support children, and improving conditions that impede their learning and development. To this, we add caring for the profession and its ability to serve children, families, and communities well.

The profession of school leadership—principal leadership, in particular— makes concern for the whole school a priority. This means that school leaders will continually need to manage tensions and dilemmas that arise among individual, group, and organizational caring (Fenstermacher & Amarel, 2013; Shapiro & Stefkovich, 2010). As we have suggested, there may be real limits of school leaders' ability to understand individuals deeply across the whole school organization and to be caring of them interpersonally. The principal of a high school or a large elementary school may be able to learn about and understand well some number of students in the school but may be unable to develop a similarly deep understanding of every student. Consider acting with regard to the entire student body, when such understanding of each individual is incomplete and imperfect. Consider also the tensions and dilemmas that may arise in caring for all at the school level when the needs and concerns of individuals and groups vary and perhaps conflict.

To these subjects of caring, we add the importance of caring for oneself and caring for the quality and effectiveness of one's professional relationships and work. This focus of caring is crucial in school leadership, as well as in other human service professions. We will explore the subject of self-care in Chapter 6.

Principled Practice

The enactment of caring school leadership is principled practice. By this, we mean three things. First, caring school leadership is propelled by principles of purpose and positive virtues and mindsets that orient the nature of one's relationships with others. These are principles that center leadership on meeting the needs and concerns of others, toward the betterment of others, and toward the fulfillment of others' human potential. In addition, caring school leadership is driven by principles of virtue: compassion, kindness, empathy and sympathy, humility, honesty, and trustworthiness, among others. Finally, it is driven by principled mindsets of motivational orientation, attentiveness, and playfulness, indeed, the principle of competent practice. Together, these principles form the foundation for caring school leadership. They are the bases of myriad concrete practices. Thus, in its enactment, caring school leadership is principled practice.

Caring school leadership is also principled practice as a moral and ethical endeavor that resides within the norms, expectations, and boundaries of profession. It also transcends the profession in certain ways. Caring school leadership evokes both general and professional orientations toward others as human beings and how we see ourselves in professional roles working on behalf of fellow human beings. We refer to principles of what it means to be human, to live in community, to be personally and professionally responsible for others and their well-being. These principles recognize both our independence from and our interdependence with others. They recognize that we cannot separate our personal happiness, success, and well-being from the happiness, success, and well-being of others. The poet Gwendolyn Brooks (1970) captures this in her ode to Paul Robeson: "We are each other's harvest, we are each other's business; we are each other's magnitude and bond." School leaders are guided and bounded by the purposes and parameters of the profession. But this does not make them any less human.

The third way to think about caring school leadership as principled practice follows from an understanding of the situational and dynamic nature of leadership. Situational perspectives, prominent in every school leadership textbook, emphasize that effective leadership requires fashioning specific actions and interactions to "fit" particular objectives, tasks, situations, persons, and contexts. Inasmuch as these conditions are continually changing, both in response to leadership and in response to other influences, leadership practice must also continually change. It is therefore very difficult, if not counterproductive, to consider leadership practice as a uniform set of discrete strategies or behaviors, as generally applicable scripts of actions and interactions. Leadership practices that are similarly effective in different situations and settings can look very different. Organization and leadership theorists emphasize that most goals may be reached through different strategies and behaviors, a principle that is called *equifinality* (Burke, 2018).

This perspective does not mean that effective leadership can be completely idiosyncratic. Instead, it recognizes the importance of thoughtfully and strategically aligning practices to situations and adapting those practices as situations change. Thoughtful and strategic alignment requires that particular principles guide action choices. Following situational and dynamic views of leadership, these principles include fit and flexibility. What also makes leadership principled practice is alignment with professional norms and expectations. And what makes caring leadership principled practice is consistency with the aims of caring, the virtues and mindsets that orient and drive the pursuit of those aims, and the principles of competency that translate intention into actions and outcomes.

When we discuss the practice of caring school leadership in the remainder of this book, we will introduce a number of specific suggestions to assist school leaders to make their practice caring. We will approach specific practices with broader principles in mind. We will not present the particulars as prescriptions. Instead, we will present them as examples of principled practice that make leadership caring.

Caring School Leadership and Educational Equity

We believe that caring leadership is an important means of promoting educational equity in schools. In Chapter 1, we pointed to a critical mass of research finding that low-income students and students of color benefit substantially from experiences of caring and the social and academic support that comes from it. When these students believe that their teachers and administrators know them and care about their success, when they believe that much is expected of them, when teachers and administrators work hard on their behalves, when they feel supported personally and academically, when they feel as if they are being heard and taken seriously, these students are more engaged in school and committed to learning. Moreover, they achieve at higher levels.

Equity does not appear as an explicit element in our model of caring school leadership because we see every aspect of the model contributing to it. To be genuinely caring of students, a school leader would be caring of each and every student, especially those students who have been marginalized, who struggle to fit in and achieve in school, who have not received support, and who have not been provided high-quality opportunities to learn. To be caring calls on school leaders to work on behalf of each student, address their needs and concerns, help them achieve their interests, move forward on their life projects, and promote their well-being and human potential.

To be caring is to be driven by virtues that require a leader to be empathetic and compassionate to each student, to be kind and fair, to be honest and authentic, to be patient, trustworthy, and respectful. To be caring demands that leaders be attentive and know and understand each student for who they are as individual learners and persons and as members of groups; of races, ethnicities, religions, and cultures; and of different socioeconomic situations, each with history and broader social and political dynamics. To be caring is to be motivated to support each and every student's success and well-being and to act in ways consistent with the knowledge and understanding derived from caring's attentiveness. The foundations of our model of caring leadership pull school leaders away from unproductive, deficit ways of thinking about some students and direct them toward more positive ways of thinking about and acting toward all students that are socially, racially, and culturally responsive and efficacious. In Chapter 1, we wrote that caring does not mean lowering expectations or demanding less. As Muhammad Khalifa (2018) argues in the context of culturally responsive school leadership: "Principals must both take the lead . . . [as] warm demanders and maintain relationships directly with students. These relationships will allow leaders to encourage students to succeed academically in ways that students will interpret through the lens of love and care" (p. 158).

Moreover, caring means that school leaders must be attentive to and address the large and small barriers that restrict opportunities to learn and constrain some students' success. The aims, virtues, motivational orientations, and authentic understanding of others that lie at the heart of caring are beacons for identifying programs, policies, and practices that disadvantage some students and for pursuing those that promote equity of educational opportunity. We will examine a number of such programs and practices in chapters to come. It is difficult to imagine any other path for leadership down which caring leads than toward equity of opportunity for every student. Moreover, it is difficult to imagine credible school leadership for educational equity that does not place caring at its core.

Questions for Reflection and Discussion

1. Test the argument that all aspects of school leadership can be viewed and enacted through a lens of caring for students. Try to think of three examples of what school leaders do that cannot be viewed and enacted through this lens.

2. Earlier in this chapter, we wrote that caring can be infused in the motivation and methods of developing and promoting a school's mission, vision, and core values. We also wrote that caring is integral to developing expectations for teaching and student learning. Think of at least three specific ways in which you could infuse caring into your school's core values and into written expectations for teaching and learning.

3. Consider how the profession of school leadership might increase the likelihood that caring in school leadership would contribute to positive student outcomes by focusing and limiting it.

4. Why is it important to think about caring school leadership in terms of guidelines and principles rather than discrete behaviors? Think of at least three reasons.

5. How can adopting an orientation of caring help one think differently about and pursue more effectively equity of educational opportunity in your school? Think about what might go unseen or become lost without an orientation toward caring.

BEING CARING IN RELATIONSHIPS WITH STUDENTS

This chapter focuses on the first arena of caring leadership practice in our model: being caring in relationships with students. We begin with this arena of practice because school leadership is at its heart relational. Leadership is often defined as a social-influence process to achieve collective purposes (Hoy & Miskel, 2012; Yukl, 2013). It is exercised through relationships (Donaldson, 2006). Leadership does not reside in the individual leader. It resides in and through interpersonal networks. Some argue that leadership is inextricably linked to followership, that the relationship between leaders and followers is what makes leadership possible (Heller & Van Til, 1983; Hollander, 1992). Leadership is conducted through actions and interactions with individuals and groups. The qualities of leader relationships, including their social-emotional dimensions, affect substantially what leaders are likely to accomplish (Goleman, Boyatzis, & McKee, 2013).

Most principals' work is conducted through actions and interactions with others. Gronn (1983) notably described "talk as the work" of school leaders. Principals interact with many people in the course of their work, from teachers to students to parents and caregivers, in brief unplanned encounters, as well as longer, planned activities. Only about 20 percent of principals' time is spent working alone, "behind the desk" (Spillane & Hunt, 2010). It is not surprising that principals emphasize the importance of cultivating good working relationships for their schools' success (Lortie, 2009).

A focus on principal–student relationships is important not only because of the interactive nature of principals' work. Relationships are important to all human service professions. As Kroth and Keeler (2009) put it, "At the heart of the work of those in the helping professions is a process of relationship that occurs time after time with numerous clients" (p. 509). Serving clients effectively depends on being in trusting, caring, and efficacious professional relationship with them. In schools, to perform the professional human service work of education effectively, it is incumbent on educators to forge positive connections with students, to know and understand them, and to serve them in ways that effectively promote their learning, development, and well-being. In other words, it is imperative to be in caring relationships with them.

We begin this chapter by examining several dynamics of relationships between principals and students. Then, we consider what makes these relationships caring, emphasizing what students say. Next, we examine four aspects of principal practice for being caring in relationships with students: (1) practices of presence, (2) practices of attentiveness and inquiry, (3) practices of effective interpersonal communication, and (4) practices of effective service, that is, acting productively on behalf of students.

Dynamics of Principal–Student Relationships

In the first two chapters of this book, we argued that caring in school leadership is grounded in and guided by the profession, its expectations for practice, its scope of work, and its norms and values. It follows that the relationships that principals forge with students—indeed, the relationships that principals forge with teachers and staff and parents and caregivers—also are grounded in and guided by the profession.

Professional Purposes and Parameters

Judith Deiro (2003) reminds us that "professionally appropriate" relationships between adults and students in schools are not the same as other types of relationships. She points to differences between *emotional-expressive relationships* and *influential relationships*. Emotional-expressive relationships encompass friendships and romantic relationships that are entered into largely for personal satisfaction or self-fulfillment. Student–educator relationships are different. Their function is to promote student learning, development, and well-being. Relationships are formed between principals and students for the purpose of affecting these outcomes.

Even as caring is rooted in basic expressions of humanness, even as it evokes emotional elements, and even as it may be personally satisfying and fulfilling, caring in professional relationships emanates from a sense of professional calling and is directed toward the accomplishment of professional objectives. Professional principal–student relationships may be friendly, but they are not friendships. Principals may perform functions associated with parenting and child-rearing—*in loco parentis*—but principals are not students' parents or caregivers. Principals' professional relationships with students may take them into areas concerning students' physical, psychological, and spiritual well-being, but principals are not physicians, social workers, clinical psychologists, or members of the clergy. A school leader's professional purposes and identity become the forge in which personal principal–student relationships form and function.

Asymmetries

Student–principal relationships, like student–teacher relationships, are asymmetrical in important ways. The student–principal relationship is an adult–child relationship. It is an educator–student, a professional–client relationship. More specifically, it is a principal–student relationship, which is likely to be different from a student–teacher relationship by virtue of the different functions associated with professional role.

In principal–student relationships, asymmetries exist with regard to cognitive, social, emotional, and moral development and maturity. They exist with regard to general and professional knowledge and life and professional experience. Also to be considered are social norms that establish the status and privilege of adults over children and the status and privilege of professional educators over students. These differences create distributions of power and influence that heavily favor the adult educator, the principal. Not only do we assume that principals are more *capable* than students of forging and managing appropriate and productive professional relationships, we also assume that principals bear the professional and ethical *responsibility* to forge and manage these relationships appropriately and to the benefit of students.

Professional Ethics

Professional purposes and parameters and the asymmetries of principal–student relationships bring to the fore ethical considerations of right and wrong. Principals bear the primary responsibility for identifying and maintaining appropriate relational boundaries. Ethical standards issued by the American Association of School Administrators (AASA), the National Association of Elementary School Principals (NAESP), and the National Association of Secondary School Principals (NASSP) each identify the education and well-being of students as the "fundamental value" of all decision-making and action. They charge school leaders with protecting the civil and human rights of all individuals, and here, we emphasize students. Moreover, they prohibit school leaders from using their positions for personal gain. The Professional Standards for Educational Leaders (PSEL) charge principals and other school leaders to act ethically and professionally in personal conduct and in relationships with others, place children at the center of education, and accept responsibility for each student's academic success and well-being.

While these standards and principles provide general guidance, the details may be difficult to identify and manage. While a romantic relationship between a principal and a student is clearly unethical and illegal, while socializing with students outside of school functions is inviting trouble, and while "friending" students on social media may be strongly ill-advised, many dimensions of student–principal relationships are fraught with ambiguity and uncertainty. They call for "Goldilocks," or "just-right," calculations. A relationship that creates emotional dependency on the part of a student may be unethical and educationally unwise (as the dependency of a principal on a student). Likewise, a relationship that creates a sense of obligation or an expectation of reciprocity on the part of a student, even though caring can be reciprocal amid the asymmetries between students and educators, also may be unethical and educationally unwise.

As Kroth and Keeler (2009) observe, professional relationships call for finding and managing appropriate balances. There is an appropriate and efficacious balance between professional attachment and underattachment. There are appropriate and efficacious balances between being dependent and being independent and between being dependent and dependable. There are calculations of revelation. A principal must decide how much to reveal of herself to be known to students both as an educator and as a person, to form a professional connection with students to achieve the aims of caring. A principal must decide how deeply to inquire, how far to go in prompting students to reveal themselves, and how far to go to learn about students' personal and family situations. A principal must consider what she should not know about a student.

The Big and Little

Caring can apply to all aspects of principals' relationships with students, the big and the little. This includes major decisions and pivotal actions and interactions. Equally important, this includes the small, routine aspects of relationships. Indeed, the everyday enactments of relationships nurture feelings of respect, trust, and dependability on which both parties draw in times of need, uncertainty, and conflict.

As former elementary school principal Joanne Rooney (2003) tells us, it is important to notice and attend to the "little things." She recounts "greeting students by name (and not confusing them with their brothers or sisters); accepting birthday cupcakes as though each was special; walking new students personally to classrooms; inquiring about the health of a . . . parent [or sibling]" (p. 76). Such small gestures can make big differences in forging caring relationships with students.

Persons in Context

In Chapters 1 and 2, we wrote about how caring in schools occurs in and is shaped by different contexts. We recall Noddings's (2013) observation that caring occurs within an interpersonal context. By this, she means the current and former characteristics of social relationships, relationships of which one may be a part and relationships among others that may be observed. The latter provide comparisons for one's own relationships. Noddings observes that past and current relationships form a foundation for caring relationships in the future. Relationships that are based on mutual acceptance, trust, and honesty and relationships that are deep, open, and revealing of self and one's vulnerabilities are particularly conducive to caring. Relationships of long duration, in which these qualities have time to emerge and relationships that consider the past and future in relation to the present are also conducive to caring.

Within these interpersonal contexts, principals and students can develop "hip-to-hip" relationships. They bring themselves—their persons. They bring age and generation, gender, race and culture, language, socioeconomic status, life experiences, and religious beliefs, among other things. They also bring personalities and likes and dislikes, as well as perceptions and values shaped by their backgrounds and experiences at home, in school, and in other settings. The backgrounds and experiences of school leaders and students function as lenses through which each will see, interpret, and act toward one another. As Tate and Dunklee (2005) remind us, "Everyone filters conversations through his or her own unique set of beliefs and experiences" (p. 7). The more sensitive principals are to these dynamics, the closer they will come to understanding the needs and motivations of students. And the better they will be able to form caring relationships with them.

Other aspects of interpersonal context are also critical. Principals are professionally responsible not only for individual students but for all students in their schools. This creates potential dilemmas in assessing and responding to students' varying needs and interests, and it poses problems of scale. Principals, especially principals of large schools, enter into interpersonal relationships with students that are governed by, among other things, decisions of how to allocate scarce time and attention. It is the same challenge that classroom teachers face but on a larger scale—how to divide time and attention among individual students and groups of students, acknowledging responsibility for each and for all at the same time.

Moreover, principals' work has been characterized by multiple, varied, and simultaneous responsibilities performed at a fast pace. Their work can be episodic, fragmented, and ambiguous and can involve competing demands from inside and outside the school. Tate and Dunklee (2005) describe the principal's work as "a tug-of-war between competing interests and multiple constituencies" (p. 57). Principals do spend long, focused periods of time on some aspects of their work, but their general responsibilities make it difficult to allocate the time and attention required to form deep interpersonal relationships that are conducive to caring, at least not with many people.

What Makes Student–Principal Relationships Caring?

Before we examine practices of caring in principals' relationships with students, we consider what makes student–principal relationships caring. We begin with what students tell us makes for caring in their schools. Then, we examine the confluence of students' perspectives and our own understanding about caring and caring school leadership.

What Students Say

When students are asked about whether their schools are caring, or if they feel cared for in their schools, they refer to their relationships with adults (Rooney, 2003). They speak of how those relationships make them feel and of the support that they receive. Students speak primarily of their teachers, those adults in school with whom they spend the most time and with whom they are likely to have the closest relationships. While they do not speak as frequently of principals and other school leaders, what is important to students in their relationships with teachers is also likely to be important in students' relationships with school leaders. Students distinguish between feeling "cared about" (feelings of concern that others hold for them) and feeling "cared for" (what others actually do to support them and provide for their needs) (Luttrell, 2013). While being cared about is important to them, students place greatest emphasis on being cared for.

Deiro (2003) highlights crucial elements of caring as defined by a third-grade student, who tells her, "A caring teacher is a teacher that is responsible and reliable and doesn't need to give candy or lemon drops or anything else. A caring teacher acts like we are older and more sensible and not just 8- or 9-year-olds. We are somebody" (p. 60).

This student and others who are noted in Deiro's essay see adults in their schools as caring when students feel respected for who they are and will be. Students feel cared for when adults act toward them in authoritative ways, that is, firmly and with dignity and respect. They don't think that "nicey-nice" is particularly caring. They do not see caring as necessarily associated with permissiveness, sweetness, or gentleness. Students can associate sternness and strictness with caring—what Antrop-Gonzalez and DeJesus (2006) call "hard caring" (p. 413) and Shouse (1996) calls "rugged care" (p. 48). They can also see caring even when adults seem somewhat detached and aloof. What matters, according to Deiro, is that teachers and other adults in school "must be respectful to be perceived as caring" (p. 62).

In their review of research on productive school cultures, Murphy and Torre (2014) identify a number of factors that students say make their schools caring. Students speak about adults—teachers and school leaders—being available to them, opening up as persons, and understanding students as students and as persons. Particular actions that students consider caring include challenging students to be actively involved in school, to achieve at high levels, and to attain personal goals. Other actions include showing concern, providing opportunities for student choice and control, acting fairly, showing respect, and valuing students.

According to Murphy and Torre (2014), students routinely associate caring with teachers who work to the best of their ability, who consistently bring their "A" games to the classroom, and who challenge students to do their best work. To challenge students in caring ways means setting clear, high, achievable expectations, including that students work actively to produce their own knowledge and understanding, not simply receive it from others. It means making classes engaging, relevant, and meaningful, and it means demonstrating palpable interest in whether students learn or not. It also means supporting students' active engagement in learning—no spectators are allowed. According to students, caring teachers are painstaking in their efforts to ensure that all students are nurtured along and successfully complete their learning journeys. Students see caring when teachers reveal themselves as persons, not solely as educators, including teachers' willingness to be vulnerable in front of their students. This helps students feel safe in sharing their own hopes, dreams, problems, and disappointments.

In the eyes of students, teachers and others are caring if they know students well and know what is unfolding in their lives. They are caring as they commit the time necessary for this understanding to form and grow. Students perceive caring when they feel that they are valued by adults and when they feel that others are taking interest and investing effort in them. Teachers are perceived as caring when they make themselves accessible to students and when they are willing to see things through the eyes of their students. Moreover, teachers and others are perceived as caring when they respect students and are trustworthy and fair to them.

Similarly, Kroth and Keeler (2009) write from their review of research that students define caring by adult behaviors that are helpful, are expressive of feelings, and build relationships. Students consider adults caring when they take time to explain things, express personal values, and show interest and concern. Students consider it caring when adults do not treat them as deficient or damaged but rather spend time with them, listen to them, and share thoughts, information, and feelings with them. Other expressions that students associate with caring include being fair, empathetic, and giving comfort and cheer. Students frequently mention love, kindness, and faithfulness as helping them feel personally understood and cared for. Kroth and Keeler point further to specific acts of support and assistance that students associate with caring. These include helping with classwork, valuing individuality, showing respect, being tolerant, explaining work, checking for understanding, encouraging, and planning enjoyable activities. Students also point to helping with personal problems, providing guidance, and "going the extra mile," such as staying after school to help students or talk about their problems.

Several recent studies provide detail about how students of color define caring. In Jeffery, Auger, and Pepperell's (2013) study, elementary school students said that teachers are caring if they attend to students' physical needs. This includes keeping them safe, making sure that they do not go hungry, and providing opportunities to play. Students also thought teachers are caring if they provide emotional support, connect on a personal level, and help them feel valued. Finally, teachers are considered caring when they provide "strategic assistance" by helping students with schoolwork and with personal issues.

The academically successful African American and Latino male high school and college graduates in Harper and his associates' (2014) study made similar observations. These former students recalled wide-ranging expressions of caring, each reflecting personalism, understanding, respect, and high expectations for academic success. Some examples include the following: A teacher introduced a student who aspired to be a physician to her own doctor. A student who ran away from an abusive father received support from a teacher at every juncture. A teacher permitted a sick student to nap at her desk during lunchtime and went to buy him hot chocolate from Dunkin' Donuts. A teacher provided tutoring from 9 a.m. to 9 p.m. on Saturdays for students who were at risk of failing algebra. A teacher visited a student's mother in the hospital after she had a stroke. Teachers calmed students before taking the SAT or Regents Examination, encouraged them not to give up when struggling academically or personally, offered students opportunities for extra credit to boost their grades, assisted them with college and scholarship applications, and gave students life-changing books to read.

Confluence With Our Analysis

What students say makes for caring in schools relates closely to our discussion of caring in Chapter 1 and to our model of caring school leadership in Chapter 2. Students see caring as a quality and function of relationships that they have with adults in school. They see it as the matter, manner, and motivation of adults' action and interaction. Students see adults as caring when they work on behalf of students, when they help students learn and succeed, and when they promote students' overall development and well-being. Students see adults as caring if adults are present, are attentive, and understand them. Students see adults as caring if adults act in ways that express empathy, compassion, kindness, trustworthiness, and respect for them as learners and as persons. Students also see adults as caring when adults not only hear but also listen, communicate well, and provide useful help and guidance. Students tell us that caring can be expressed in multiple ways, not through one set of behaviors.

Moreover, students tell us that they see caring related to the manner in which adults in schools fulfill their professional roles and responsibilities. They acknowledge, indirectly and implicitly, the asymmetry of the adult–child, or the educator–student, relationship. They also seem to recognize that caring relationships are defined by professional boundaries. While students might consider "friendliness" to be an indicator of caring on the part of a teacher or principal, nowhere in the literature do we find students referring to caring relationships with teachers and principals as friendships. One way to interpret this is that students consider their teachers and principals caring if they do their jobs well and in ways that students consider helpful and respectful. The elementary students in Luttrell's (2013) study considered principals caring if they were "good at [their] jobs," especially "getting special things for the school" and "taking care of students who have problems" (p. 299). Like Eugene Peterson (1994) argues with regard to the helping professions, "If we do not keep our assignment, we do not care" (p. 71).

We now examine four types of practices to promote caring in principals' relationships with students.

Practices of Presence

A common aphorism suggests that the first step to success is just showing up. Indeed, it is difficult to imagine principals being able to be caring in their relationships with students unless they show up in a personal way. Practices of presence are necessary first to form and then to nourish student–principal relationships. Both *physical presence* and what we call *mindful presence* are important and can be seen as acts of caring. We can imagine a principal being physically present in conversation with a student or a group of students, but her attention lies elsewhere. She hears but does not listen. Students will detect this lack of presence immediately. We can also imagine a principal thinking deeply and sincerely about a student or a group of students while sitting at his desk, caring much about the problems they are experiencing but failing to be physically present to convey his concern, to offer understanding, or to provide assistance. Without physical presence, the principal is unable to convey his caring, and students will likely remain unknowing and feel uncared for.

Physical Presence

In order for principals to lay a foundation for caring in their relationships with students, they must be physically present and visible to students in and around the school, even in the community where students reside. They must put themselves in the presence of students. They must make themselves known. They must show up at events that matter to students and to the school. They must put themselves in places that are important to students, be they halls and classrooms, the stage or athletic field, or the community.

We recall a leadership practice described years ago by business and management consultants Tom Peters and Nancy Austin (1985) as *management by walking around* (MBWA). This practice of presence calls on managers to get out of their offices and move around the workplace to be in touch and make connections with employees. The three major activities of MBWA are listening, teaching, and facilitating. Peters and Austin write that by engaging in these activities, managers develop firsthand knowledge of their workers, their interests, goals, needs, and perceptions. They develop firsthand knowledge of issues in the workplace and problems in conducting the work. In their book on strategic listening for school leaders, Tate and Dunklee (2005) consider MBWA a useful way for principals to make themselves present in their schools, to be seen and known by students, faculty, and staff alike. They observe that "as a principal, you never know what you'll discover as you roam around the school" (p. 6).

To be present, principals must make themselves available to students who seek them out. They must be accessible, both making time for students and being welcoming and approachable. Being mindful of professional boundaries, principals need to figure out effective ways to span distances that separate them from students, distances that are associated with the principal's professional roles and responsibilities, the principal's power and status, and the physical and symbolic barriers that school offices often erect. Being present does not only mean being available and accessible when students reach out. It also means taking initiative, reaching out to students. It means learning names and something personal about students. It means expressing personal and professional interest in what students are doing, what interests them, and their aspirations for the future. It means not allowing students to fall through the cracks or fail to reach school goals. It means asking questions, getting to know students as learners and as persons.

As we mentioned earlier, there are real limits to practices of physical presence for many principals. Principals cannot attend all student plays and musical performances, all athletic events (home and away!), all science fairs, all debate and robotic team competitions, or all spoken-word performances and poetry slams. Principals cannot be accessible all the time—there is too much other work. Yet principals can continually remind themselves that students are their first priority, that sometimes all else must wait while an important student need is addressed. Principals can establish and manage expectations for their availability. Often, a student need is immediate, and all else must wait. Otherwise, principals can be clear when they are available to students, what they are able to do for them, and when they may be able to do those things. Then principals must do as they say. Students and others should understand that school leaders may not be able to keep an "open door" or may not be able to drop what they are doing at a particular moment. Students should be able to count on their principals to keep their appointments, to respond to them according to set expectations, and to explain and apologize when interruptions caused by pressing matters cannot be handled by someone else. Dependability is a hallmark of presence and accessibility.

Mindful Presence

Principals also need to be mindfully present. This means keeping students foremost in thought and intention and directing everything a principal does toward student success and well-being. It means continually asking how decisions will affect students, both positively and perhaps negatively and not just students generally. Principals should think about how individual students and particular groups of students might be affected, as well as the student body as a whole.

Being mindfully present means being wholly attentive to students in moments of interaction. It means being attentive to students when they are physically absent. Noddings (2013) calls this mindful presence *engrossment*. She writes of engrossment as absorption and occupation in the one being cared for, in that person's needs and interests, and in that person's success and well-being. Noddings tells us that engrossment carries with it strong emotions. Yet emotional feeling does not completely define engrossment. When solving problems, an appropriate mode of mindful presence includes rationality and objectivity. Yet engrossment orients and moves rationality and objectivity toward the person cared for. It moves the principal's rationality and objectivity toward the student.

Practices of Attentiveness and Inquiry

Central to caring in general and caring in relationships with students is developing an authentic understanding of students as learners and as persons, and of students' needs, interests, joys, and concerns. To develop such understanding requires practices of attentiveness and inquiry. Attentiveness is more than observing and noticing, although these are important ways of attending. Attending involves more proactive and interactive practices of engaging with students. After we take a brief look at observing and noticing, we examine practices of strategic listening and humble inquiry.

Observing and Noticing

One way of being attentive to students is to observe them and notice things that are meaningful to them. *Student watching*, much like people watching, can be an important source of learning about them. It can be informative to watch students in activities in different places in the school—in classrooms, halls, the school cafeteria, and other public places. It can be informative watching them interact with adults and with their peers. It can be informative to watch students outside school in the community.

It is also important to take notice of students and let them know that they are noticed. Principals should make effort to learn students' names and learn something about them as learners and as persons. It is important to find out something meaningful and of value to a student and, when together or in passing, to acknowledge both the student and that which is meaningful. Even small gestures make students feel that they are noticed and are known. Principals can greet students by name. When they do not know their names, principals can offer a supportive comment that recognizes something they enjoy or value—a bright smile, the name of a college or a national park on a T-shirt, or a book or project being carried to class. Principals might recognize work that a student has been doing or a particular accomplishment. They might acknowledge a key event in the student's family. Noticing even the smallest things can be construed as caring.

The Practice of Strategic Listening

In their book *Strategic Listening for School Leaders*, Tate and Dunklee (2005) argue that in order to be effective, principals must be able to understand the concerns and interests of others. They propose a practice of *strategic listening* that goes beyond hearing to listening for understanding. Through listening strategically, principals are able to "understand the day-to-day experiences of . . . faculty, staff, students, and parents. Principals know what they worry about; what motivates them; what frustrates them; and what they think, feel, and need" (p. 5).

In order to listen strategically, principals must "sincerely want to listen . . . and attend to the emotions, needs, and concerns of those who are trying to communicate" (p. 5). They must listen to what students want to say, not what they want to hear. They need to see things through the eyes of students. Principals need to understand that words alone are not the complete message. According to Tate and Dunklee, "To understand another's feelings and sentiments, you need to find the context for them by looking for referents to the speaker's words in life events and social situations to understand the full meaning of those words" (p. 54).

Tate and Dunklee (2005) maintain that principals who engage in strategic listening effectively listen for more than information and knowledge. They listen respectfully to create shared meaning and shared understanding. They adapt to the communication styles of students and are mindful of how meaning may differ from student to student and situation to situation—indeed, how meaning may change for the same student from one situation to another. They recognize that points of view are usually related to "layers of past experiences, influences, and generalizations" (p. 9). By inquiring and reflecting effectively, principals are able to "dig deeply into the matters that concern [others] and create breakthroughs in [their] ability to solve problems." Moreover, "when you try to see the world through the eyes of [your students], [you] acknowledge the values of your [students'] perspective. This is a powerful act of respect and value" (p. 10)—and of caring.

Tate and Dunklee (2005) argue that strategic listening takes thought and effort and recommend that principals prepare themselves for listening. This means to open one's ears and mind when a speaker opens their mouth. It means being prepared and conjuring the willpower to bear a speaker's emotions, emotions that center on one's actions or inactions. Tate and Dunklee recommend adjusting to the particular listening situation. They point out that no two listening situations are exactly the same and that the environment, the speaker, and the message all change. They recommend being aware of the listener and the situation, and "play the reality" (p. 107). Finally, Tate and Dunklee recommend letting some intuition into the listening process. They caution not to prejudge what a student has to say, but at the same time, they encourage principals to make use of life and work experiences and their gut reactions. Intuition, or *smart guessing* as they call it (p. 107), can contribute to listening and making meaning.

To be an effective strategic listener, a principal should be aware of and combat defenses that can limit listening and understanding. One such defense is entering a conversation with a predisposition toward evaluation and judgment and, even worse, a negative mindset. A second defense is a predisposition toward the meaning of a conversation and what may be the best way to respond to it. A third defense is a stance of superiority, a sense that you as the listener, for whatever reason, possess superior knowledge, understanding, or insight. Last but as important, a disposition toward control can block effective listening. This reflects a need to influence and direct conversation toward a particular outcome. To this we would add the problem of always "going by the book," unthoughtfully applying rules and regulations.

Other, more supportive stances can enhance listening. These include adopting a nonjudgmental and problem-solving orientation, being supportive and empathetic of the speaker, and showing respect for what the speaker has to say. Strategic listening is enabled when the listener remains open to new ideas and accepts that their own ideas might need to be reconsidered. Finally, strategic listening is enabled when the listener listens to themself as well as to the speaker, attends to their own feelings, and recognizes that the sense they are making and the emotions being felt may be due to myriad factors including but extending beyond the speaker and what is being said. Effective strategic listeners also are attuned to sources of miscommunication and misunderstanding, which may be related to differences in generation and gender, language and culture, and religion. Race and socioeconomic status also can be sources of miscommunication and misunderstanding.

Tate and Dunklee (2005) propose seven basic principles for the practice of strategic listening. In addition, they offer specific suggestions about how to listen strategically to students. Together, these practices are summarized in Figure 3.1.

Figure 3.1 • Practices of Strategic Listening

Basic Principles

1. Give 100 percent of your attention to the speaker. Limit the amount of talking you do.

2. Use both verbal and nonverbal responses to demonstrate that the message has been received, understood, and has had an impact.

3. Pay attention to nonverbal signs of the speaker's inner feelings.

4. Consider the other person's views, concerns, or questions seriously. Recognize your own personal biases.

5. Recognize that there are cultural barriers to strategic listening that can lead to misunderstanding.

6. Read your audience and use this ability to form a constituent following.

7. Consider communication as a *people process*, not just a *language process*. Recognize that strategic listening is a relationship.

(Continued)

Figure 3.1 • (Continued)

> **Suggestions for Listening to Students**
>
> 1. Understand phases of human growth and development.
>
> 2. Keep up with current trends, fads, entertainment, language, and ways of thinking of childhood, adolescence, and young adulthood.
>
> 3. Be aware of students' relationships with peers, family, and others.
>
> 4. Be aware of and respond to students' physical and emotional needs.
>
> 5. Listen carefully and explore what students are thinking, how they make decisions, and how they reach conclusions.
>
> 6. Remember that younger children are just learning words and are constantly searching for the "right" ones. Be patient.
>
> 7. Recognize that students like to give advice and share opinions if they feel respected. Listening to them can help you see the school through their eyes.
>
> 8. Eliminate distractions in the environment around your conversations.
>
> 9. Be aware that children of all ages can be strongly affected by your tone of voice and nonverbal expressions. Manage them accordingly.

Tate and Dunklee (2005) remind principals that students may be hesitant to communicate openly with adults and with you as principal in particular. They remind principals that students are young people who exist in their own world and speak their own language: "If you're not tuned into their world, you may misunderstand or misinterpret what they're saying" (p. 59). This does not mean that a principal must adopt, like, or approve the perspectives, social behaviors, language, and tastes of students. Rather, it means that principals should be aware of and understand such things if they are to communicate effectively with students and understand them authentically. Principals need to be generationally and culturally competent. They need to understand the *law of importance*: What is important to students is what is most important (Murphy, 2016b).

Finally, Tate and Dunklee (2005) remind us of the relationship between strategic listening and trust. Trust is a critical antecedent to open and perhaps difficult conversations. It is important to making oneself vulnerable. Without trust, it is unlikely that students will share enough information for principals to develop full and authentic understanding of them or to help principals provide meaningful assistance and support. While trust is an important antecedent for strategic listening, strategic listening can be an instrument for building trust. How effectively a principal listens, coupled with the principal's demeanor and deportment, can communicate to students whether that principal is trustworthy. Trustworthiness is developed through accumulated impressions over time, impressions about whether what students say will be heard accurately, with respect and understanding, and will be responded to in meaningful manner. Principals who understand this can actively manage interactions toward trust, monitoring and adjusting the ways in which they listen and respond to what students have to say.

The Practice of Humble Inquiry

Another approach that principals can use to be attentive and to understand students is the practice of *humble inquiry*. Humble inquiry is an approach to interaction introduced by Edgar Schein (2013), who refers to it as "the gentle art of asking instead of telling." Schein defines humble inquiry as the process of "drawing someone out, of asking questions to which you do not already know the answer, of building a relationship based on curiosity and interest in the other person" (p. 2) and as a desire to be helpful.

Schein (2011) argues that assistance and support that are genuinely helpful depend on an authentic understanding of the person seeking or being offered help and a true understanding of that person's needs, problems, and concerns. Such understanding, in turn, depends on what is learned from inquiry that also seeks to build up the person's status and confidence; create a situation in which it is safe to reveal anxiety, information, and feelings; gather as much information as possible about the situation; and involve the person in the process of diagnosis and action planning (Schein, 2011, pp. 69–70). Such inquiry may be particularly important in developing understanding of others who are in different situations and of other cultures. Schein observes that abstract knowledge about others' situations and cultures is useful but insufficient compared with authentic understanding that can be derived from personal experience and inquiry. In short, what builds strong, positive relationships; what evokes useful knowledge and understanding; and what solves problems and moves things forward is "asking the right questions" (p. 4).

Key to the practice of humble inquiry is humility. Schein (2013) stresses *here-and-now humility*, which results from recognizing that from time to time, we depend on someone else to accomplish tasks to which we are committed. In order to be caring in relationships with students and to provide them help and assistance, principals are dependent on students to provide information about themselves; their interests, problems, needs, and concerns; and their situations. Principals are dependent on students to provide feedback, be it direct or indirect, about how they perceive and receive principals' actions and interactions as caring and helpful, information that could help principals discern whether to persist or adapt in more positive directions. These are things, among others, about which school leaders cannot know fully on their own or from other sources.

Coupled with attitudes of interest and curiosity, humility dictates the primary method of humble inquiry—the art of questioning. While humble inquiry is defined by questions, not every question establishes humble inquiry. Schein

(2013) contends that most people do not consider how questions should be asked in the course of daily life, in ordinary conversations, and in work. Few people consider complexities arising from asking questions across cultural and status boundaries, gender and generational lines, races and ethnicities, and various intersectionalities. Schein observes that few people distinguish questions of humble inquiry carefully enough from other forms of questions, such as leading questions, rhetorical questions, accusatory questions, embarrassing questions, or statements in the form of questions. These other questions can be deliberately provocative and function not to elicit information unknown to the questioner or to elicit authentic knowledge and understanding about the respondent. Instead, they have the effect of affirming the perspectives and advancing the status of the questioner, damaging trust, and doing little to develop the sort of knowledge and understanding conducive to caring. Instead, humble inquiry calls for questions that are open and evocative of what the other person truly wants to say and how the other person truly feels. Such questions do not presume a priori answers. As such, these questions communicate respect and value of the other person and what this person has to say. They make the questioner vulnerable to a response that is not presumed. In the process, trust is built, and as trust is built, relationship is built.

Schein (2013) offers several "lessons" for conducting humble inquiry drawn from specific situations, mostly involving managers and coworkers engaged in task-related matters. These lessons are readily applicable to principals and their relationships with students. Indeed, they are applicable to principals' relationships with teachers, other staff, and parents and caregivers. Some of these lessons are presented in Figure 3.2. To these lessons, we would add bringing an asset-based, positive mindset to the conversation—not a negative and deficit-based mindset.

Figure 3.2 • Lessons for Conducting Humble Inquiry

1. Humble inquiry is conveyed by a whole attitude, not just specific questions asked.

2. Questions often most important in establishing relationships are personal ones.

3. Accessing one's ignorance, allowing curiosity to lead, is often the best guide to what to ask about.

4. A timely open question, one that does not presume an a priori or a socially correct answer, is sometimes what is needed to open up a conversation.

5. Asking for examples is one of the most powerful ways of showing curiosity, interest, and concern and developing shared understanding.

6. Do not jump to conclusions or presume you know what the other person has to say. Keep asking open questions and asking for examples.

7. Resist the inclination to slip into telling. Resist shifting to leading or other assumptive questions.

8. Reflect on your role and status as the one asking questions and seeking information and understanding.

9. Consider carefully the kind of questions that would evoke the knowledge sought. Consider the medium and in what settings these questions should best be asked.

10. Where there is the choice between *you or me*, explore *us*, the relationship itself.

11. When too busy with one's own work but when one wants nevertheless to acknowledge and respect the other person, what often works well is a small gesture, perhaps seeking some initial information, validating the concern, affirming the relationship, inviting a follow-up, and taking a first step in joint problem solving.

Interpersonal Communication With Students

We turn now to examine practices of effective interpersonal communication. These practices go beyond strategic listening and humble inquiry and apply to student–principal interaction generally.

Educational administration researchers Wayne Hoy and Cecil Miskel (2012) observe that communication permeates every aspect of school life. They place interpersonal communication among many forms of formal and informal communication. Communication involves verbal elements of speech and writing, as well as nonverbal elements of body language, gestures, and touch. It also involves physical elements or artifacts with symbolic and other communicative value. Much of what we discuss below relates to spoken communication, as well as to written and electronic communication.

Hoy and Miskel (2012) identify three important areas of skills and practices for effective interpersonal communication. The first consists of ways to *send* messages in ways that make oneself understood by others. The second consists of ways to *listen* and understand others. The third consists of ways to convey *feedback* of recognition and effects of communication. Feedback is also part of *active listening*, which is the ability to reflect back to the speaker the content, feeling, and meaning of what is heard.

Sending Skills and Practices

Sending skills and practices concern relaying messages to make oneself understood by others. Hoy and Miskel (2012) identify five practices for sending messages effectively. We focus these practices on how principals might communicate effectively with students in spoken or written form and summarize them in Figure 3.3.

Figure 3.3 • Sending Practices for Communicating With Students

1. Use appropriate, direct language, avoiding jargon and complex concepts when simpler words will do.

2. Provide clear, organized, and complete information that helps promote understanding and shared meaning.

3. Minimize noise and interruptions from the physical and psychological environments of the conversation. Put away electronic devices.

4. Employ multiple media matched to situation and communication needs to increase the chances of being understood.

5. Use face-to-face communication and redundancy when communicating, especially complex or potentially ambiguous messages.

Listening Skills and Practices

Listening skills and practices focus on the ability to understand what others are saying. Particularly effective is active listening whereby the listener reflects back to the speaker what is heard. Such reflection relates to the content spoken, the meaning the content is to convey, and the feelings that surround the interaction. Much of what Hoy and Miskel (2012) include in practices of listening overlaps with practices of feedback, which we will discuss shortly. Moreover, these practices have much in common with aspects of strategic listening and humble inquiry. These practices are summarized in Figure 3.4.

Figure 3.4 • Listening Practices for Communicating With Students

1. Be attentive and focused, and concentrate on the student and what that student is saying.

2. Ask clarification, elaboration, and explanatory questions to listen and develop understanding.

3. Be encouraging of the student and their message, including the content, meanings, and feelings of the message.

4. Paraphrase and summarize what is being heard to focus listening, communicate to the student that they are being heard and understood, and create opportunities for the student to correct, clarify, or elaborate the message.

5. Reflect the feelings, emotions, and motivations that surround a particular communication to promote understanding of the whole message.

To these practices, we add that principals should bring a positive, asset-based perspective to listening. Focusing on critique, deficiencies, and problems can hurt productive communication. Principals should be alert to the effects of communication. After some time has passed, the principal should check with students to see if their conversations had any impact. Real-time reactions and effects should also be monitored.

Feedback Skills and Practices

The third category identified by Hoy and Miskel (2012) are skills and practices of feedback that convey understanding of messages and the effects of communication on the listener. Feedback can be sent verbally and nonverbally. It can be positive, neutral, or negative. Indeed, providing no explicit feedback is itself a form of feedback that may communicate lack of understanding or ambivalence about the speaker and the message.

Hoy and Miskel observe that we often seek feedback from those with whom we are speaking to gauge their attentiveness and understanding of what we are saying. We try to understand how our messages are being received and perhaps reasons why they are being received in particular manner. Ways to seek feedback from students include attending to their listening behaviors, inquiries, and responses. Their feedback can come through verbal and nonverbal signals. Seeking feedback can involve direct inquiry about how students perceive the principal as the speaker, the message, and the emotions and manner of conveying the message. Ask the student directly what they are hearing and sensing and what meaning the student makes of it. Principals can also gain feedback by monitoring the environment of their interactions with students, by observing students' peers and how they are responding. Observing how the behavior of other adults affects students also can be helpful.

In our discussion of listening, we mentioned several ways in which feedback can be given by a listener to a speaker, in particular by a principal to a student. These ways include questioning, encouraging, paraphrasing and summarizing, and reflecting feeling. Giving feedback to a student can include direct statements conveying understanding or lack of understanding of what the student is saying—"I'm not sure I understand what you mean." It can include observations about how an interaction makes one feel—"I'm so sorry to hear that this happened" or "I'm delighted by your news!"

Acting on Behalf of Students

The last area of practice we examine in this chapter concerns acting on behalf of students. Recalling the language of caring we explored in Chapter 1, this involves practices of care giving—that is, the actions school leaders might take to address students' interests, needs, joys, and concerns. These are actions to promote students' learning, development, and well-being, and they include practices of helping. Acting on behalf of students—giving of care—can be motivated by self-interests or by an intention to serve students' best interests. We understand that what we do to give care can be done in a caring or an uncaring manner. We know that because of inappropriate choices of action or poor enactment, even the most well-intended care may be not particularly beneficial and may even be harmful.

Guiding Principles

Earlier, we introduced several principles that concern how principals might act on behalf of students and do so in caring manner. We recall that caring in school leadership is a professional endeavor, one that is both guided and bounded by the norms, values, and roles of the profession. How principals act on behalf of students should be consistent with their roles and functions as school leaders. They should understand their professional value and their limitations and be willing and able to engage appropriate others to provide needed aid and support. We recall the importance of knowing and understanding the student from attentiveness, inquiry, and communication.

Also important is the complex but necessary ethical discernment of students' needs and interests, including the students' best interests. Crucial to acting on behalf of students is the principal's knowledge and understanding of appropriate and effective courses of action. To act effectively on behalf of students requires that principals have access to a repertoire of strategies that may be responsive to what they know about students, students' needs and interests, and students' situations. Principals should be able to assess and identify those most efficacious for the student and the situation, adapting them accordingly. Moreover, principals should have in mind a logic—a *theory of action*, in the words of Argyris and Schön (1974)—that can help them think through why a particular action might lead to a desirable outcome under particular circumstances. School leaders should be able to reason why they believe that acting in a particular way rather than another might help a student and promote that student's success and well-being. School leaders must also be concerned with the ethical dimensions of the actions they consider and take.

Being knowledgeable about different actions and their potential efficacy is necessary but insufficient to act on behalf of students. School leaders must also possess capabilities of enactment. That is, they must possess the knowledge and skills to put potentially efficacious strategies into action and to do so in a caring manner and in ways that achieve their intended effects. This is what Argyris and Schön (1974) refer to as *theory in action*. It is the need to act on behalf of students with procedural competence. This competence includes mindfulness of student reaction and response, as well as the ability to reflect, adapt, forego, or replace the action with a more well-received and effective one.

Discerning the Needs and Interests of Students

Related to practices of attentiveness and inquiry are practices to discern the needs and interests of students. Like developing authentic understanding of students as persons and learners, discernment of their needs and interests is complicated matter and involves skills of communication. It involves different sources of knowledge and continual calculation of factors, including ethical considerations when discerning students' best interests. It also involves critical self-reflection to distinguish what may be the true and best needs and interests of students rather than principals' own presumptions and self-interests. Such self-reflection can help principals understand that they can be empathetic and caring of students without personally approving what students' needs are or interests should be.

Sources of Information and Understanding

Students are vital sources of information. What they say through humble inquiry and strategic listening is crucial in principals' discernment. At the same time, it is important to recognize that students may not always have a full and accurate understanding of their own needs and interests. Nor might they be able to adequately distinguish wants from needs. And we cannot assume that students will always be forthcoming or able to communicate clearly their needs and interests, especially if trust is lacking.

While it is incumbent on principals to ask and listen to what students say about their needs and interests, principals can draw on other sources of information as well. Principals can reflect upon their direct experiences with and observations of particular students. They can seek information and insight from others who have knowledge of these students. Teachers, parents and caregivers, and even student peers can be useful sources. Students' school records also might provide useful information.

In addition, principals can draw on their knowledge of students generally and students who are similar to those individuals and groups who may be of current attention. From their experience working in schools, principals may have a general sense of students' needs, interests, problems, and concerns. Moreover, principals can draw on research and wisdom of the profession about students, their learning and development, the contexts in which they live and grow, and particular issues that they may confront. Principals can refer to professional literature, the practice-based insights of teachers and fellow school leaders, and conversations with students, parents, and caregivers. From such sources, principals may be able to flesh out and validate students' self-expressed needs and interests. They may be able to determine that those self-expressed needs and interests are not necessarily in students' best interests. In such situations, it is important for principals to help students understand why a particular self-expressed need or interest is not likely to be in their true interest.

It is important to recall that principals work within the boundaries of their profession. Their value to students comes from the professional roles, knowledge, and school leadership experience and perhaps classroom experience. Principals must understand that students' needs and interests may extend beyond the boundaries of the profession. They may extend beyond the ability of an individual principal or principals generally to understand adequately and to address effectively and ethically. Such recognition is an expression of professional humility. It is an act of caring to acknowledge one's personal and professional limitations, to seek the expertise and understanding of others, and to refer students to others who may be better able to care for and be caring of them. Of course, the principal should continually gather feedback to ensure that the student sees such interventions as helpful. Principals cannot just assume that they will be.

Discerning Best Interests

In caring, it is not enough to identify students' needs and interests. According to Jacqueline Stefkovich and Paul Begley (2007), scholars of ethics in leadership, it is incumbent upon school leaders to do their best to make decisions and take actions that genuinely reflect the true needs and best interests of students. They must do so without the guidance of a settled, shared meaning of *best interests*. Moreover, they must do so understanding that adults in schools possess a great deal of power in determining students' best interests and realizing that it is easy to ignore the voices of those who have the most at stake—students.

Stefkovich and Begley (2007) propose a framework that school leaders might use to discern the best interest of their students. This framework consists of three interrelated factors: (1) rights, (2) responsibilities, and (3) respect. *Rights* are moral or legal entitlements due to persons or groups, including universal human rights, rights of children, and basic legal rights, including freedom of religion and speech, privacy, due process, and freedom from unlawful discrimination. There are also rights to dignity and protection from humiliation. According to Stefkovich and Begley, the exercise of these rights is not unfettered. Conflicts can occur between two or more rights, as well as between individual and group rights. Therefore, when considering individual and group rights, school leaders must also consider a second factor, *responsibilities* toward the rights and interests of others and the community as a whole. The third factor, *respect,* recognizes the intrinsic importance and value of self and, accordingly, the intrinsic importance and value of others. Respect, considered this way, creates a path toward equity and tolerance and a commitment to finding common ground in discerning and acting to achieve best interests.

Stefkovich and Begley's (2007) model directs principals toward concurrent consideration of rights, responsibility, and respect in discerning the best interests of students. These factors should be considered a part of active inquiry into students' needs and interests and critical self-reflection to distinguish a leader's self-interests. They should be considered along with knowledge and understanding from multiple sources. Because there is no common definition or shared meaning of the *best interest of students*, there is also no hard-and-fast formula to reveal it. Our use of the word *discernment* is intentional to describe an inexact, dynamic process of comprehension and consideration.

Practices of Helping

In his book *Helping: How to Offer, Give, and Receive Help*, Schein (2011) examines helping, giving particular attention to it as an element of organizational leadership. Many of his insights and lessons are useful to principals when they take action on behalf of students.

Schein (2011) defines helping as an element of human relationship that "moves things forward" (p. ix). Help includes not only what we ask for but also the "spontaneous and generous behavior of others who recognize when we need help even if we have not asked for it" (p. 4). Helping occurs in and through relationships, and the provision and effects of helping depend on the type and dynamics of relationship. Like our earlier discussion of how the characteristics of interpersonal relationships create a context for caring, so too do such characteristics shape the provision, reception, and effects of help. Schein contends that we must be aware of relational dynamics in helping. He reminds us that helping, as with other aspects of relationships, occurs in the broader context of the "powerful rules" of cultural and social norms that govern relationships (p. 9).

Schein (2011) argues that helping is highly complex and complicated. Like caring generally, helping involves perceptions and attitudes, values and mindsets, and competency. According to Schein, it often goes wrong:

> As helpers we often feel that well-meaning help is refused or ignored. As [recipients of help] we often feel we do not get the help we need, we get the wrong kinds of help, we feel overhelped, or worst of all, we discover too late that we are not aware of some of the best help we got and then feel guilty. (p. 144)

Because of its complexities and because it often is difficult to help in ways that are actually helpful, Schein offers several lessons to increase the chances of successful helping. We present these lessons subsequently, adapting them to relate to the help that principals may provide students.

First, Schein observes that effective help occurs when both principal and student are ready. Simply put, for help to be helpful, the principal must be ready to help the student, and the student must be ready to receive it. By ready, Schein (2011) means that the person giving help—the principal—must be clear about their true intentions, must understand the needs and desires of the student to receive help, and must have a good sense of the form of help that might be helpful. The principal must consider all these things in relation to the *cultural rules* for helping that are associated with the profession, the school and its community, and social norms generally. The person to be helped—the student—can also try to be clear about their emotions and intentions about receiving help. The student, to the best of their ability, should be aware of the cultural rules for helping. It is unlikely that students, particularly young students, will be able to understand these things, so the duty of readiness falls primarily to the principal. The principal helps by readying the student to be able to receive help.

Schein tells us that effective help occurs when the helping relationship is perceived to be equitable. His idea of equity relates to our argument that despite asymmetries in their relationships, both principals and students can be helpful to and caring of one another, perhaps in different manner and proportion. In making help helpful in student–principal relationships, open two-way communication is important. Principals may need to ask students what they really want or need and what might be the best help to provide. Principals need to check from time to time whether students are getting the help they need. This is particularly important when helping involves others. Likewise, it can be useful for students to give principals feedback about what is and is not helpful and for principals to acknowledge the usefulness of this information. However, for students to provide honest feedback, they must trust that their principal will use sensitive information carefully and without judgment. If students are unable or unwilling to provide such feedback, principals might look for evidence elsewhere and then check in with the student.

Schein also tells us that effective help occurs when the helper—the principal—is in the proper helping role. Role here refers the form of help. The principal should never assume that a specific form of help is needed without checking first. Even if a student has asked for help or if the principal perceives a clear need, the principal should look carefully to see if that type of help is appropriate. In an ongoing helping situation, the principal should check periodically to ensure that the student still perceives the support as helpful. As situations change, the principal should be prepared to alter the type of help. Principals will need to be aware of the forms of help that appropriately fall within their professional role and those forms that fall beyond and might best be provided by others (e.g., a social worker, a clinical psychologist). Indeed, a critical type of help that principals can provide is to link students with other appropriate helpers, including teachers, professional staff at the school, parents and caregivers, and perhaps professionals in the broader community. To reiterate, principals should not simply "hand off" a student to another source of help and think that a one-time problem has been solved. Continual monitoring and engagement are necessary.

Moreover, Schein reminds us that everything said or done in a relationship is an "intervention" that shapes the future of the relationship. As helpers, principals should assess everything they say and do before and after the fact, not only for their direct impact on needs or problems but also for their potential impact on the student–principal relationship. In Schein's (2011) words, "No matter what you do or don't do, you are sending signals, you are intervening in the situation and therefore need to be mindful of that reality" (p. 151). Not providing enough help, overhelping, or helping in unproductive ways can have consequences for addressing the reason help is provided in the first place. These shortcomings also can affect the student–principal relationship, as can the manner of providing help. For example, a principal should avoid allowing conversations and solutions that proceed from a focus on deficiencies, defects, and problems. Such a focus will damage relationships and harm helping efforts.

To Schein, effective helping begins with pure or humble inquiry. Accordingly, the principal should reflect before deducing the need for help or responding when asked for help. The principal should ask open questions that characterize humble inquiry before deciding how to respond. No matter how familiar a request for help sounds, no matter how common a need for help appears, the principal should treat it as a new request never heard or seen before. This does not mean that prior knowledge and understanding of a student are irrelevant. It means that such prior knowledge and understanding, while potentially valuable, should be continually questioned and adjusted.

Schein reminds us that it is the one helped—the student—who owns the problem. This is not meant to be dismissive or to relieve a principal of the professional responsibility to provide help when asked by a student or when need surfaces. Instead, it is a reminder to the principal that it is ultimately the student who must determine what is helpful and what to do with the help. While a principal needs to see things through the eyes of the student, they can never fully understand a problem or need as the student understands it. Going beyond humble inquiry, principals may find it useful to involve students in designing or choosing among different forms of help, being careful to offer potentially effective alternatives neutrally. Steering students toward particular options becomes problematic when a principal acts out of self-interest, has a limited repertoire of insights, is an expert on the problem, or the need at hand and falls into what Schein calls a trap of *content seduction*. This trap is reflected in the adage "when your only tool is a hammer, everything looks like a nail." While principals' expertise is a relevant and important source for assessing students' needs, interests, and ways to address them, principals should resist reflexively framing students' problems and needs in terms of their own expertise, of seeing only through their own eyes. Principals should inquire and access their own shortcomings and ignorance to understand students' needs and interests and to assess helpful ways to address them.

Finally, Schein cautions that no one has all the answers. It is appropriate to close this section with Schein's own words on humbleness in helping:

> The older and more experienced I get, the more I leap to the conclusion that I know how to help. It is only when I slow down and pay attention that I realize how often the client or situation produces new dilemmas for which I am not prepared. Because I am in the helper role, it is very tempting to assume that my experience will provide a solution. I fall into the trap of believing that I am omniscient, and then I invent solutions because I feel it is expected. Yet that produces unhelpful help in almost every case. I have learned that sometimes the correct alternative is to "share the problem." (p. 156)

In humbleness, principals should feel no disgrace to admit when they are stuck and when they need help from others to be of genuine help to students. Principals should turn to teachers, to parents and caregivers, and to professional experts to share their problems of helping students and learn to be more helpful. Of course, principals should always turn to students themselves to address problems of helping and to become better helpers.

Bending the Rules

Sometimes, the actions that principals take on behalf of students, to promote students' best interests, rub up against policies and procedures of the district or the school itself. Principals may find themselves in gray areas or in direct conflict with a particular policy or procedure. They may face what community psychologist John Glidewell (1970) calls a *choice point*. That choice point may call on a principal to act in favor of the student and his best interests in "questionable interpretation" of policy and procedure or to act according to policy and procedure and not fully in the best interest of the student (e.g., assigning a district-mandated out-of-school suspension when the school believes that being out of school during the day might put the student in harm's way).

While we do not condone wanton disregard for or encourage violation of rules, policies, and procedures, we urge principals to consider, within the broader calculus of care, whether strict adherence to policies and rules enable or restrict their ability to act on behalf of students, to address their best interests, and to care for and be caring of them. We recognize the forces in schooling that push principals to make the safest choices possible, to protect themselves from criticism and from the ire of district office authorities. Some principals understand how to skate close to the edge, to work artfully at the boundaries of rules, policies, and procedures to serve individual students and their student bodies best. They choose to bend the rules to the student rather than bend the student to the rules.

Confronting such choice points takes principals to an important question posed by ethicist Thomas McCollough (1991): "What is my personal relation to what I know?" (p. 13). This question calls on persons to consider how they should think and act given knowledge they possess and knowledge that they can and should possess. Through practices of attentiveness and inquiry, through practices of discernment, principals come to know students as learners and as persons. They come to know students' situations and their needs and best interests. Principals know what it means to be caring and the value of caring. They know the relevant rules. They know that there may be consequences for their students and themselves for bending the rules. They know that to comply with the letter of policies and procedures that they may fail to work in the best interests of their students. What is a principal's relation to knowing these things when she must decide how to act on behalf of a student? What will she do with knowledge of these things? To be caring in relationships with students means that this question cannot be avoided. To avoid it is to answer it. To answer it by avoidance is not caring.

Questions for Reflection and Discussion

1. Think of the particular barriers that may make it difficult for you to form caring relationships with individual students in your school. How might these barriers be surmounted?

2. How present and accessible are you to students in your school? Look at the full schedule of your day. What messages might your presence and accessibility—or lack thereof—send to students? What specific steps might you take to become more present and accessible to your students?

3. Think about the ways in which you interact with students and with teachers, staff, and parents and caregivers in terms of Edgar Schein's distinction between *asking versus telling*. How might your assessment help you think about the idea of *humility* in your relationships with students and with others? Be specific.

4. How do you discern the *best interests* of the students in your school? The best interests of individual students and the student body as a whole? How do you manage instances when your assessments of individual students' best interests are inconsistent with your assessments of the best interests of the school as a whole or of district policies and rules? Think of specific examples from your work.

5. Imagine that, through practices of attentiveness and inquiry, you are able to develop deep and authentic knowledge and understanding of students, and imagine that this understanding tells you of need and concern that transcends the professional parameters of your role as principal. Think of specific examples from your experiences. What do you do with this?

Chapter 4

CULTIVATING SCHOOLS AS CARING COMMUNITIES

In this chapter, we examine the second arena of caring school leadership practice in our model—cultivating schools as caring communities for students. We begin by exploring the concept of *community* and the idea of the school as a *caring community*. We examine *cultivation* as a metaphor for leadership that is itself caring and that is well suited to developing schools as caring communities. By beginning with these images, we hope to evoke a sense of an ideal toward which principals might work. Following this opening discussion, we present an overview of different approaches for developing caring and community. From this presentation, we explore two foci of leadership practice: (1) developing capacity for caring community among teachers and students and (2) developing organizational conditions conducive to caring community.

Before we begin, a few observations are in order. First, there are many things that schools can do that help build caring community. Christopher Spence (2009), director of education for the Toronto District School Board, lists numerous examples, including spirit weeks, pep rallies, student buddy systems, peer-support networks, interschool athletic competitions, mixed sport teams, dances and other social events, mixed-grade homerooms, house leagues, and awards and recognition events. A group of principals and heads of independent schools with whom Murphy worked identified many things that they had put into place to create caring communities in their schools, including academic monitoring, support, and safety net programs; counseling, mentoring, and student advisory programs; programs of student recognition and encouragement; opportunities for student voice and participation in school decision making; and care teams for students and their families. While these and other programs and activities can make a difference, we believe that cultivating caring community depends fundamentally on concerted efforts to develop underlying knowledge, skills, and attitudes for caring and community. It furthermore involves systemically shaping organizational conditions to animate members' capacity for relationships that brings caring community to life.

Second, while we treat practices for developing capacity separately from practices for developing enabling organizational conditions, the two are intertwined. Efforts to develop capacity for caring and community will likely contribute to organizational conditions that support caring community. Likewise, efforts to develop organizational conditions to support caring community may also contribute to capacity for it.

Third, we argued in earlier chapters that caring school leadership is not defined by any one pathway or particular set of practices. Similarly, education scholar Thomas Sergiovanni (1994b) told us that there is "no recipe for building community. . . . There is no list available to follow, and there is no package for trainers to deliver" (p. 218). And Peter Block (2018), an expert on community, reminds us that community building is always "a custom job . . . born of local people, with unique gifts, deciding what to create together in this place" (p. 5). So we present approaches, programs, and practices and encourage you to examine them for relevance and usefulness. We encourage you to build your own *custom jobs* in a manner consistent with the principles of caring and community and according to the distinct approach to leadership suggested by the metaphor of cultivation.

Finally, while our attention is on principals, cultivating schools as caring communities should also involve students, teachers and staff, and parents and caregivers. We are particularly mindful of student voice and involvement. Students can bring valuable perspectives to the work of cultivation. Their engagement can motivate others and galvanize commitment. And it can contribute to students' learning, development, and sense of community citizenship. We are mindful of the importance of teacher involvement, not only for the ideas and insights they may bring but also for the commitment and accountability for action that engagement can promote. Parents and caregivers can also be vital partners, bringing ideas, commitment, and accountability to the endeavor.

It is difficult to imagine the committed engagement of teachers in cultivating caring communities for students if they do not feel part of the school and if they do not feel cared for themselves, especially by principals and other school leaders. It is important for principals and other school leaders to apply the caring principles and practices discussed in earlier chapters to their relationships with teachers and staff. It is important for principals to consider teachers as persons as well as professionals, to be caring and supportive of them in their personal and professional lives. It is important for principals to be trusting of teachers, to honor the professional autonomy and discretion required of them to do their work with students effectively. And it is important to provide teachers with what they need to do their work well. The essential point here is that principals need to be caring of teachers in the ways that they expect teachers to be caring of students. As we will discuss later, it is vital for principals to be caring of parents and caregivers and to engage them as full-fledged members of the school community. This may be particularly important for parents and caregivers who attended noncaring schools themselves.

The Meaning of Caring Community

In much of his writing on schools and school leadership, Sergiovanni (1994b) asserted that the idea of community is the best, most appropriate way to understand "what is true" about how schools should be organized and function, about what motivates teachers and students, and about what school leadership is and how it should be practiced (p. 217). Understanding schools as communities highlights their moral purposes and the fundamental relational nature of teaching and learning in ways that more conventional understandings of schools do not. Community is a compelling way to think about schools as caring places for students.

Most contemporary definitions of *community* proceed from psychologist Seymour Sarason's (1974) description of community as a sense of relatedness born of shared understanding and values. This sense comes from "an acknowledgement of interdependence with others, a willingness to maintain this interdependence by giving to or doing for others what one expects from them" (p. 157). In a strong community, Sarason maintains, this sense is a quality of social relationship strongly woven into the simple realities of everyday living.

Following this line of thinking, community psychologists David McMillan and David Chavis (1986) define community as "a feeling that members have of belonging, a feeling that members matter to one another and to the group, and a shared faith that members' needs will be met through their commitment to be together" (p. 9). McMillan (1996) later extended this definition to include emotional safety, intimacy, trust, mutual benefit, and transcendent values around which members bind and bond.

Similarly, sociologist Amitai Etzioni (1996) defines community as "a web of affect-laden relations among a group of individuals, relations that often crisscross and reinforce one another" and "that require a commitment to a set of shared values, norms, and meanings, and a shared history and identity" (p. 5). In community, Etzioni observes, is "a relatively high level of responsiveness to the 'true needs' of its members" (p. 5).

In education, the concept of community has been defined in similar ways. Sergiovanni (1996) wrote of it as a

> [collection] of individuals who are bonded together by natural will and who are together bound to a set of shared ideas and ideals. This

bonding and binding is tight enough to transform them from a collection of "I's" into a collective "we". As a "we", members are parts of a tightly knit web of meaningful relationships. This "we" usually shares a common place and over time comes to share community sentiments and traditions that are sustaining. (p. 48)

Other education scholars have defined community in schools according to particular ideas, ideals, values, and norms. For example, Beck and Foster (1999) observe that the word *community* is frequently associated with a strong sense of belonging experienced by students and adults. Community arises from a system of values that is commonly understood and shared by members of the school, a common agenda of activities that demarks membership, and relationships among members characterized by mutual care and support. Similarly, Murphy and Torre (2014) define community according to "a distinctive pattern of social relationships embodying an ethic of care" (p. 49).

We affirm these authors arguing that schools become communities when they are organized around a particular set of ideas and ideals, values and norms understood and shared by students, staff, and parents. Schools become communities when they engage members in common activities to achieve collective purposes, in particular, student learning and development, academic success, and well-being. Further, schools become communities as they support a system of strong, positive social relationships that meets members' needs, that fosters a sense of belonging and a sense of *we*, and that promotes shared responsibility for oneself, other members, and the community as a whole. Importantly, school communities become *caring* as they are grounded in and guided by caring as a way of being in communion.

The "sharedness" of community can imply exclusivity and homogeneity, an assumption of a *unitary we* that can be problematic. Community psychologist Esther Wiesenfeld (1996) challenges the assumption of a unitary we as a definitional quality of community. Like others, she views community as a group of people who share common features, including the specific environment in which they live, work, enjoy themselves, help each other, and meet the needs they encounter. The collective nature of community is built upon individual members' needs, their social relationships, networking, and the exchange of material, social, and emotional resources. However, Wiesenfeld argues,

> The "I" of that collectivism . . . is made up of many distinct identities. . . . Acknowledging that everyone possesses multiple identities allows one to recognize that belonging to a community is but one of an individual's many roles and that events occur in each of these roles, which affect one's emotional and physical conditions, social relationships, etc. Such events are what lead a person temporarily to set himself apart from the other members of the community. (p. 340)

Wiesenfeld maintains that belonging to and feeling part of a community should not conflict with other aspects of one's life. It is incumbent upon the community, in support of its members, to value and protect differences among members so long as those differences to not compromise the community as a whole. Such differences provide the community with a range of skills and resources while also creating the potential for tension and conflict among members. Community, then, becomes a totality that is "joined by common features" and, at the same time, embodies "the individual aspects of its members" (p. 341).

Sergiovanni (2000) addressed the *unitary we* in terms of forces that might suppress and exclude individuals, lead to "rigid centers that divide," and promote stifling "sameness" (p. 69). He argued that communities of "relationships, heart, and mind" need not and should not be built upon narrowly defined, all-encompassing rules but should rest on more broadly construed purposes, norms, and values. Sergiovanni advanced the idea of principled decentralization that would embrace different voices and interests as part of a "larger coalition built around common goals and ideas and bounded by a framework of mutual respect" (p. 70).

Sergiovanni (2000) evoked Etzioni's image of a mosaic to describe community characterized by principled decentralization. A community as a mosaic is composed of elements of different shapes and colors held together by a frame and glue. The mosaic symbolizes a community in which individuals and groups maintain their *cultural particulars* while they are also integral parts of an encompassing whole. Individuals and groups have commitments both to their uniqueness and to their communion. Community members have *layered loyalties* not simply to one's self and group but to the whole.

This image of community as mosaic is particularly compelling when considering schools as complex places, often serving diverse student populations and families and employing diverse teaching faculties and staff members. School community as mosaic encourages individual and group differences—racial, ethnic, cultural, gender, generation, language, religious, identity, and affiliation—to flourish, to be assets for the school community as a whole. At the same time, a frame of common purposes, norms, and values would bind these "pieces" together with the glue of strong, trusting social relationships, of which caring would be a defining element.

Leadership as Cultivation

As community is an effective way to think about schools as caring places for students, cultivation is an effective way to think about leadership by which caring community is developed and nurtured. Cultivation is a metaphor for leadership focused on growth and development. Leadership as cultivation recognizes school community for its dynamic, innately human, and relational qualities. It acknowledges that neither caring nor community can be commanded or willed into being.

Louis, Toole, and Hargreaves (1999) write that to cultivate is to teach and enable, to be a steward, a servant, a model, a friend, and an advocate. Cultivation, they continue, recognizes that growth is fed by arranging and rearranging its facilitating conditions and contexts. Education scholar Robert Starratt (2003) continues this line of thinking, arguing that school leadership as cultivation involves engaging the talents and interests of people in the school—students, faculty, and staff and parents and caregivers alike. It involves understanding their learning and development, their conditions and contexts, and their cultures, languages, traditions, and histories. It requires understanding things that can engage them with the school community. In these ways, cultivation as a metaphor for leadership embodies the matter, manner, and motivation of caring.

Cultivation recognizes that change in schools—in this case, growing caring community—is more than a technical process of initiation, implementation, adaptation, and institutionalization or of *plan-do-check-act*. It is a human enterprise of learning, growth, and development, a relational, psychological, and emotional process inevitably connected to aspirations, ambitions, interests, fears, and insecurities. Change—even change we say we desire—introduces uncertainty that can trouble us and unsettle our experiences and the meanings given to them. It can challenge long-standing social arrangements and interpersonal relationships. While technical processes remain important, to be caring in change leadership means to be aware of and attend to others' hopes and concerns, to understand and provide for the additional time and energy required for change, and to be mindful of unintended personal, interpersonal, and organizational consequences.

So what might leadership as cultivation look like, especially when directed toward developing schools as caring communities? What might principals do? To these questions we now turn our attention.

Approaches to Cultivating Caring and Community

Both educational and noneducation literatures point to ways of cultivating caring community. We begin with one general approach to community building and then examine three approaches to developing schools as communities. In each approach is a strong theme of caring and a range of leadership practices to promote it.

Structuring the Experience of Belonging

Margaret Wheatley (2002) and Peter Block (2018), community and organization development experts, argue that the way to develop community is to focus on creating relationships of belonging. Block refers to efforts to shape the form, purpose, and direction of a community as *structuring* while Wheatley calls on leaders to *host*, which is a particular approach to structuring. Both argue that the essential challenge for leadership is to transform the isolation and self-interest within a place into connectedness and caring for others and for the whole. Block writes that one thing that leaders can do is shift attention and orientation from the problems of community to the possibilities of community once developed. He and Wheatley make the argument that it is only when members are connected and care for one another's well-being and for the well-being of the whole that we can achieve collective, pro-social purposes.

Wheatley and Block point to a second task for leaders: to attend to and help others attend to the small but important ways of being together. Block (2018) writes that these ways become visible when everyone begins to notice "each invitation we make, each relationship we encounter, and each meeting we attend" (p. 10), while Wheatley (n.d.) notes that "when we begin listening to each other, and when we talk about things that matter to us, the world begins to change" (para. 14). Both agree that after all the thinking about mission, policy, strategy, and operations, the structure of belonging features engaging others in how we will be in relationship.

A third thing that leaders can do to promote community is create a productive mindset about the nature of connectedness among people. Such a mindset would draw attention to gifts individuals bring into relationships, the nature of associational life, and the ways in which change happens through language and conversation. It would also draw persons into a view of a community-based future.

From this, a fourth thing leaders can do is promote community-building conversations that "citizens" of community hold among themselves. In this regard, conversation refers to the ways in which people listen, speak, and communicate meaning to each other. Block (2018), for example, along with Schein (2010), points to how the symbolism of contexts, including the arrangement of physical spaces, allocations of time, and rules and procedures, can enter into conversation and "speak" as they evoke an organization's culture. Block calls on leaders to ask questions and direct dialog from problems to possibilities, from faults and fears to gifts, generosity, and abundance. He charges leaders with the responsibility of shifting the center of their organizations to associational life, reducing dependency on hierarchical rules and oversight, and moving toward mutual responsibility, accountability, and caring. He charges leaders with shifting the focus that might be on them to organizational members and the meaning and value of belonging. This, Block contends, advances the idea of organizational membership as citizenship, which further promotes community.

Promoting Positive Relationships

Educational researcher Gordon Donaldson (2006) speaks to the cultivation of caring community through his writing on building positive relationships in schools. He argues that it is crucial that leaders validate the importance of relationships in the work of schools and support their development. He argues that it is important for leaders to be present—"being there" face to face (p. 70)—and in their presence affirm those around them, promote openness and trust, and generate a sense of optimism about the future.

Donaldson (2006) argues that principals can foster positive relationships in schools in four ways. The first is promoting processes to bring people together. They can create opportunities for faculty and staff members to gather for positive purposes, for personal rejuvenation or professional development and problem solving. Staff members can be assigned to work groups and spaces to spur collaboration and teaming. Principals can schedule common planning time and foster mentoring and critical friend relationships. Meetings can be organized around discussions of issues and decision making rather than around reports and presentations designed simply to impart information. Sharing food—"breaking bread"—can bring people together, as can setting aside time for social interaction. Principals can create opportunities for students to gather with teachers and staff, as well as with peers, in ways that build relationships and community.

A second way that principals can foster positive relationships in schools is by honoring how students, teachers, and staff feel about their work and one another. They can recognize emotional and personal realities and can constantly reinforce the message that "we all count here" (Donaldson, 2006, p. 131). Principals can inquire about how people are feeling and can model empathy and compassion. In doing so, they acknowledge the psychological and emotional aspects of schooling, as well as the personhood of others beyond the roles they occupy. Elevating the affective and affirming persons beyond their roles builds a foundation for forging positive relationships.

A third way that principals can foster positive relationships in schools is to help others clarify their formal work roles and their role-based relationships with others. To help people understand their formal roles and relationships is to help them see interdependencies in their work, discover prospects of joint action, and allocate talents and energies to address collective opportunities and challenges. It also is to identify areas of ambiguity, points of conflict, and problems with power and influence that might inhibit positive relationships and restrict effort toward achieving collective purposes—and should be addressed accordingly.

Finally, Donaldson (2006) tells principals that they can promote positive relationships by helping groups develop their capacity to work together and avoid overextension, frustration, and potential failure. Principals can monitor groups' collective capacity to succeed at the challenges they take on. They can watch groups' energy and morale and can help them stretch without overreaching. Principals can honor real limits of groups and, in helping to manage their work, be caring of them and their members.

Administering Community

Beck and Foster (1999) contend that creating positive communities in schools requires that principals perform several functions they call the work of *administering community* (p. 351). First and foremost, principals need to rethink "deeply engrained administrative and organizational assumptions," reconsider their understanding of education's purposes, and redefine their roles accordingly (p. 351). They need to understand that many of the values that relate to caring and community are not reflected in the current structures and practices of schooling. Beck and Foster argue that "such *rethinking* must also be accompanied by *reacting*" (p. 351, italics in the original). This means that leaders need to retool organizational structures and practices in schools to promote caring, community, growth, and development.

Moreover, Beck and Foster (1999) call on principals to see their schools as social settings in which students, faculty and staff, and others develop intellectually but also morally, emotionally, socially, and physically. They call on school leaders to embrace the metaphor of the school as community. Accordingly, the prospects for cultivating schools as caring communities are enhanced when leaders think about their schools as social-moral contexts for learning, when their concern includes but extends beyond student academic success to the idea, the norms, and the commitments of the caring community that promote that success.

According to Beck and Foster (1999), principals need to recognize the importance of efficiency, impartiality, and equity in their schools but should not let rules and procedures replace commitments to caring and the well-being of individuals and the community. Making caring a guiding principle does not require principals to abandon rules and procedures. Instead, principals are challenged to set priorities so that commitment to people and values takes precedence over reflexive application of rules and procedures. The normative standard of care is to anchor the school community, guide the administration of justice, and provide for forgiveness and redemption (p. 353).

Beck and Foster (1999) also challenge principals to "work diligently and strategically" to foster organizational conditions conducive to caring community (p. 354). Principals should reform school structures to provide for the emergence and protection of community. Beck and Foster suggest creating more socially intimate settings—such as small schools, schools within schools, and school family groups—to provide opportunities for students, faculty, and staff to know each other well and form strong social bonds. They suggest keeping students and teachers together longer, for several years perhaps, and grouping students according to criteria other than age or perceived academic ability. Principals should also *reculture* their schools, shifting norms, assumptions, and beliefs toward those of community. This means replacing the language of individualism, efficiency, and impartiality with the language of compassion, humility, wisdom, and loyalty. This also means envisioning schools according to images of family, community, and congregation. Beck and Foster speak further about the importance of shifting the politics of schools from pursuing self- and group interests to fulfilling collective moral purposes. They suggest moving from adversarial to consensual politics, politics that employ power and influence to build community rather than create winners and losers.

Building Community in Schools

Sergiovanni wrote extensively about schools as communities and about leadership for building community in schools. Foundational to building community is the orientation of leadership itself. Sergiovanni (1994a) argued that to build community, school leadership must flow from shared norms and values, moral authority, and strong, trusting social relationships rather from a positional, role-based, bureaucratic, or personal orientation. The relationship of leadership to followership should be *covenential*, not contractual and transactional. By covenential, Sergiovanni (1992) referred to relationships based on "solemn and binding agreements between two or more parties that provide reciprocal rights, duties, and obligations on the one hand, and guidelines for action on the other" (p. 103). Covenential relationships define how one should live as an individual and as a member of a community.

Sergiovanni (1996) described leadership for building community in schools as ministerial. He considered the primary functions of principals to include purposing, building relationships and maintaining harmony, and institutionalizing values. Accordingly, leadership embodies a commitment to ad*minister* to the needs of the school by serving its purposes, serving those who struggle to embody these purposes, and acting as a guardian to protect the institutional integrity of the school as a caring community.

Continuing, Sergiovanni (1996) also saw leadership as pedagogical, according to its historical meaning. In the ancient Greek, *pedagogue* referred not to a teacher but to a watchful "guardian whose responsibility it was to lead the [child] to school" (p. 92). The pedagogue was an adult whose job it was to accompany the child, to be with the child, to care for the child. The pedagogue's job was to provide the child with protection, direction, and orientation. It was a role shared with parents and exercised in their absence. Sergiovanni argued that principals practice pedagogy by facilitating growth to adulthood and by ensuring that the interests of children are served well. A key part of such leadership is to mobilize people to face the problems children experience and address them. The pedagogy of principal leadership proceeds from the moral authority of community-oriented leadership, an authority that ensures that people fulfill their responsibilities for children, that they make good decisions on behalf of children, and that things work out well for children. Merging with the ministerial, principals practice pedagogical leadership when they engage in the tasks of purposing, when they act as stewards, and when they commit themselves to serving, caring for, and protecting the school, its purposes, and its students.

These orientations have important implications for principals' work. According to Sergiovanni (2000), they direct principals to develop shared understanding and commitment to ideas, ideals, virtues, and values around which teachers, staff, students, and parents and caregivers can form "tightly knit communities of mind and heart" (p. 70). They direct principals to foster a view of the school as a system of ideas, values, and relationships rather than a place of brick and mortar. They also call on principals to build and manage mosaics of varied commitments, layered loyalties, and nested communities.

These orientations also lead principals to examine how school structures, processes, and practices promote or suppress the shared values and strong social relationships of community. Like Donaldson and Beck and Foster, Sergiovanni (1996, 2000) pointed to the potential of small social settings and to keeping students and teachers together longer to build strong student–teacher and student–peer relationships and to promote learning. Sergiovanni (1994a) also argued that these orientations would move principals toward collective problem solving and decision making, which would foster mutual accountability and responsibility to the community. Moreover, Sergiovanni (1996) recommended that leaders shift the criteria for addressing conflict and discipline problems toward moral principles and the values of the school community. Resolution would be oriented toward inclusion and restoration of relationships rather than individual punishment and exclusion. Moreover, reward systems would include collective and intrinsic rewards consistent with the norms, values, and purposes of the school community.

Developing Capacity for Caring Community

We now turn to practices that principals can use to develop capacity for caring community among students, teachers, and staff. In the first part of our discussion, we focus on developing teacher and staff capacity through leader modeling, leader coaching, formal programs of professional development, and professional community. In the second part, we focus on developing student capacity for caring community through programs and practices related to academic instruction and classroom learning environments, social-emotional learning, positive conduct, conflict resolution, and school safety. We recognize that efforts to develop student capacity for caring community can also develop teacher and staff capacity, as teachers and staff members serve as instruments of student capacity development.

While our attention is on what principals do to develop capacity for caring community, we again recognize the power of student and teacher peer learning and development. In complex social settings like schools, capacity development is a systemic, interconnected process. The capacity of persons and groups can be shaped as much by aspects of the organization as by modeling, coaching, and professional development. We will note as we proceed opportunities for student peer and teacher peer capacity development and how developing aspects of school organization can contribute.

Because we cannot explore all relevant avenues of capacity development, we will not address how the broader range of human resource development practices might contribute. We refer to recruitment and hiring, assigning faculty and staff to students and work, supervision and evaluation, rewards and compensation, and retention. Such practices should not be overlooked in a comprehensive approach to capacity development for caring.

Developing the Capacity for Caring Community Among Teachers and Staff

Leader Modeling

Modeling is a potentially effective leadership practice for cultivating caring community. It can communicate and reinforce norms and values and strengthen social bonds around which caring school communities form and function. Leader modeling can contribute to developing capacity for caring among students, faculty, and staff. It can also help develop capacity for caring among parents and caregivers.

Principals are important models for faculty and staff by virtue of their roles and positional authority in schools. Indeed, principals' modeling is likely to be influential whether intended and purposeful or not and whether it attends to matters of caring and community or not. In fact, all that principals say and do—indeed, all that principals do not say and do not do—have potential to influence. And so, it is important that principals be mindful, if not strategically intentional, about their modeling influence.

Research demonstrates how important principal modeling can be for cultivating caring community in schools. Rutledge, Cohen-Vogel, Osborne-Lampkin, and Roberts's (2015) study of academically effective and socially supportive high schools shows that the visible presence and modeling behaviors of school administrators are crucial to developing strong personalized connections with students and a strong sense of caring community. "Leading by example" (p. 1078) is vital to students' sense of caring and support in their schools. In her review of research, Riehl (2000) also emphasizes principal modeling in creating schools that are inclusive and supportive of all students.

The literature on organizational leadership considers modeling to be "an essential leader behavior" (Brown, Treviño, & Harrison, 2005, p. 119). Leader modeling can influence pro-social behavior positively or negatively, and it can facilitate ethical behavior (Brown et al., 2005; Brown & Treviño, 2014). Leader modeling can affect organizational citizenship behavior—that is, collective action among members of an organization to help and support one another and work on behalf of the organization as a whole (Ogunfowora, 2014).

We get a good sense of what principals can do to be effective models for cultivating caring community from literature on ethical leadership. Michael Brown and Linda Treviño (2006) define ethical leadership as "the demonstration of normatively appropriate conduct through personal actions and interpersonal relationships, and the promotion of such conduct to followers through two-way communication, reinforcement, and decision making" (pp. 595–596). According to Ogunfowora (2014), ethical leaders engage in moral conduct, actively communicate high ethical standards, and uphold these standards through rewards and punishments. Through these actions, members of an organization perceive leaders as credible sources of acceptable behaviors.

There are many persons who can be regarded as models, including leaders outside of one's setting, one's peers, and inspiring persons from all walks of life (Brown & Treviño, 2014). Even as we focus on the principal as a source of modeling, we should consider a principal's modeling influence in a context of other potential models and their influence. Modeling can occur formally, through purposeful presentation of particular behaviors. In many instances, however, modeling occurs informally and vicariously through observations in day-to-day life, sometimes without conscious awareness on the part of the observer or the model (Ogunfowora, 2014). Leaders—in our case, principals—can make themselves purposeful presentations to others and be aware that even when not purposefully modeling, teachers, students, and others are watching, listening, and learning.

What can a principal do to be an effective model generally and for cultivating caring community in particular? Again, we find several lessons in the literature on ethical leadership, lessons summarized in Figure 4.1 (Brown et al., 2005; Ogunfowora, 2014).

Figure 4.1 • Lessons for Leader Modeling

1. "Walk the talk" of caring and community in personal and professional behavior. Be continual, active sources of messages promoting caring and community.

2. Be visible to others. Engage *practices of presence*.

3. "Talk the walk" by making messages known through explicit communication, including telling and open and frank discussion.

4. Encourage and reinforce expectations for attitudes and behaviors modeled through consequences—rewards, redirection, and punishment—that are consistent with norms of caring and community and that communicate benefits of engaging in modeled behavior and costs of engaging in contrary behavior.

Coaching

A more direct and active way that principals can help develop the capacity for caring community among teachers and staff members is coaching. Coaching helps develop particular attitudes and ways of acting and interacting. It focuses primarily on thinking, behavior, and job performance. It is, according to Ellinger, Ellinger, and Keller (2003), "a day-to-day, hands-on process of helping employees recognize opportunities to improve their performance and capabilities" (p. 438). Most of the work on principal coaching is associated with the work of Jim Knight (2009), who focuses on instructional coaching. However, principals and other leaders perform many coaching roles in addition to improving instruction, particularly where it is focused on cultivating caring communities.

While there are many different ways to define the role of leaders in coaching, we distinguish between two: (1) employee-centered coaching, such as helping teachers understand and address problems that they identify in their practice, and (2) performance coaching, which might center on more assertive assistance to help a teacher meet certain expectations of the job. This distinction is not hard and fast—indeed, the lines between the two approaches are often blurred.

Ellinger and her colleagues (2003; Ellinger & Bostrom, 1999) identify practices that exemplary managers use to coach their employees that align with employee-centered coaching to increase caring. These practices are summarized in Figure 4.2 and are modified to make them applicable to how principals might coach teachers and staff members on caring and forming strong relationships with students. Coaching strategies can be more directive where expectations for caring are clear and the person's performance in relation to them is also clear.

Figure 4.2 • Practices of Leader Coaching

1. Personalize learning situations with specific examples, analogies, and scenarios.

2. Start with the persons being coached. Ask questions that allow them to define issues in their situations that they would like to improve to increase caring.

3. Encourage employees to think creatively and see other perspectives.

4. Provide observations, reflections, and feedback.

5. Seek feedback from employees on how they see themselves developing.

6. Pose open-ended questions (how, when, what, where) that allow the coach to understand how the person being coached understands caring in their situation.

7. Pose outcome-oriented questions or context-specific questions to encourage employees to think through and reflect on issues related to caring.

8. Set goals and expectations, and agree on their importance.

9. Provide resources, information, and material for learning and remove roadblocks in the way of caring (which may require engaging other aspects of practice).

10. Step into the employee's shoes to better understand their perspectives and experiences in work and in the coaching relationship.

Florence Stone (2007) of the American Management Association identified practices that are tied directly to developing particular aspects of employee job performance and meeting specific performance expectations. Applied to caring, these practices include modeling the caring performance desired, clarifying expectations about particular tasks and the organization's overall mission and vision for caring community, and providing regular feedback about how employees' behaviors represent improvement.

Whether a principal uses teacher-centered coaching or performance-focused coaching, access to professional development opportunities that will help teachers and others improve is critical. Both styles of coaching should emphasize the positive. Stone (2007), for example, argues that effective performance coaching hinges on employee motivation. She emphasizes that a crucial aspect of coaching is "praise, praise, and praise . . . to reinforce positive performance" (p. 19). For a principal, this is likely to involve noticing small caring gestures when conducting walkthroughs or making other observations.

Lancer, Clutterbuck, and Megginson (2016) present an expanded view of employee coaching that begins with developing a strong and trusting relationship between the leader and employee. Neither performance coaching nor a self-discovery improvement model will work without trust in the principal's capacity to coach and maintain fairness. This involves building rapport, promoting readiness, and even contracting the "terms" of the coaching relationship. Coaching needs to be grounded in staff members' work, while concurrently helping them articulate issues and opportunities for caring. This can involve exploring beliefs and values related to the focus of coaching for caring. Once this foundation is laid, coaching can proceed to setting and pursuing specific goals. Because caring is emotionally laden, any efforts to promote it through coaching will involve engaging emotions and managing the coaching relationship itself. The principal as coach may need to spark the employee's willingness to address caring through coaching and to be open to guidance from the principal. And the principal as coach may need to help the teacher cope with setbacks in a process that is rarely linear.

Formal Professional Development

Another way to develop teacher and staff capacity for caring community is through formal programs of professional development. These programs can be helpful in developing mindsets and competencies of caring, including attentiveness to others, motivational orientation to others' well-being and success, knowledge of groups and their situations, knowledge of strategies to address the needs and concerns of others and to promote their interests, and knowledge of oneself and one's capacity for caring. Formal professional development can promote community by focusing on knowledge of community norms and values and knowledge and skills for promoting caring relationships with students. Collective learning opportunities can become forms of community themselves. Later in this chapter, we will discuss additional strategies for teacher and staff professional development for implementing programs and practices for developing students' capacity for caring community.

Research identifies several qualities and characteristics of formal teacher professional development that make it effective (Garet, Porter, Desimone, Birman, & Yoon, 2001; Wei, Darling-Hammond, Andree, Richardson, & Orphanos, 2009; Yoon, Duncan, Lee, Scarloss, & Shapley, 2007). These qualities and characteristics are summarized in Figure 4.3. They are elaborated in standards for effective professional learning issued by Learning Forward (learningforward.org/standards) and in a companion analysis of the role of school leaders in promoting those standards (Louis, Hord, & Von Frank, 2016).

Figure 4.3 • Qualities and Characteristics of Effective Teacher Professional Development

1. Focus on the concrete tasks of teaching and teachers' work.

2. Sustained, active learning (e.g., observation, discussion, presenting/writing), with opportunities for sense making and hands-on experience.

3. Relevance to teachers' needs and interests.

4. Alignment with other learning opportunities and school improvement activities.

5. Collaborative learning and participation of teachers from the same school, grade levels, or subject areas.

6. Extended duration.

7. Opportunities for modeling, practice, and reflection on new strategies.

8. Sufficient, sustained material and fiscal resources and support from school leaders.

Most research on effective teacher professional development focuses on instructional improvement and, more specifically, teaching to academic content standards. Yet because they are derived in large part from principles of adult and professional learning, the characteristics and qualities that make professional development effective for improving instruction are also likely, perhaps with variation, to make them effective for developing individual and collective capacity for caring and community.

Professional Community

Finally, yet importantly, teacher capacity for caring community can be cultivated by nurturing professional communities in their schools. Professional communities are considered critical sources of individual and peer learning, motivation, improvement, and shared accountability. There are a number of resources that can help principals develop and support teacher professional communities. For example, Kruse, Louis, and Bryk (1994) identify five critical areas for development and support, shown in Figure 4.4.

Figure 4.4 • Critical Areas for Developing and Supporting Professional Community

1. A collective focus on students' learning, driven by the premise that all students can learn at reasonably high levels and that teachers can be careful and help them succeed.

2. Deprivatization of practice through sharing, observing, and discussing each other's work.

3. Collaboration to develop shared understandings of students and to improve classroom practice (including caring).

4. Shared norms and values concerning the purpose of teachers' work, critical educational issues, and the priorities of the school.

5. Reflective analysis and dialogue among teachers.

Louis and Kruse (1995) identify several structural and social conditions of schools that should be addressed in order for professional communities to grow and function. These conditions are shown in Figure 4.5. Several were discussed earlier in relation to caring communities for students.

Figure 4.5 • School Conditions for Growing Professional Community

1. Time to meet and talk.

2. Physical proximity of teachers to one another, including space for gathering.

3. Interdependence in teachers' work to promote communication, shared knowledge, and joint planning and decision making.

4. Communication channels that encourage the development and exchange of ideas.

5. Discretion and autonomy to make decisions regarding one's own work.

6. Trust and respect.

7. Cognitive and social capacity to engage in joint work.

8. Openness to improvement.

9. Norms and values that support the development and function of professional communities.

10. Supportive leadership from the principal and other school leaders.

Schools should organize as professional communities in ways that promote teacher capacity for caring community for students and become sources of caring for teachers themselves. The social bonds created among teachers in professional community should be grounded in norms and values of caring communities.

Developing Capacity for Caring Community Among Students

There are countless things that schools can do to build strong relationships and cultivate caring community for students. Many opportunities for building caring community can be planned. Other opportunities arise serendipitously. In this section, we examine several types of programs and practices that principals can promote to develop capacity for caring community among students. We focus primarily on programs and practices for which evidence of effectiveness exists. We look first to practices that create strong learning and caring communities in classrooms. Before we do, we recall our earlier discussion of leader modeling and its contributions to developing teacher capacity for caring community. We will not repeat the main points of that discussion here. Instead, we ask you to revisit that discussion (pp. 83–84) and think about the contribution of leader modeling to developing student capacity for caring community.

Classroom Learning Communities

There are a number of practices that principals can promote to create strong, productive caring classroom learning communities for students. Many are identified in research on the effective teaching of diverse, underserved student populations. This research finds that these teacher practices can strengthen social relationships among students and teachers and develop collective capacity for both caring and community. By doing so, they facilitate student academic engagement and success.

In the elementary school classrooms he studied, Howard (2001) found that African American students gave more effort and were more engaged when teachers formed caring bonds and displayed caring attitudes toward them, when teachers established positive classroom environments, and when teachers made learning relevant and fun. When students were asked what made for an optimal learning environment, their most frequent answers were teachers' willingness to care about their students and ability to bond with them. Showing care and empathy, emotion, and affective and nurturing behavior were all important to students. Students were more highly engaged when teachers brought their best selves to the classroom; when teachers showed respect for students through high expectations and follow-through; when teachers showed that they had students' best interests at heart, even when interactions were strict and tough; and when teachers did not allow students to withdraw from activities. Also important was teachers' ability to create positive classroom environments that "make school seem like home" (p. 141). These classrooms exude a positive family atmosphere, where children and adults gather around common interests, histories, and experiences. In these environments are daily rituals and traditions that reflect school norms and values. These are classrooms where teaching and learning are enthusiastic, filled with imagination and excitement.

From their study of classrooms serving Latino, African American, and Asian American high school students, Wallace and Chhuon (2014) also speak to the importance of student–teacher relationships to building classroom community and student engagement. They emphasize what teachers do to ensure that students feel that they are being heard. Important are teachers' willingness to listen to students and address their learning needs. Also important are how much teachers invite student critique of their teaching and of classroom activities and adapt on the basis of such feedback. Often, feeling heard comes from opportunities teachers provide for student choice and autonomy, which help students feel that they contribute to the success of lessons—indeed, to classroom community.

Wallace and Chhuon (2014) also emphasize how teachers demonstrate to students that they are "going all in." Students look for genuine commitment and enthusiasm from their teachers. They look for teachers to reveal their thinking, to reveal themselves as "real people," and to find commonalities with students. Also important is what teachers do so that students feel that they are taken seriously. Students want to be respected by their teachers and acknowledged as partners in teaching and learning. Offering truly helpful support to students is one way of taking students seriously. So too is knowing a student as a person, not simply as a learner. All these things go far to create strong social bonds between teacher and student and build community in classrooms.

Similarly, in her study of teachers who were exceptionally successful with African American students, Ladson-Billings (2009) found that students were much more engaged and performed better academically when teachers nurtured social relationships in their classrooms. These teachers created communities of learners, rather than idiosyncratic connections with individual students. These teachers used deliberate strategies to build community. They treated all students like family members and emphasized collective responsibility and collective rewards. Efforts to build classroom community were closely related to teachers' instructional approach. These teachers did not believe that teaching was simply transmitting information, and they did not want their students to just "receive or consume knowledge" (p. x). Instead, they wanted students to produce and demonstrate new understandings to others. Although specific teaching methods varied among these effective teachers, all sought to develop cultural competence and cultivate sociopolitical awareness, which became hallmarks of classroom community. Likewise, de Royston and her colleagues (2017) document how middle and high school teachers fostered positive relationships with African American male students by being intentional about positively influencing these students lives, by pushing back against racialized and hegemonic structures of schools, and by making concerted efforts to know, rather than stereotype, each student and work to develop each student's full potential.

Reese, Jensen, and Ramirez (2014) identify similar teacher practices that create highly supportive classroom communities for Latino students. These practices fall into two categories: (1) practices of emotional support and

(2) practices of cultural responsiveness. Emotional support is expressed in teachers' warmth and enthusiasm and in comfort they provide students. In highly supportive classrooms teachers communicate verbal and physical affection and help students feel comfortable in expressing their ideas and seeking guidance and support from others. They hold high expectations for students and show students that they can meet these expectations—and form even higher expectations for themselves. Teachers are aware of and respond to students' individual academic and socioemotional needs and lived experiences. Supportive classroom communities develop when teachers demonstrate care and respect for students and their languages, families, and communities and when this respect is reflected in instruction. In these classroom communities, teachers encourage students to ask questions, seek clarification, assert their needs and concerns, and take an active role in their own learning.

Culturally Responsive Teaching

The classroom practices discussed previously are consistent with practices of culturally relevant or culturally responsive teaching (Gay, 2010; Ladson-Billings, 1995, 2014). Culturally relevant teaching can be described by four "markers" (Aronson & Laughter, 2016): (1) constructivist methods to connect students' cultural references to academic concepts and skills; (2) inclusive curricula to promote critical reflection among all students in school and classroom, by which students consider their own lives within those cultures; (3) strategies to develop all students' cultural competence, to help students learn about and develop pride in their own and others' cultures; and (4) strategies to promote student critique of discourses of power and oppression in the classroom, in school, in the community, and in society generally and to actively pursue justice for all members of society. Often, culturally relevant or culturally responsive teaching is thought to be pedagogy for students of color. To the contrary, its principles and practices benefit classrooms of all racial, ethnic, social, and cultural compositions. Some studies have found that culturally relevant teaching contributes to developing community by fostering motivation and belonging in school, indeed, by fostering critique and care for the school itself (Aronson & Laughter, 2016). For students and teachers, reflecting on how dominant culture can perpetuate "acceptable" knowledge and inequities fosters understanding, empathy, and connections among all students (Allensworth et al., 2018).

One notable example of a systemic, critical approach to classroom practice is Teaching Tolerance (2016). This approach integrates intellectually rigorous, culturally relevant instruction; building classroom community; and strengthening family and community engagement. Teaching Tolerance emphasizes critical engagement of subject matter, differentiated instruction, socially constructed learning, relevance and meaningfulness, making connections between subject matter and real-world experiences of students, mastery learning, and values-based assessment and grading. Particularly relevant to building classroom community are instructional practices that create opportunities for students to learn about each other; examine critically issues of identity, power, privilege, and bias; share multiple perspectives; and exchange ideas and analyze each other's work. Practices of collaborative and cooperative learning, in particular, allow students to learn from peers with different backgrounds and work with partners they may not reach out to as friends. Practices that connect subject matter to students' real-world experiences can help students deepen their understanding of and empathy toward one another. Teaching Tolerance recommends that student assessment focus not only on academic learning but also on social skills and relationships, including collaboration and conflict management.

Central to Teaching Tolerance (2016) are practices for developing a classroom community and inclusive culture that honor student experience, focus on relationship building, promote multiple viewpoints through shared inquiry and dialogue, provide for social and emotional safety, and prioritize values-based behavior management. Key to relationship and community building is a "thoughtful" classroom setup (p. 9). Classrooms should be *student centered* in the arrangement of furnishings, in access to materials and supplies, in students' roles and responsibilities for care of the classroom, and in the decorations and work that adorn the walls and ceilings. The setup of the room creates opportunities for interaction and social learning and sends messages that relationship building is a priority. As students' races, ethnicities, and cultures are honored through classroom texts and materials and as students' experiences are honored through telling student stories and community studies, students can better understand each other, develop the ability to take multiple perspectives, and establish stronger social relationships around common school values and understandings. Shared inquiry and dialogue create similar opportunities, especially as they prompt openness to new ideas and collective learning.

Classroom community and inclusive culture are also promoted through practices that establish social and emotional safety. Creating a safe and respectful classroom community involves helping students develop social-emotional competencies: attention to positive peer relationships, bullying prevention and intervention, explicit focus on understanding and appreciating differences, meaningful conflict resolution, restoration of damaged relationships, protocols that allow students to challenge biases and exclusion, and *upstander training*, whereby students can learn how to stand up for others. We will examine several of these practices in more detail shortly. Teaching Tolerance (2016) contends that developing classroom community and inclusive culture cannot simply focus on empathy and kindness. It also must focus on social differences and biases that underlie unsafe and exclusionary behaviors. In addition, acknowledging and understanding multicultural perspectives are critical for both teachers and students when trying to build relationships and community in classrooms.

Finally, practices of values-based behavior management can contribute to developing inclusive classroom community. These practices emphasize the dignity of every person and the values of community, particularly equity, fairness, inclusion, and respect. Values-based behavior management enforces high standards for respectful interaction, incorporates student-generated discipline policies, teaches conflict resolution, and actively addresses instances of bias, bullying, exclusion, and disrespect. Addressing disciplinary incidents should go beyond consequences and be treated as opportunities for growth, restitution, and relationship and community building. Instead of zero tolerance, Teaching Tolerance promotes *zero indifference* (p. 12). Values-based behavior management recognizes that in some cases, inappropriate behaviors may reflect a cultural mismatch between norms of the school and norms of a home or community. The possibility of missing or responding inappropriately to such mismatches can be reduced through greater self-awareness and cultural competency.

Finally, Teaching Tolerance (2016) contends that inclusive classroom community can be promoted through positive practices of family and community engagement that build social bonds and promote classroom and school community. We discuss parent and community engagement at the end of this chapter and in Chapter 5.

Social-Emotional Learning

Principals can develop caring community by promoting programs of student and teacher social-emotional learning (SEL). These programs help develop mindsets, skills, and dispositions that promote positive and caring social relationships. By doing so, they contribute to the development of community.

According to Durlak, Weissberg, Dymnicki, Taylor, and Schellinger (2011) at the Collaborative for Academic, Social, and Emotional Learning (CASEL), SEL is "a process of acquiring core competencies to recognize and manage emotions, set and achieve positive goals, appreciate the perspectives of others, establish and maintain positive relationships, make responsible decisions and handle interpersonal situations constructively" (p. 406). Accordingly, SEL promotes self-awareness, self-management, social awareness, relationship skills, and responsible decision making. By developing these competencies, children and youth will be better able to act according to internalized beliefs and values, express caring and concern for others, make good decisions, and take responsibility for their actions.

According to Richard Weissbourd and Stephanie Jones (2014b) of the Making Caring Common Project at Harvard University, helping children and youth develop such competencies and, in particular, helping them become more caring, depends on the opportunities they have to practice caring and helpfulness, often with guidance from adults. It also depends on opportunities for them to learn and practice taking perspectives of others, observing peer and adult models, and managing negative and destructive feelings, such as anger, envy, and shame.

A number of factors contribute to the success of SEL programs for students (Durlak et al., 2011; Elias, Arnold, & Hussey, 2003; Jones, Boffard, & Weissbourd, 2013; Weissbourd & Jones, 2014b). These factors are summarized in Figure 4.6.

Figure 4.6 • Factors Contributing to the Success of SEL Programs for Students

1. Embedded into the daily life of the school for everyone, adults and students alike.

2. A multiyear commitment, not a single event.

3. Strong, consistent guidance and support of school leaders.

4. Shared responsibility for the program throughout the school, with specific tasks assigned to individuals with time and capabilities to be successful.

5. Active participation of teachers, families, and community members in collaborative decision making, in implementation, and in support of students' SEL activities.

6. Explicit curriculum focused on specific SEL competencies, rather than general positive development or general social skills, that progresses in developmentally appropriate ways from lower to upper grades.

7. Active, not passive, forms of student learning.

8. Recognition of specific needs of the school and its students.

9. Effective professional development and ongoing support for teachers and staff to develop their social-emotional competencies and practices and to support implementation of SEL programs for students.

10. Sufficient sustained resources and supportive organizational conditions.

11. Provisions for assessing implementation and outcomes and adapting and improving the program as necessary.

There are many examples of promising SEL programs for students. Stephanie Jones and her colleagues (2013) identify several of them, including emotion-focused training, relationship building, mindfulness training and stress reduction, and SEL routines. The Making Caring Common Project provides guidelines for programs that seek to strengthen empathy and caring school community (Jones, Weissbourd, Boffard, Kahn, & Ross, 2014). The Collaborative for Academic, Social, and Emotional Learning (2013, 2015) has catalogued a large number of effective, research-based SEL programs for preschool, elementary, middle, and high schools. Among them are the 4Rs Project (Morningside Center, n.d.), the Listening Project (Way & Nelson, 2018), Roots of Empathy (Gordon, 2018), and the Ruler Approach (Nathanson, Rivers, Flynn, & Brackett, 2016).

Social-Emotional Literacy Programs for Teachers

Most SEL programs focus on students. While many contain professional-development components to support implementation, few provide much explicit instruction to foster social-emotional literacy among teachers

(Powell & Kusuma-Powell, 2010). There are, however, some notable exceptions. For example, the 4Rs Project, a student SEL program noted previously, joined with the MyTeachingPartner (MTP) Project to provide teachers direct instruction in SEL, coaching, and classroom support (Curry School of Education, 2015). The Caring School Community Project and the Alternative Thinking Strategies (PATH) curriculum and the Emotionally Intelligent Teacher (EIT) professional-development program provide specific opportunities for developing teachers' social and emotional competencies (Jennings & Greenberg, 2009). The EIT program is designed to develop teachers' emotion-related awareness and skills and promote their application to SEL initiatives for students. It helps teachers recognize, label, understand, and regulate emotions in situations with students, colleagues, and families.

Jennings and Greenberg (2009) note other approaches for developing teachers' social-emotional competencies that are theoretically promising but lack research on their effectiveness (see also Weissbourd & Jones, 2014b). Among them are contemplative practices and practices for developing mindfulness. The logic of these practices is to increase teachers' awareness of their experiences and promote reflection, self-regulation, and caring for others. Other approaches include programs of personal development, not only professional development, of teachers. These programs are designed to develop teachers' knowledge and understanding of one another and develop more trusting and caring relationships with colleagues and with students. Finally, Jennings and Greenberg note that teachers can develop their own social-emotional capabilities from implementing SEL programs for students and from helping students act on those capabilities.

Positive Conduct and Conflict Resolution

Principals can cultivate caring community by promoting positive student conduct and productive conflict resolution. A number of programs and practices address misconduct and conflict, prevent future problems, and, at the same time, build positive and caring relationships (Allensworth et al., 2018). In this section, we explore three types of such programs and practices: (1) positive behavior interventions and supports (PBIS), (2) restorative practices, and (3) peer mediation. Following this discussion, we examine practices of student safety and security, including antibullying programs and ways of preventing cyberbullying.

Positive Behavior Interventions and Supports

Positive behavior interventions and supports use data and a continuum of evidence-based interventions to develop and reinforce positive student conduct (Children's Defense Fund, n.d.; Welsh & Little, 2018). This approach emphasizes behavior supports and building positive school culture and climate. In most iterations of PBIS, school personnel receive training to help them identify circumstances surrounding particular student behaviors, establish and communicate clear behavioral expectations, tailor and align consequences with particular infractions, and develop ways to reinforce positive behaviors (Welsh & Little, 2018). Depending on the school and the student conduct issues at hand, PBIS can support a wide variety of proactive and positive programs and practices. Among them can be restorative and peer mediation practices, to which we now turn.

Restorative Practices

Restorative practices focus on establishing safer school environments through responsive reintegration (Welsh & Little, 2018). These practices address misconduct, conflict, and delinquency by fostering community, establishing and mending relationships, and forming a more inclusive, caring, and supportive school culture. Restorative practices do not focus primarily on punishment (although they may include it) but instead seek to repair harm through dialog and accountability, uniting persons wronged with the persons responsible. This approach considers misbehavior to be a violation of relationship, either between an offender and a victim or between an offender and the school community (Payne & Welsh, 2015). In order to address the harm, the offending and offended student must reconcile, thereby mending and building their relationship. Restorative practices emphasize mediation and conflict resolution, restitution, and service to the school community. Payne and Welsh (2015) recognize that gender, racial, income, age, and cultural differences can affect relationships, their repair, and their development. In addition, restorative practices can be particularly helpful to address equity concerns associated with more punitive, exclusionary methods to shape student behavior.

Peer Mediation

Related to restorative practices is peer mediation, a cooperative, relationship-oriented approach to conflict resolution (Johnson & Johnson, 1996). Peer mediation focuses on long-term integration and reintegration of parties. Conflict resolution is constructive to the extent that disputants can coordinate their efforts to maximize joint gain and establish or reestablish a relationship that allows them to work together in the future. Typically, peer mediation programs prepare students as neutral third parties to assist other students to resolve and manage interpersonal disputes. Student mediators encourage their peers to explore issues systematically and engage in cooperative problem solving. According to Burrell, Zirbel, and Allen (2003), the goal is to generate agreements acceptable to everyone and to develop a strategy to handle similar problems in the future.

There are many ways to design peer mediation programs. Some are embedded in broader conflict resolution programs that promote "open, trusting, democratic relationships" (Lindsay, 1998, p. 87). Most peer mediation programs involve teaching an entire student body the principles and strategies of negotiation and conflict resolution, including listening, communication, and cooperative problem solving. Teams of teachers, counselors, and administrators are also prepared. Students are selected to become peer mediators and to receive more in-depth preparation. Mediators work in teams to help peers resolve disputes, and a group of teachers is often designated to support student mediators and address issues that require adult intervention (Noaks & Noaks, 2009).

Several factors contribute to the success of peer mediation programs (Daunic, Smith, Robinson, Miller, & Landry, 2000; Lindsay, 1998). There must be committed leadership from school administrators and from groups charged with implementation. School leaders should understand the philosophy and processes of peer mediation, provide adequate and sustained resources, and encourage teachers to adopt similar practices in their classrooms. Multiyear commitment is crucial, as is the degree to which programs are incorporated into the life of the school and into classroom practice. Students should be continually taught and given opportunities to practice constructive approaches to dispute resolution. There needs to be quality professional development for teachers and staff who teach peer mediation and conflict resolution and who coordinate these programs. And all students in a school need to learn the purposes, principles, and general strategies of these programs.

The success of peer mediation also depends on the performance of the peer mediators. Students selected to become peer mediators should not be the highest-achieving students in the school but rather, to promote acceptance and fairness, should be representative of the student body (Daunic et al., 2000). Students who are selected should learn the aims, principles, and practices of peer mediation and conflict resolution. Schools should monitor peer mediators' performance and provide them adequate and sustained support. Daunic and her colleagues argue that the effectiveness of peer mediation also depends on establishing a clear referral process and schedule, allocating sufficient student and staff time and providing adequate resources and space. It is important that schools establish processes for check-in and follow up to find out how disputants are doing, how they view the process, and whether they find the outcomes of mediation satisfactory. Finally, schools should continually keep peer mediation and conflict resolution before students and staff. School leaders can provide regular announcements of referral processes and schedules, recognize the contributions of peer mediators and staff, and provide indicators of accomplishments, such as reductions in disputes, referrals, and disciplinary actions, and recognition of mediators and disputants successes.

Student Safety and Security

There is substantial evidence that strong social bonds and support associated with caring community can go a long way to create physically and emotionally safe and secure schools for students (Murphy & Torre, 2014). Safety is promoted through authentic, supportive relationships between students and teachers and among students themselves. Impersonality, individualism, lack of belonging, and alienation work against efforts to create safe and secure learning environments. The Centers for Disease Control and Prevention

(2018) include strong social connections between adults and students and engagement of students in school as important factors in preventing violence. The recent report of the Federal Commission on School Safety (2018) recognizes "a culture of connectedness" as an important source of school safety and violence prevention.

Developing and maintaining a safe and secure school environment is one of the principal's most important responsibilities (Murphy, 2017). The strategies principals employ to ensure students' safety can help cultivate caring community and, at the same time, can lead to greater safety and security. Asset-based programs and practices that promote school safety by developing personalism, sense of belonging, and feelings of mutual responsibility and support can help develop caring community. So too can practices for safety and security that promote attentiveness to students' problems and needs and positive, preventative action to address those problems and needs. Moreover, programs that emphasize positive, nonexclusionary, and restorative approaches, such as those discussed earlier, can contribute to safety and security and to caring community. And efforts to promote student engagement in school can contribute to school safety and caring community.

Bullying and cyberbullying have become growing threats to student safety and security. Efforts to prevent and respond to them are good examples of practices that can contribute concurrently to student safety and security and to caring community.

Antibullying Programs

In the past twenty-five years, bullying has been recognized as a serious problem in schools, and programs to prevent it have proliferated. Bullying is a "physical, verbal, or psychological attack or intimidation that is intended to cause fear, distress, or harm to the victim" (Ttofi & Farrington, 2011, p. 28) or to hurt and shame peers. It involves an imbalance of psychological or physical power with a more powerful child (or children) oppressing less powerful ones. It involves related incidents between the same children over a prolonged period of time (Merrell, Gueldner, Ross, & Isava, 2008). Bullying is antithetical to student peer caring and community, so efforts to prevent and address it become important parts of improving school safety and cultivating caring community.

Antibullying programs can include a number of elements, such as conflict resolution strategies, accountability measures, and referrals to the juvenile justice system (Polanin, Espelage, & Pigott, 2012). Effective approaches include promoting understanding; communicating consistent, high expectations for student behavior and interaction; focusing on positive behavior; emphasizing development of relationships and community; restoring relationships in response to harm; and applying such approaches universally. Antibullying programs can promote caring and community by reducing bullying and victimization. By fostering empathy and responsibility for others (bystander behavior), they can also develop *organizational citizenship behavior* (OCB), that is, prosocial actions that ultimately benefit the school community as a whole (Goess & Smith, 2018).

Several factors make antibullying efforts effective. Ttofi and Farrington (2011) write that effective programs take a whole-school approach, institute antibullying policies, provide teacher professional development in antibullying strategies, and integrate antibullying strategies into classroom practices. In addition, these programs can be particularly effective when they include cooperative student learning, student supervision on playgrounds and other places where bullying might occur, and parent education, school–family communication, and parent–school conferences. The greater the number of these elements in a program and the greater intensity and longer duration of the program, the more likely it will reduce bullying behavior and victimization and restore positive relations and community. The largest positive effects occur when antibullying programs are culturally focused, rather than developed for generic student populations (Evans, Fraser, & Cotter, 2014).

Anticyberbullying Practices

Donlin (2012) argues that cyberbullying awareness, prevention, and intervention should be required as part of a school's ongoing bullying prevention and intervention efforts. Like preventing and redressing bullying, effective approaches to preventing and redressing cyberbullying focus primarily on building community, nurturing positive and supportive relationships among students in school and online, and fostering positive and supportive relationships among students, teachers, and parents. Donlin emphasizes developing *cybercitizenship* among students, that is, an understanding of both the freedoms and the responsibilities toward others in school and online communities.

Experts on anticyberbullying recommend a comprehensive approach of age-relevant strategies and resources that relate to students' actual relationships and online experiences, that help build those relationships, and that develop students' knowledge and skills for safe and productive online experiences (Hinduja & Patchin, 2015; Walker, 2012). According to Donlin (2012), principals must resist *the assumption of nonoccurrence* in their schools and recognize that cyberbullying occurs everywhere, whether or not it is reported. He cautions that scare tactics, "just say no" approaches, and one-shot "inoculations" do not work. Comprehensive, ongoing, schoolwide, and community-based efforts are required, as are the coordination and cooperation of educators, students, parents and caregivers, and members of the larger community.

Successful anticyberbullying efforts are usually embedded in systemic antibullying programs and incorporate prevention strategies that reduce the chances and risks of cyberbullying, employ strategies for confronting and combating instances of cyberbullying, and buffer against the negative impact of cyberbullying (see, e.g., Perren et al., 2012). Prevention strategies should involve the whole school, as well as individual students and groups of students who may be at risk of becoming bullies and victims (Donlin, 2012). These strategies can include anticyberbullying curricula, instruction in *netiquette* (etiquette for using the internet; Perrin et al., 2012, p. 286), and technical solutions, such as monitoring and filtering software, firewalls, and other online security measures. However useful they may be, technical strategies will not address the educational, social, developmental, and emotional situations that might lead to cyberbullying (Donlin, 2012). According to Hinduja and Patchin (2015),

> Prevention is all about relationships. Even though many [students] are not deterred by the threat of formal punishment, they are dissuaded from . . . behavior that they know their friends, parents, or other valued adults would frown upon. When [students] are emotionally attached or socially bonded to others, they internalize their norms and values and do not want to disappoint by behaving in a way that is contradictory to those principles. (p. 153)

According to Hinduja and Patchin (2015), the best general response to cyberbullying will always be educative and restorative, rather than negative and strictly punitive. Generally, cyberbullying can be addressed using many of the same strategies used to deal with bullying generally and student conflict and harm. Schools must exercise due diligence, monitoring to determine if the response "took" and if follow-up interventions are required. Crucial to buffering the negative impact of cyberbullying are systems of social, emotional, and instrumental support from peers, educators, parents, and community organizations. Students can be helped to develop psychological and emotional coping strategies to confront cyberbullying, as well as ways of redefining and focusing on growth elements of stress that come from cyberbullying (Perren et al., 2012). At the bottom line, prevention and response strategies must rest on positive caring relationships developed within a school community among students and adults. Like antibullying efforts, such anticyberbullying efforts can contribute to the development of capacity for caring community.

Promoting Enabling Conditions

Cultivating caring community in schools depends not only on developing the capacity for caring and community among students, faculty, and staff but also on promoting organizational conditions that support putting this capacity to work. In this section, we examine practices for enriching three aspects of school organization to support the cultivation of caring community: (1) school culture, (2) structural supports, and (3) authority relationships, governance, and politics.

Cutting across this organizational work is what principals do to shape the mission and vision of the school to make caring and community priorities and foundational anchors for all else. It will be important to seek active participation of students, teachers and staff, and parents and caregivers in shaping mission and vision and in developing shared understanding of, commitment to, and engagement with them. The mission of the school—its purposes, what it exists to achieve—can make clear that caring is an important educational outcome, on the same plane as other outcomes, including academic achievement. As Noddings (2005) stresses, schools should be organized around and promote the themes of caring. "Such an aim does not work against intellectual development or academic achievement," she argues. "On the contrary, it supplies a firm foundation for both" (p. 173). Likewise, Weissbourd and Jones (2014a) contend that even as educators say that developing caring for others is a valued educational purpose, they should prioritize caring in practice.

Similarly, with the participation of others, principals can set forth school visions that incorporate caring. Such visions would be aspirational, future-oriented portraits describing what schools would look like and what students, faculty and staff, administrators, parents and caregivers, and others would be doing if they are functioning effectively as caring communities. Such visions would speak to the programs and practices that we have described earlier in this chapter and to the aspects of school organization to which we now turn.

Creating a Culture of Caring Community

Creating a supportive organizational culture lies at the heart of cultivating caring community. By organizational culture, we refer to the norms, values, and taken-for-granted assumptions that form the basis for individual and collective meaning and behavior (Schein, 2010). Organizational culture performs several functions essential to cultivating caring community. Through its expression in stories, symbols and artifacts, language, rituals, ceremonies, and routines, culture can communicate and "teach" members of an organization what is "good and true." It can provide the normative lenses through which members interpret and give meaning to their work and experiences. Culture can communicate expectations, including expectations for how members of an organization are to work together and relate to one another. Culture can create standards by which members can hold each other responsible and accountable. A school culture anchored in the norms and values of caring and community can provide strong support for cultivating the relationships, actions, and interactions that bring caring community to life.

Principals play a crucial role in developing school culture. We recall that everything that a principal might say and do contributes to culture building, as the principal's words and actions reflect and reinforce particular norms and values or contradict and compromise them. With this in mind, there are particular practices that principals can use to build culture for caring community in their schools.

Principals can clearly define, continuously communicate, and promote the norms, values, ideas, and ideals that define caring and community to students, faculty and staff, parents and caregivers, community members, and other stakeholders of the school (Sergiovanni, 1994a, 1994b). Principals can communicate, model, and reinforce these norms and values through their actions and interactions. Rutledge and her colleagues (2015) explain how principals can communicate norms and values of caring and community by building strong relationships with students. They can get to know their students and their students' backgrounds and work to create a positive sense of family in their schools. To students, faculty, and staff, principals can establish personalization and positive social relationships as explicit goals of their schools. They can also encourage students to connect with their schools through relationships with teachers and peers.

Similar practices can be seen in research on culturally responsive leadership and leadership for developing inclusive schools. In their work on culturally responsive school leadership, Khalifa, Gooden, and Davis (2016) point to the importance of leveraging resources in ways that reflect inclusivity and create welcoming, safe spaces for all students. They speak of principals acting as *warm demanders*, maintaining high expectations while developing relationships and being supportive and caring of all. Riehl (2000) also identifies leadership practices that can contribute to developing community-oriented, inclusive school cultures. These practices include adopting a personalizing approach to relationships with students, appreciating the cultural knowledge that students bring to school and using it to help teachers work with students, and promoting high levels of cooperation among students, teachers, and families. They also include holding high academic and behavioral expectations for all students and providing the supports necessary for students to attain them; encouraging teachers to examine their practices for possible biases; developing strong caring relationships with parents, caregivers, and families; and maintaining an environment of assessment and critique of overt and implicit practices that might marginalize and exclude particular students and their families.

Principals can use language reflecting the norms and values of caring community. As mentioned earlier, principals can replace language of individualism, efficiency, economy, and impartiality with language of relationships, compassion, forgiveness, wisdom, humility, mutual responsibility, and loyalty. They can use language and examples that convey images of community, home, and church, which can help students, teachers, staff, and others envision the school as a caring community. Rutledge and her colleagues (2015) encourage principals to use language of personalism and relationships, a language that encourages teachers to know their students as more than academic learners, to gain personal knowledge of students' cultural and academic backgrounds, aspirations, and home life.

In addition, principals can develop cultures of caring community by translating experiences through the norms and values of caring and community. Community psychologist John Dunne (1986) explains this point in his writing about l'Arche communities. Founded in France and now located across the world, these are service communities in which persons with disabilities and nondisabled persons make their home together. They are organized around beliefs that everyone has the capacity to grow and mature and make contributions to society, and that personal growth and service are best achieved in the context of community. Dunne observes that the cultural cohesiveness of these communities is promoted as community leaders translate experiences, particularly moments that are painful, through the "common ideal and practical goal" of the community. Such translation gives "a unifying focus to the community effort and [identifies] and make[s] more meaningful the struggle to overcome difficulties and differences" (pp. 49–50).

Principals can further promote a culture of caring community by communicating and reinforcing norms and values through symbols, artifacts, rituals, routines, and similar mechanisms. Dunne (1986) describes collective celebrations, acts of forgiveness, and habits of fun and laughter as ways to communicate and reinforce norms and values in l'Arche communities. In her study of a small urban high school serving a predominantly Latino student body, Curry (2016) illustrates how rituals communicate and reinforce the norms and values of *authentic cariño*, or *heartfelt care* (p. 884). She describes the *firewalk*, a transformational rite of passage, which calls on each sophomore and senior to testify publicly about their personal and academic development. Students face a circle of caring peers and adults and contemplate their journeys toward graduation and beyond in a safe, confidential, but brutally honest environment. The rite ends when the witnesses stand to indicate their confidence that the firewalker has reflected deeply and demonstrated the commitments and habits needed for advancement. If witnesses choose to not stand, the firewalk continues until a remediation plan is negotiated.

Principals can also develop, communicate, and reinforce norms and values through the collection and dissemination of data and through mechanisms of accountability. Data and accountability can contribute to caring culture if focused in a supportive way on the appropriate norms, values, and behaviors and if directed toward bringing those norms and values to life. Rutledge and her colleagues' (2015) study of high schools found that data collected to identify and monitor students in need of support became important means of promoting the norms of personalism and collective responsibility for student success.

Last but not least, principals can promote a culture of caring community through storytelling. Storytelling can be an effective way for principals to communicate the norms and values of caring community and how to bring those norms and values to life. Stories can convey both positive and negative examples and lessons. Kruse and Louis (2009) tell us that stories bind people together and can persuasively teach. Stories can communicate experiences, aspirations, expectations, and identities. They can help preserve elements of the past but also bridge the past and present to the future. Stories can promote understanding and direct attention to and reinforce norms, values, and aspirations. They can share knowledge and perspective and can spark action and change. Stories can make the abstract concrete, create common understanding, and promote common purpose. Indeed, stories can illustrate how students, teachers, and staff might act and interact if they live according to the norms and values of a caring community. (See the companion to this volume, our *Stories of Caring School Leadership*.)

Establishing Structural Supports

Principals can also cultivate caring community by establishing structural supports that create opportunities for developing strong social bonds, attending to and understanding others, and caring. While the overall goal is to promote caring community, it is also important to establish structural opportunities for positive one-on-one relationships between teachers and students. Each student should have a special caring adult to whom they can go for guidance and sharing. Every teacher, in turn, may be similarly responsible for a manageable number of students, covering the full age span of the school. These crucial "hip-to-hip" relationships can last for several years.

From their study of different types of organizations forming communities, Putnam and Feldstein (2003) stress the importance of structures for developing relationships and promoting social interaction. They found that structures that create opportunities for multiple and "redundant" contacts foster "human connectivity" (p. 271) and "virtuous circles of mutual responsibility" (p. 277).

When establishing such supports, leaders can confront a number of challenges. According to Putnam and Feldstein (2003), one challenge is the *dilemma of size and scope*. They believe that, generally, "smaller is better" for forging and sustaining social connections, arguing,

> Listening and trusting are easier in smaller settings. One-on-one, face-to-face communication is more effective at building relationships and creating empathy and understanding than remote, impersonal communication. Smaller groups enable members to get to know one another more easily. . . . [T]he more extensive interchange that is possible in smaller groups makes it possible to discover unexpected mutuality even in the face of difference. Small size also makes individual responsibility for maintaining the group intensely clear. (p. 275)

Putnam and Feldstein (2003) observe that larger social settings are usually better for accomplishing ambitious objectives and promoting diversity. Moreover, community-building efforts often benefit from a sense of being part of something important and growing, a sense that can be more difficult to achieve in small settings.

Putnam and Feldstein (2003) suggest that one way for leaders to manage the dilemma of size and scope is to adopt strategies of *federation* (p. 278), such as nesting small groups within larger groups. They reason that linking smaller groups together and nesting them within the larger organization—a strategy akin to creating a mosaic, discussed earlier—can foster social relationships that would not be so readily formed within the larger organization. This strategy can be especially effective when members participate in more than one small group, are able to weave interpersonal ties among groups, and reinforce relationships and a sense of identity within the larger whole.

CHAPTER 4

Another challenge that Putnam and Feldstein (2003) describe is the *dilemma of cohesion and diversity*. Akin to the idea of a mosaic, while small groups promote strong social cohesion—"birds of a feather" (p. 279)—linking structures and strategies are necessary both to support diversity across small groups and to bring coherence to the whole. This may require leaders to craft *cross-cutting identities* and emphasize similarities on which cross-group bonds can form. These similarities become part of the frame and glue of the mosaic. As culture and structure reinforce each other, these similarities take root in and reinforce norms and values of caring community. In l'Arche communities, structures function in the service of people, of carrying out community objectives, and of shared emotional connections that define these communities (Dunne, 1986).

Most scholars who write about developing schools as communities point to the importance of structure. Beck and Foster (1999) write that "administrators must participate significantly in the reformation of structure to provide conditions for the emergence of community" (p. 354). What this often means is creating small social settings that create opportunities for interaction and for social bonds to form, for students and teachers to come to know each other more authentically, and for caring to emerge. It also means creating opportunities for students and teachers to stay together longer to continue to develop those social bonds and deepen the experience of caring. As mentioned earlier, Beck and Foster recommend creating smaller schools, schools within schools, and family groups within schools. They recommend recasting age-graded classrooms; assigning teachers, students, and support personnel together for several years (i.e., looping); and grouping students according to criteria other than age or perceived academic ability.

Similarly, Rutledge and her colleagues (2015) recommend developing *deliberate* structural systems that support meaningful conversation, interactions, understandings, and relationships among students and adults. These include times, places, and activities for bringing students and their peers, as well as students and adults, together. They also include smaller classes and looping to sustain adult–student relationships over multiple years. Sergiovanni (1994a, 1996) also recommended smaller schools and schools within schools, *kinship groups*, and looping to keep students and adults together longer. He recommended organizing schools into multiaged "families" rather than age-specific grades and classes, and longer class periods to create more sustained contact. Schools also can bring students, teachers, and staff together through advisories, block scheduling, before- and after-school tutoring, small-group seminars, clubs, sports and other teams, and other extracurricular activities. Principals can arrange and appoint the physical spaces of their buildings to be warm and welcoming and exude a sense of connection and community: warm colors on the walls, places designated for congregation and conversation, and student work, symbols, and artifacts reflecting the values of caring community on the walls and in display cases.

Structural supports for cultivating caring communities in schools extend beyond those that promote proximity and sustained opportunities for developing social bonds and caring. They include fiscal and physical resources necessary to implement programs and practices of the sort that we have discussed throughout this chapter. They include time and space for developing capacity for caring and forming community.

In Chapter 1, we observed that educators generally understand the importance of caring and strong social relationships to the learning and development of students. But many work under the *assumption of care*, believing that because teachers and school leaders are among youngsters that caring is present. It would be a mistake to assume that all educators are similarly capable and motivated. For this reason, an additional structural support—incentive systems of reward and accountability—should be considered. We have discussed how principals can communicate, encourage, recognize, and reinforce expectations for caring and community. And we have noted how data could promote responsibility and accountability. To go one step farther, principals, with teachers and staff, can explore ways to introduce caring and community as formal criteria for school assessment and personnel reviews. They can consider ways that contributions to caring community can be recognized and rewarded and how behaviors that do not focus on caring can be reset. Behaviors that impede caring should be eliminated. Consistent with the norms and values of caring community, these decisions and the ways in which they are carried out should be caring of the school community, consistent with redefinitions of authority, governance, and politics.

Redefining Authority Relationships, Governance, and Politics

Caring community in schools is further cultivated by redefining authority relationships, governance, and politics. This begins by shifting the basis of authority in schools from roles and rules to professional and moral norms and values that define the school as a caring community (Sergiovanni, 1994b). In Dunne's (1986) words, this is the authority that comes from the community's organizing values. As Beck and Foster (1999) observe, it is the moral purpose of the school community that forms the basis of authority. A principal, teacher, or other member of a school community has authority to the extent that they call upon, promote, and embody these norms and values. This shift in the basis of authority comes about as principals make decisions, exert their power, and explain their actions in ways that are consistent with the norms and values of caring community.

Principals can promote the relational bonds of caring community by making school governance a more participative process and by creating opportunities for student, teacher, and parent and caregiver voice and influence. To promote and live in community calls for adopting processes of collective problem solving and decision making (Sergiovanni, 1994b). Riehl (2000) argues that problem solving and decision making should become more inclusive and more democratic and examine distributions of benefit and loss.

In school governance, there are many ways in which principals can turn problem solving and decision making into a community process. These include forming leadership teams, problem-oriented study and work groups, task forces, advisory bodies, and governance councils. Other mechanisms include the sort of problem-oriented learning groups that Etienne Wenger (1998) and Wenger, McDermott, and Snyder (2002) call *communities of practice*, ad hoc voluntary groups that convene around a shared problem or concern to learn, create solutions, and bring their work to the organization as a whole. Principals can convene schoolwide forums, engage in informal conversations with individuals and groups, and develop channels of two-way communication by which they can seek input and feedback from students, teachers and staff, and parents and caregivers. While participation can take various forms and can be motivated by different reasons, participation in problem solving and decision making will contribute to caring community to the extent that it arises from motivations of caring community and is enacted according to the norms and values of that community.

As governance shifts toward meaningful participation, school politics will need to shift. By politics, we refer to the exercise of power and influence within formal problem-solving and decision-making processes, as well as outside of them (Slater & Boyd, 1999). All schools—indeed, all organizations—have politics. Good and useful politics is not the absence of politics; rather, the positive nature of the politics is what makes it good and useful.

Conducive to the cultivation of caring community are politics that are cooperative and consensual rather than competitive and adversarial (Mansbridge, 1983). Cooperative and consensual politics emphasize common perspectives, shared interests and values, and interdependencies, all of which increase the likelihood that different views will be expressed directly and honestly, that opposing positions are open-mindedly explored, and that differences are integrated or bridged into new solutions that participants commit to implement. In the process, there are opportunities for strengthening social bonds and for developing situated understanding of others that promotes caring. Competitive and adversarial politics, on the other hand, create the prospects of winners and losers and contribute little to commonality and community.

Likewise, focusing politics on collective or organizational-level interests is more conducive to caring community than politics focused on individual or group interests (Etzioni, 1996). The latter has potential to create division while the former creates greater prospect for community. The active engagement of conflict, rather than its avoidance, also holds prospect for creating politics conducive to caring and community (Achinstein, 2002; Tjosvold, 1998). Consistent with a cooperative and consensual orientation to political strategy and restorative approaches to conflict, active engagement of conflict can strengthen the social bonds of community. Last but not least, as suggested by our discussion of participation in school governance, expansion of power among many is more conducive to community building than consolidating power in a few (Slater & Boyd, 1999). Expansive distribution creates greater prospect for promoting mutual responsibility and accountability and for decisions that serve the interests of the community, as well as its individual members. It also creates stakes for individuals in the well-being of the whole.

Additional Thoughts

Making organizational changes to promote caring community can be difficult. There are always too many things to do and not enough time or resources to do them. Many forces conspire against cultivating caring community. It is difficult to step back from daily routines, buffer competing expectations, and engage in the long-term work of cultivating caring community. But, as we argued in Chapter 1, caring is not always about additional work. It is much about the matter, manner, and motivation of what educators already do, the many actions that teachers and leaders perform each day. It is about the matter, manner, and motivation of being in relationship, of being in community. Cultivation is, in large part, a matter of making caring community a priority, of bending structures and systems to fit the student, rather than changing the student to fit structures and systems.

We are not so naïve as to suggest that the work of cultivating caring community will not require additional time, energy, and resources. It is not unreasonable for principals, teachers, and students to challenge each other to recognize this possibility and to reprioritize and reallocate time and resources accordingly. It is not unreasonable to challenge principals to take away demands and activities that are of lower priority or that work against cultivating caring community. We have met few principals who strategically follow the course of "addition through subtraction." We have met a few teachers who tell us that their principals support the implementation of new initiatives by taking away old, less useful, and competing ones. Nevertheless, bringing students, teachers, staff, and administrators together to inventory and assess what they currently do that can be recast in the mold of caring community might go a long way toward cultivating caring community. The process becomes a model of collaborating on caring for one another. It might also help to identify those aspects of "how we do things around here" that can be abandoned because they have become barriers to creating caring community.

Engaging Parents and Caregivers

We conclude this chapter by returning to our argument that cultivating caring community in schools is not only the work of principals. It is work that calls upon the engagement and contributions of many. Throughout this chapter, we have discussed ways of engaging teachers, staff, and students in cultivating caring community. Now, we focus briefly on engaging parents and caregivers.

As we observed at the beginning of this chapter, it is unlikely that parents and caregivers will become engaged in school and contribute to its development unless they are welcomed as members of the school community and feel respected and cared for, especially by school leadership. Principals should make their schools welcoming and friendly places for parents and caregivers. It should be easy for parents and caregivers to become involved. Principals can remove barriers—literal and symbolic—that make it difficult or uncomfortable for parents and caregivers to participate in the life of the school. Principals should approach their relationships with parents and caregivers as a two-way, mutually supportive partnership. They should not view parents and caregivers as outsiders or simply as resources to be captured and enlisted into service. This may mean creating inclusive spaces, as did nearly five hundred schools in Los Angeles that dedicated at least one room to parents, often comfortably furnished and with computers. One low-income school installed pay washing machines and dryers in the basement, which allowed staff to meet with parents and younger siblings while parents completed a necessary household task.

Parent and caregiver engagement can be promoted through caring actions and interactions that they experience with the principal and teachers and, importantly, through the caring their children experience in school. As they experience caring directly and indirectly and as principals model and communicate the norms, values, and expectations of caring community, parents and caregivers are more likely to become engaged and feel part of the school community. As with teachers and staff members, principals can apply practices from Chapter 3 to relationships with parents and caregivers. If parents and caregivers are to be in two-way partnership with schools, if they are to be full-fledged members of a school's community, they can be invited into the workings of the school, for example, into programs and activities for students, into classrooms, and into school governance. They can be asked for information, feedback, and advice not only about their children and how to serve them well but also about matters of importance to the whole school community. They can be asked for direct assistance on subjects of interest to them and to which they may make substantive contribution. Importantly, they can be asked to participate in developing a vision and a strategy for cultivating caring community in the school. By these and other means of engagement, parents and caregivers are afforded opportunities for mutual responsibility that are part of community membership.

There is an extensive literature on parent involvement in schools and an extensive array of practices that can promote it (Epstein & Associates, 2019; Khalifa, Arnold, & Newcomb, 2015). Among broad areas of practice are clear and regular communication, opportunities to help parents and caregivers develop parenting skills and ways to support their children at home, volunteer opportunities at the school and classroom levels, learn-at-home activities that parents can engage with their children, participation in school and classroom decision making, and efforts of schools to work with community organizations and agencies. Some who advocate for parent engagement write about educating parents to better support student academic learning at home and foster a *family educational culture* that supports the school (Murphy &

Torre, 2014). This school-centric culture can manifest itself in a number of activities, such as tutoring children, reading with them, taking them to community and cultural events, helping with homework, engaging them in academic discussions, and supervising them within and outside the home.

Parent engagement can be promoted in other more family-centric ways, too. Principals' efforts to be visible and active in their schools' surrounding neighborhoods and efforts they make in neighborhoods to support and advocate for families can demonstrate caring and promote parent and caregiver engagement in schools (Khalifa et al., 2015). Moreover, principals can show caring by considering family circumstances and work and life demands borne by parents and caregivers. Murphy and Torre (2014) encourage principals to be mindful of and address causes of limited involvement. They identify a number of parent-related reasons, including lack of time and resources, work schedules and family obligations, limited knowledge and skills of how to interact with and participate in school, language barriers, transportation problems, discomfort associated with cultural and class differences, lack of trust, misperceptions, and histories of bad experiences. Some school-related reasons include negative and unwelcoming attitudes, limited physical and other resources, tendencies to "buffer" unwanted intrusions and influence, and lack of knowledge and skills about how to engage parents and caregivers.

There are many ways that principals can surmount these barriers. Murphy and Torre (2014) suggest that principals can provide options for participation and engagement that would take into account differences in family organization, culture, language proficiency, educational attainment, employment, and home educational milieu. As Khalifa and his colleagues (2016) suggest, principals can pursue strategies that are culturally sensitive and responsive, setting a tone of caring, respect, and inclusivity. They can focus on family needs, not just student needs and not just school needs. Importantly, principals can promote a vision and comprehensive strategy for engaging parents and caregivers, work that should meaningfully involve parents and caregivers themselves.

More specifically, there are myriad practices that principals can use to be caring of parents and caregivers and promote their engagement in cultivating school community. They can provide translators and translations to non–English speakers. They can meet parents and caregivers in their homes and workplaces, public libraries, churches, and community centers. They can develop opportunities to help parents and caregivers develop knowledge and skills to participate effectively in the life of the school, from volunteering in classrooms to engaging in leadership activities. Principals can locate activities that involve parents in their schools and also in homes and in other places in the community. They can hold community meetings and facilitate parent–teacher discussion groups. Regardless of the specific strategies principals use, it is important that the goal of cultivating caring community for students is central and those strategies be coherent and consistent with this goal.

Questions for Reflection and Discussion

1. How would you compare the *ideal* of caring community portrayed in this chapter with the *reality* of your school? In what ways is your school a caring community for students, and in what ways is it not?

2. How do you see yourself as a model for students and teachers of caring and of caring school community? What aspects of your leadership serve as positive modeling for caring and community? What aspects of your leadership might work against such positive modeling?

3. What programs and practices do you have in your school now that are helping to develop student and teacher capacity for caring and community? How are they helping? Where might you need to consider additional programs and practices to develop student capacity? What ideas might you have?

4. What organizational aspects of your school create opportunities for you to promote caring community? What aspects are barriers? What steps might you take to use these opportunities and to overcome these barriers?

5. What strategies might you use to engage students, teachers and staff, and parents and caregivers in cultivating caring community in your school? Think about strategies of engagement that might themselves reflect caring and contribute to the cultivation of caring community.

FOSTERING CARING IN FAMILIES AND COMMUNITIES BEYOND THE SCHOOL

In Chapter 1, we advocated for systemic consideration of the full range of sources and outcomes of caring for children and youth. This system includes relationships in school with teachers, staff, administrators, and fellow students, and it includes relationships in families and communities. How children and youth experience caring across these relationships determines caring's contributions to their development, learning, and well-being. Therefore, we follow our discussion in Chapter 4 of what principals can to do cultivate caring within their schools to consider what they can do to foster caring beyond their schools—in families and communities.

We recognize that parents, caregivers (those nonparent adults who raise children), and members of communities care about children and youth and care about their learning, development, and well-being. We know that parents and caregivers want their children to be happy, healthy, safe, and successful in school and beyond. And we recognize that while caring about their children, parents and caregivers may sometimes find it difficult to be caring of them. Sometimes, parents and caregivers may not have developed crucial competencies of caring, such as skills of attentiveness and inquiry, of asking and listening, of communicating and helping. They may not understand child and youth development or issues that affect children and youth to be caring in beneficial ways. Moreover, parents and caregivers may confront stresses, experience fatigue, and encounter myriad obstacles that make caring difficult. They may work multiple jobs and bear financial burdens. They may have health issues or experience relational or marital stress. Parents and caregivers may lack caring and support from others, which may compound these stresses and strains. Indeed, international research makes clear that socioeconomic stress and weak social connections are major factors affecting parents' and caregivers' capacity for caring.

Fostering caring in families and communities is often not part of principals' work—or at least an emphasized aspect of it. Kruse and Louis (2009) observe that one of the weakest and least prioritized components of principals' work is developing parent and community engagement *in* the school. Fostering caring *beyond* the school in families and communities is likely to be even less prioritized. Moreover, principals' orientations are often school centric rather than parent or family centric and thus not very responsive to what is happening in families and communities (Baquedano-López, Alexander, & Hernandez, 2013; Khalifa, Arnold, & Newcomb, 2015). We recognize the possibility that paternalistic and presumptive efforts by principals to support parents and families may be unresponsive and erode relationships. So, we present this arena of caring leadership as a challenge and encourage principals to consider how they might engage in it.

Nature of the Work

One way to think about this arena of caring school leadership is in terms of strengthening the social resources of families and communities to support the learning, development, and well-being of children and youth in general and their success in school in particular. In the words of Kruse and Louis (2009), it is work to "build social capital within communities, engaging schools to collaborate to promote community well-being" (p. 136), to make communities healthier and safer places for children and youth to learn and grow.

This aspect of caring school leadership is reminiscent of work ascribed to the principalship in the 1970s. According to Beck and Murphy's (1993) history of school leadership, a defining theme of the principalship that decade was leadership *in* and *of* the larger community. Principals were expected to lead their schools, but they were also expected to provide leadership within the community. They were to be educators of the community to help others understand and address social problems. They were responsible for ensuring that schools and communities connected in meaningful ways. Such civic leadership was an obligatory part of principals' work. Principals were to "lead in educating the public" (p. 141), especially with regard to educational matters, and involve the community in school activities. Principals were to "concern themselves with the totality of life within a given community" and to "improve the community by offering educational opportunities to its members" (p. 141).

Principals were also to provide leadership and resources so that community problems might be addressed through the "meaningful and real" involvement of "a familiar and generally accepted institution"—the school (Beck & Murphy, 1993, p. 141). This meant that principals worked closely with social agencies and community organizations to better support children and families. The principal was "an involved person" in the lives of families and communities (p. 118), visiting homes, providing direct support to families, and serving on committees to develop community initiatives to better support families and their children.

In many ways, this work is akin to the work of *public ministry* for members of the clergy. As we discussed earlier, public ministry is considered ministry to the public, in the public, and for the public on matters that transcend a particular congregation. This work fulfills the calling of service to the world, to make the world a better place. Willimon (2002) writes of the pastor as "the community prophet—moving about town agitating for reform, speaking out on justice issues, engaging the powers that be" (p. 64). It is an image of the pastor as *resident activist*. Willimon invokes Charles Gerkin's notion of pastoral care as "giving caring attention to concerns that reach beyond the individual to the community . . . and the larger society" (p. 37).

In similar manner, Jinkins (2014) writes about public ministry in terms of what the clergy does to guide and support a congregation's service to the community and the world. Theologically, the church is meant for proclamation and enactment of scripture in the world (Willimon, 2002). The pastor is to equip, engage, and guide the congregation in this work. In Judaism, this obligation belongs to all, and clergy guide. Couture (2014) describes this work as "theology-in-action" (p. 160). Work at the intersection of ministry and social policy may involve engaging government, supporting community activism, and using privilege and influence of the profession on behalf of the marginalized and oppressed.

Willimon (2002) observes that few pastors today are community opinion makers and community consciences. "Sadly," he writes, "most of us pastors . . . see ourselves as maintainers of equilibrium in the congregations that we serve; controllers of damage, soothers of ruffled feathers, rather than agents of social change" (p. 64). So too have the priorities of the principalship shifted toward leadership within the school in the forms of instructional leader, facilitator of professional community, even cultivator of caring communities for students, largely to the neglect of leadership in the outside community. The exception, perhaps, being principals' engagement of parents and community in the work of the school.

By focusing on this arena of caring school leadership, we challenge principals to consider the analogy of public ministry and the idea of civic leadership, community education, and advocacy as parts of their work. We challenge principals to consider how they might foster caring for children and youth beyond school in families and communities. Principals have a lot to do and the job can easily become all-consuming and overwhelming. Our challenge is not for them to take on this work outside their schools alone. Engaging this work may mean reallocating time and energy. It may mean relying more on others, such as teacher leaders, to perform some of the school-level functions of administrative leaders. Similar to the call of clergy to engage their congregations in public ministry and service, it may mean finding ways to make family and community support and development a project of the whole school. As we will see, our challenge is not for principals to perform the work of caring for families and the community alone. Instead, our challenge is for principals to consider how they can participate in the work of others, to contribute to and support it, helping others outside the school do better in caring for children and youth.

We proceed with a word of caution. With regard to public ministry, Willimon (2002) warns that in their strong desire to do something useful in the world, clergy must guard against being *surrogate social activists* or anything other than being clergy (p. 66). To do so would compromise their professional calling and primary responsibilities, including preparing and engaging their congregations to fulfill their theological functions of public ministry. We issued the same caution for principals in Chapter 1, where we emphasized the importance of professional boundaries and professional identity. It is important for principals to be realistic and humble in their expectations for this work. Yet, while their efforts may be limited, principals should not be agnostic about caring for children and youth outside the school. Nor should they be dissuaded by the enormity of the task to foster it. Even small efforts can make a positive contribution.

We now examine practices that principals might use to foster caring in families and communities. We consider how principals might work through their district central offices. Then, we discuss several ways to foster caring in families by working with parents and caregivers. We conclude by discussing several practices for fostering caring in communities. Because of a paucity of practice-based education literature to inform us, we turn to other professional fields—community organizing and community development—for guidance. Akin to our observation about cultivating schools as caring communities, principals' efforts to foster caring in families and communities are best understood as "custom jobs." We remember that it is not only the focus of this work that makes it part of caring school leadership, it is also the caring motivation and manner in which it is pursued.

Working Through Central Office

School district central offices play a key role in effective school–community relations and in the contributions that schools might make to support families and community development. Sanders (2014) argues that it is important for districts to think of schools, families, and communities as parts of a system that influences the learning, development, and well-being of children and youth. She states that central offices can perform crucial leadership functions, notably communicating clear messages of vision and value, setting expectations, creating opportunities for learning and development, providing resources, and coordinating relationships among schools and between schools and the families and communities they serve.

Principals can make important contributions by encouraging, supporting, and participating in this district-level work. Principals can act independently or perhaps, more effectively, in networks and coalitions they might form. Principals can encourage district-level leadership to make caring of students, as well as caring in families and communities, a central priority for the district as a whole. Principals can encourage central-office leaders to include as part of strategic plans and budget initiatives support for caring schools, families, and communities. Principals can help develop and implement districtwide policies and programs that foster caring in schools, families, and communities. Importantly, they can be watchdogs and help district leadership be mindful of how programs and policies affect district-level and school-level efforts to promote caring, positively or negatively.

Moreover, principals can help central offices support their own school-based efforts to cultivate caring in schools, families, and communities. With other principals, they can lobby central offices to support similar efforts in schools across their district. Principals can call on their central offices to bring resources and other influences to bear on forming and supporting partnerships with community agencies and organizations. Principals can encourage their central offices to engage in public informing about the importance of caring in schools, families, and communities. This can include helping families and the public better understand issues in the education, learning, and development of children and youth and the promise and limitations of particular pathways to address these issues. Finally, principals can encourage district-level leaders, notably superintendents, CEOs, and school boards, to be civic leaders in advocating for municipal and state-level programs, policies, and resources that promote caring in schools, families, and communities.

Fostering Caring in Families

In this section, we examine several practices for fostering caring in families. We begin with modeling and vicarious learning. These practices reflect the idea that caring and the experience of being cared for begets caring. We turn to practices that provide opportunities for parent education and support, build connections among families for mutual assistance, and facilitate family access to educational and support services available in the community.

Modeling and Vicarious Learning

As we discussed earlier with regard to students and teachers, principals can foster caring among parents and caregivers and other members of families by modeling caring behavior. Through their actions and interactions, principals can demonstrate the knowledge and understanding they have of individual and groups of students, their families, and their situations. Principals can express empathy, sympathy, and compassion, three critical virtues of caring. They can show caring in the ways that they communicate with parents and caregivers about how they are helping their children in school. Equally important, they can demonstrate skills of caring, including inquiry and attentiveness, communicating, helping, advocating, and acting in other ways on behalf of parents, caregivers, and families. Principals can model caring when parents and caregivers come into the school, and they can show caring when they go into communities to meet and work with parents and caregivers. Indeed, principals who make the effort to go into homes and communities, to work with parents in ways that acknowledge their circumstances, may be seen as being caring. Such opportunities for modeling can also come as parents and caregivers observe and interact with their children's teachers. Principals can model caring when parents and caregivers witness principals interacting directly with their children in school or in home and community settings. Modeling can occur as children share with their parents and caregivers the caring actions and interactions they experience with principals and also with teachers.

Another way that parents and caregivers can learn caring is through their experiences in schools that have become caring communities for students and through their participation in cultivating these communities. They can see caring when experiencing schools as welcoming and caring places for students and adults. As full-fledged members of these communities, parents and caregivers can witness examples of caring among adults and students. They are exposed to information that may help them better understand their children and issues they confront. They have abundant models of how to act and interact in caring ways. Moreover, membership in caring school communities provides parents and caregivers opportunities to be caring themselves, to practice and to receive feedback as they develop their own capacity for caring.

Education and Support

Principals and their schools can provide education and support directly to parents, caregivers, and perhaps other family members in the form of courses and workshops, among other formal learning opportunities. According to Epstein and Associates (2019), these activities can increase families' understanding of their children's growth and development. They can inform parents and caregivers about children's health, safety, and nutrition and other topics of child and youth development. They can provide guidance for creating home conditions conducive to children's health, learning, development, and well-being. And they can offer ideas about what parents and caregivers can do to support students' schooling at home. Moreover, these educational opportunities can directly foster parents' and caregivers' capacity for caring by developing the competencies, mindsets, and virtues of caring. They can nurture parenting and caregiving skills, as well as social-emotional competencies. As we will discuss shortly, these opportunities can provide information and strategies for parents and caregivers to engage support services in the community.

To be effective, these educational opportunities should focus on meeting the particular needs and interests of families and students in school and at home (Epstein & Associates, 2019). According to Murphy and Torre (2014), such programs should be concrete rather than abstract and provide specific strategies for parents, caregivers, and families. These programs need to be accessible. This means that they should be available at times and in places—including sites in the community—so that parents and caregivers can participate in them. They need to be in languages and at levels that connect with parents and caregivers. Educational opportunities need to be culturally relevant, and they should be designed and delivered in ways that reflect how parents and caregivers learn and put such learning to use. Moreover, these educational opportunities are perhaps better attended and more effective if planned and led with parents themselves.

Epstein and associates (2019) provide numerous examples of ways in which schools can extend support and assistance to parents and caregivers. They can conduct workshops, provide summaries of information on parenting, set up websites, sponsor panels, and hold classes on specific subjects directly related to parenting, caring, and family well-being, such as physical and mental health, nutrition and exercise, family finances and budgeting, and computer technology and use.

Connections Among Families

Principals can foster connections among families so that they can support each other. According to Epstein and associates (2019), principals and teachers can organize parent support groups and parent networks. The educational activities discussed previously can create opportunities to build supportive relationships among parents and caregivers themselves. Teaching Tolerance (2016) emphasizes the importance of promoting strong connections among families so that they may be sources of support for one another. In addition to the activities that Epstein and her colleagues recommend, Teaching Tolerance suggests developing user-friendly contact lists and directories, instituting family service projects that can bring families together around joint activities in the school and community, sponsoring film and speaker series, and linking families together and with the school on social media.

Access to Community Support Services

Another way that principals can foster caring is to promote parent, caregiver, and family access to support services in the community. Schools can be places where a range of support services can be located. Schools can host job fairs and food banks, sponsor GED programs, and provide spaces for social service and physical and mental health care providers to render services. If not in their buildings, schools might sponsor such services in other locations, such as churches, public libraries, or community centers. Moreover, schools might become delivery hubs of family resources and support services. They can be banks of information to direct parents and caregivers to services in and around their communities. Schools can provide information about the particular services that different providers offer and contact information, even information about how to pay for such services, including what types of financial assistance might be available. In these ways, schools can serve as "optimal distribution points for social services" (Murphy & Torre, 2014, p. 187).

That schools can be focal community institutions for children and families is part of the logic behind coordinated children's services projects in schools and community–school initiatives. Central to this logic is that collaborative efforts can increase access to services and enhance the efficiency of service provision. These efforts can lead to an overall expansion of services available to children and families and, perhaps, increase their effectiveness. In these projects and initiatives, schools enter into partnerships with community organizations and agencies, local businesses, and service providers to support the schools' educational objectives and to provide direct caring support services for children and families. Through these partnerships, principals and schools can "broker" access to caring services beyond those that the school alone can provide (Murphy & Torre, 2014).

There is a useful body of literature to guide principals who might be interested in pursuing coordinated children service projects and community–school initiatives (see, e.g., Comer, Haynes, Joyner, & Ben-Avie, 1996; Dryfoos & Quinn, 2005), as well as a national association—Coalition for Community Schools (www.communityschools.org). These resources contain important insights into the dynamics of working relationships among schools and professional agencies, community organizations, businesses, and individual service providers. It also contains insights into the managerial complexities and resources required to develop and sustain coordinated service provision— and to keep caring as the center of gravity.

Murphy and Torre (2014) summarize some of the things that principals will need to do when forming relationships with community organizations and service providers. First, they should assess the capabilities, will, and interests of potential partners. They should seek input from parents and caregivers, teachers, students, and community members about their hopes, resources, and needs. Many community organizations seek involvement with schools, but principals should investigate the attitudes of teachers and parents toward particular agencies and their potential contributions. It is unwise to assume that even though a service provider is in the community that it would be welcomed and supported in the school. With this information, principals can prepare their schools and promote buy-in. Principals would need to locate and secure requisite human, fiscal, and material resources. They would need to prepare for problems that might arise, including communication problems, issues of mistrust, clashes of professional perspectives, conflicting expectations, and maintaining a balance of benefits. With others in the school, including parents and caregivers, principals and prospective partners would set clear goals and develop a *collective vision* for joint work. They would set clear expectations for working together.

Once in partnership, principals need to monitor, maintain, and adjust joint work. According to Murphy and Torre (2014), principals need to promote the vision of the partnership and ensure that joint goals and expectations are met. Principals need to make and adjust rules and procedures as coordinated work evolves. They also need to ensure that the right people are involved and empowered to make decisions. Because of the demands and complexities of making these interorganizational efforts successful, principals may wish to start with small manageable projects and use them to build trust and confidence and hone relationships to undertake more ambitious projects in the future. Principals also may realize that they need to hire or assign staff or volunteers to coordinate these initiatives—few principals can add monitoring outside agencies to their already full work agenda. But we caution that delegation still requires staying informed and involved to ensure that community linkages do not sit at the periphery of the school organization. Principals are responsible for integrating them into the life of the school.

Fostering Caring in Communities

In this section, we present several strategies that principals can use to foster caring for children and youth in the communities that surround their schools. As we discussed earlier, many of these strategies focus on what principals can do to guide and support, even challenge, community organizations and members in their work with children and families and in making communities more caring places. We begin with involving schools in community-based projects and turn to public informing, advocacy, and developing the capacity of community organizations.

Community-Based Projects

One way that principals can foster caring in the communities surrounding their schools is by engaging their teachers and students in community-based projects. Such projects can be developed and conducted by partnering with community agencies, associations, and organizations of all types (e.g., government, nonprofit, business). Or they may be conducted by the school alone. Many schools have implemented service-learning initiatives, some making them a curricular requirement. While there is not extensive research on the outcomes of service learning for K–12 students, some evidence suggests that it can have positive effects on students' personal and social development, sense of civic responsibility, engagement in school, and academic achievement (see, e.g., Billig, 2000; Furco & Root, 2010). Service learning can also lead to improved student–teacher and student–peer relationships. There is less research about the impact of service learning on communities, except that it can lead community members to have more positive perceptions of schools and participating youth. Community members who participate in service learning with schools are likely to see youth as valued resources and positive contributors to the community (Billig, 2000).

It is likely that greater community impact can be achieved through focused, large-scale action projects involving critical masses of students and school personnel. Community action projects are described in Teaching Tolerance (2016) as a powerful way for students to develop and exercise care, address important social issues, and contribute to the development of their schools and local communities. Principals can play an important role in initiating these projects and in recruiting teachers, other staff members, and volunteers from the community to organize and lead them. Principals can help teachers enlist students and make connections to community members and organizations.

To make meaningful contributions, these projects should address real needs of communities. With regard to our focus, these needs would relate to the care and support of children, youth, and families. Conversations with community leaders and their constituents can help identify these needs. Programs like service learning are likely to have more impact if they are implemented for extended periods of time, even as students who might have helped initiate them graduate or turn to other activities and other students take their place. These efforts are more likely to have a positive impact if they engage schools and students in work *with* rather than *for* community members.

Public Informing

Another way that principals can foster caring for children, youth, and families is through public informing and advocacy. As we argued in Chapter 2, principals should not be agnostic or silent about caring and its importance to the learning, development, and well-being of children and youth. Through public forums, social media, and communications with local newspapers, radio, and television outlets; by being available to the press; and by pursuing publicity for caring-related initiatives in their schools, principals can inform the public about the meaning and importance of caring in schools, homes, and communities. They can inform the public about how caring in its many forms can contribute to the learning, development, and well-being of children and youth, as well as promote their success in school. Principals can help the public consider caring as a responsibility of the whole community. Through public informing, principals can encourage community thinking about different ways to foster caring, challenge practices that may impede caring, and build public support for community-based initiatives.

Advocacy

Riehl (2000) and Khalifa, Gooden, and Davis (2016) argue that public advocacy for community-based causes is crucial to address issues of educational and social inequity. Moreover, advocating for community-based causes is important to earning trust and credibility among families and community members, which can help leverage political and other resources to address both school-related and community-related issues, including building capacity for caring. Moreover, as Khalifa and his colleagues observe, "Perhaps the most effective way for educators to understand parental needs is by advocating for some of them" (p. 24). As community-based advocacy inspires parent rapport and trust, parents may feel more comfortable helping to promote school-based needs and interests. Advocacy becomes key, Khalifa and his colleagues conclude, for making schools part of—rather than apart from— the communities they serve.

Principals can engage in targeted advocacy for specific programs and policies that provide care for children, youth, and families and that develop capacity for caring in families and communities. They can develop relationships with civic and municipal leaders and advocate for programs and policies through local governance processes. They can work with departments of parks and recreation, safety and law enforcement agencies, businesses, religious organizations, and social-service and health care providers to advance programs that serve children, youth, and families and that foster caring in families and communities. Khalifa and his colleagues (2015) identify several true examples: a retired principal attending and speaking at a community-based rally against racism, a principal speaking at a rally against immigration-focused racial profiling, a principal marching against poverty, a principal advocating for refugee students, an assistant principal feeding hungry community residents, and a principal publicly standing against violence and drug abuse.

Such advocacy fits within a broader agenda for developing social resources for children and families in community. We will say more about advocacy later in this chapter when we discuss insights and suggestions for principals from community organizing and development.

Developing the Capacity of Community Organizations

Principals can help develop the capacity of community agencies and organizations to serve children, youth, and families better. Either as volunteers or through partnership arrangements, principals can advise and consult with children and family-oriented agencies and organizations. They can provide knowledge and understanding from the profession of education and educational leadership, as well as from experiential knowledge and understanding developed within schools to help these agencies and organizations better understand the children and families they serve. From their work as leaders of complex organizations, principals can be a source of insight and assistance in helping community agencies and organizations organize themselves to more efficiently and effectively provide service (Murphy & Torre, 2014). Finally, principals can help community agencies and organizations serve and be caring of children and families by assisting them to better communicate and coordinate with each other to improve their services.

Insights From Community Organizing and Community Development

As we mentioned at the beginning of this chapter, the education literature does not provide much practical guidance for this arena of caring school leadership. However, a number of insights and suggestions are found in literatures on community organizing and community development. By looking to these literatures, we are not suggesting that principals become community organizers or full-time social activists. Nor are we suggesting that principals forego their professional responsibilities as educational leaders to become community developers. As we have mentioned several times, the contributions that principals make to their schools and to the learning and development of children are advanced by operating within the parameters of the profession. Still, scholarship on community organizing and community development offers principals some useful ideas.

While community organizing and community development are both focused on social change and addressing problems in communities, the former is often distinguished for its focus on political power and conflict. According to social work scholars Robert Fisher and Eric Shragge (2000), community organizing assumes that social problems exist in large part because of oppressive power and conflicting interests that can only be addressed by confrontation and oppositional power. Community organizing assumes that empowerment, which is necessary for effective confrontation and change, is built on the strength of interpersonal relationships that can only be realized through organizing (Speer & Hughey, 1995). Community development, on the other hand, proceeds from the assumption that change comes through shared interests, political moderation, and common pursuit of the well-being of the whole community. Some experts see ways of integrating community organizing and development. For example, Brady and O'Connor (2014) think about the professional practice of community organizing as involving purposeful activities that challenge unjust systems and policies politically and also help communities develop through interconnections among diverse members who may not agree on all goals or strategies.

There are many models and strategies of community organizing (e.g., Rubin & Rubin, 2008; Weil, 2005). According to organization development scholars Brian Christens and Paul Speer (2015), different models typically share four elements or phases. The first is assessment and relationship building, during which community members identify and define critical issues affecting them. The second is participatory research with knowledgeable community members and representatives of relevant community entities and interests. The third is mobilization and action through strategy development and exercise of social and political power developed through organizing. The final stage is evaluation and reflection. Often these phases are integrated into cycles of mutually informing learning and action, or as Speer and Hughey (1995) put it, a dialectic of action and reflection. These phases and specific actions associated with them are shown in Figure 5.1.

Figure 5.1 • Phases and Actions of Community Organizing

1. Assessment and relationship building

   - Identify and define critical community issues

   - Small-group meetings to assess issues, connect individuals, and deepen relationships among community members

2. Participatory research

   - Examine causes and correlates of issues

   - Study possible solutions and likely effects

   - Investigate how distribution of community resources affects issues

   - Investigate how individuals and organizations exercise social and political power around issues

3. Mobilization and action

   - Engage large numbers of disciplined, focused community members to take action

   - Strategically use media

   - Engage public officials

   - Work with other organizations concerned with the same issues

4. Evaluation and reflection

   - Examine effectiveness of strategies

   - Identify and assess problems and lessons, including power dynamics

   - Calculate future directions in strategy, organizing, and leadership

In their work to develop a *formal practice theory* of community organizing, Shane Brady and Mary Katherine O'Connor (2014) describe these four phases somewhat differently and, in the process, suggest additional actions. For example, in the first stage, they emphasize the goal of relationship building, where organizers and community members engage in various activities that help them get to know one another and develop trust to move forward in organizing. Crucial to this process is learning about the community, raising awareness about oppression, and identifying mutual issues and needs.

From relationship building, Brady and O'Connor's (2014) practice theory moves to planning. During this stage, organizers and community members develop an organizing plan with explicit goals and strategies. Once a plan is developed, community members and organizers come together in a mobilization stage to enact the plan and achieve the goals. Key to the success of this phase is whether enough collective power has been generated and exercised to achieve the plan's goals. Much like Speer and Hughey (1995), Brady and O'Connor close the cycle with evaluating organizing's processes and outcomes. They contend that the particular activities undertaken within each phase should be contingent upon the context of the community, its members, and the people who become involved in organizing. Community organizing is thus best considered a "custom job."

A potentially useful set of strategies comes from a guidebook for community organizers by education reform and community-organizing experts Kavitha Mediratta, Seema Shah, and Sara McAlister (2009). While this guidebook focuses on what community organizing can do to improve schools, there are a number of insights that principals can use to develop community-based caring for children and families. Even if principals are not leaders in organizing activity, they can participate in and guide activity led by others. They can identify and define issues and needs. They can work with organizers and community members to identify causes of problems and search for potentially effective solutions. They can lend their credibility and influence to the process. Of course, principals must be aware of their professional responsibilities and sensitive to possible consequences of assuming a visible role in community organizing involving political confrontation.

Mediratta and her colleagues (2009) advise organizers to begin with the strategic development of relationships among people who are directly affected by and concerned with a particular problem. They should invite these people into a group process in which they can discuss and analyze causes of the problem. Such groups would assess who has the institutional authority to make decisions concerning needs and who has the political power to influence those decisions. From these analyses, coalitions to achieve particular goals will emerge and principals might choose to become involved with those that are directly related to creating caring in their communities and in their schools. Mediratta and her colleagues contend that the power and influence of organizing comes from the number of people involved in making demands and also from members' knowledge of issues, their credibility, the strength of proposed solutions, relationships with influential allies, and the legitimacy of demands. Principals may have interpersonal and professional resources that they may offer to other community members. By tapping into their connections, principals may help develop a growing base of members and supporters that enables organizers to take on more complex issues.

Mediratta and her colleagues (2009) suggest a number of specific strategies for building relationships and mobilizing community members. These include one-on-one conversations and home visits, potluck meals, public speaking, and other community events. These strategies should not be "one-offs" or disconnected from one another. Moreover, strategies need to be connected in a mutually reinforcing *system* of action. This kind of principal engagement is not new. Organizations, such as the Search Institute (www.search-institute.org), have brought principals into community organizing. And Ann Ishimaru (2013) and Dennis Shirley (1997) have written case studies of principals engaged in successful community-organizing activities to benefit students and families.

Should principals consider community development rather than community organizing to foster caring of children and families in communities, they can find guidance in the Search Institute's work on asset-building communities (Benson, 2006), which focuses on organizing to fill the *relationship gap* that spans community and school. In a new asset-building approach, Search Institute has initiated a national partnership with youth-serving organizations "to study and strengthen relationships in five sectors—schools, out-of-school time programs, mentoring programs, peer-to-peer programs, and programs that work with families" (Pekel et al., 2018, p. 499).

Central to growing asset-building communities is the cultivation of "developmental nutrients" that children and youth need to grow up successfully (Benson, 2006, p. 13). These include consistent support and care provided by one or more parents or other caregivers, sustained relationships with other nonparent adults, and a neighborhood where adults know, respect, protect, listen to and hear, value, and engage children and youth. Other nutrients include opportunities for children and youth to participate in developmentally responsive and enticing clubs, teams, and organizations; access to child-friendly public places; and intergenerational relationships in which children and teenagers bond with adults of many ages and with each other. Additional nutrients include peer groups motivated toward mutual support and success; caring schools, religious congregations, youth-serving organizations, corporate sponsors, and other community institutions; and opportunities for frequent acts of service to others.

Building on Benson's work (2006), Kent Pekel and his colleagues (2018) are building asset-based communities by working with and through youth-serving organizations and schools to examine the caring relationships that occur within families, schools, and communities and by providing learning opportunities for adults to strengthen their ability to work with each other to promote caring for children. The focus is on increasing developmental relationships outside of school, but they also focus on school calendars and programs, among other things, that "facilitate substantive and sustained interaction between young people and adults" and ways of assessing existing and future staff members' capacities for contributing to developmental relationships in school (Pekel et al., 2018, p. 499).

The general strategies of this work focus first on identifying and developing community readiness, energy, and commitment. They focus second on creating operational infrastructures (programs and people) to support the work of community building. And third, they focus on actions to build specific community and school assets. Examples of strategies within each are shown in Figure 5.2.

Figure 5.2 • Strategies for Community Development

1. Developing community readiness, energy, and commitment

   - Developing and mobilizing a public vision and the will to bring that vision to life

   - Nurturing relational trust and social bonds among community members

   - Promoting individual and collective efficacy to engage in the work

   - Gathering data and monitoring to identify community assets and weaknesses

2. Creating an organizational infrastructure to support community building

   - Identifying and assessing human, material, and fiscal resources

   - Organizing networks of participants and stakeholders

   - Creating communication systems and strategies

   - Developing processes of planning, decision making, and governance

   - Securing tools and establishing connections for training and technical assistance

   - Developing processes of assessment and documentation, management and coordination, and recognition and reward

3. Actions to build specific community assets

   - Community education programs for parents and families

   - Corporate and community service programs (e.g., peer mentoring, tutoring)

   - Opportunities for youth development through youth organizations, teams, clubs, arts programs, and parks and recreation programs

   - Mobilize and use media

Benson (2006) argues that it is important to "activate" different sectors of the community to engage in this work, including local businesses and government, religious institutions, health agencies, neighborhood organizations, community centers, libraries, and schools. It is also important to press for alignment of civic decisions with asset-building goals and strategies. In each of these, principals may have both a presence and a voice because of their expertise and understanding of children and youth. Community development and developmental relationships are linked: "Young people need essential economic resources *and* essential developmental resources" (Benson, 2006, p. 17). Addressing issues of poverty and discrimination and building developmental assets in mutually reinforcing ways is essential.

1. How might you see yourself as a leader in your school's community? What responsibilities do you feel you may have, personally and/or professionally, to promote the interests and well-being of students beyond the walls of your school and to help families and communities be more caring and supportive of children and youth? Where do you draw professional parameters for this work? Why do you draw them here?

2. How might your school district's central office promote caring of students in schools, in families, and in communities? What might you do to help?

3. Think about ways that you and your school could help parents and caregivers be more caring of their children at home? What role might modeling play? What role might educational programs, networking initiatives, and access to community services play?

4. How might you and your school help families and members of your community better understand the importance of caring for the learning, development, and well-being of children and youth? In what forms of public informing and advocacy might you engage?

5. How might you work with community organizations, businesses, and agencies to help them better serve children and families? What value might you add as a school leader?

DEVELOPING CARING SCHOOL LEADERSHIP

If we aspire to more caring in school leadership, how might we develop it? What might we do to bring the practice of caring school leadership to life so that students, teachers, and parents and caregivers see it as commonplace? Answers to these questions are the subject of this, our last chapter.

We begin by reviewing the foundational elements of caring school leadership to identify key points of leverage in developing it. We recall the potential problems and pitfalls of caring to argue that helping principals avoid, mitigate, and learn from them is an important part of caring school leadership development.

Following this review, we describe a number of activities and experiences that can help develop caring school leadership. Some are recommended for developing positive, ethical, and authentic approaches to leadership akin to caring school leadership. We also consider recommendations for developing the relational aspects of leadership and school leaders' social-emotional capabilities. We focus on the role of learning from experience, looking particularly at reflective practice and vicarious learning. We conclude with a discussion of self-care, that is, what school leaders can do to care for themselves and thus enhance the prospects of being caring of others in their leadership. Our discussion is informed by research and professional expertise on the importance of job embeddedness, collaboration, and systematic information in professional learning. We emphasize the importance of group learning and learning with the support of others.

There is little written about developing caring school leadership as we have presented it in this book. Much of what we can learn comes from professional literatures on developing related forms of leadership. Guidance also comes from literature on how to develop relationship aspects of leadership generally and leaders' social-emotional intelligence in particular. None of these literatures are particularly well advanced, but they offer insights and lessons that can be useful. We also find guidance from literatures of other human service professions, such as medicine, nursing, and ministry.

As we stated at the beginning of this book, we recognize that principals and other school leaders care deeply about the students in their schools and about their success and well-being. We assume that many principals already possess some measure of the values, mindsets, and competencies that undergird the practice of caring school leadership. So, as we explore how to develop caring school leadership, we assume that we are not starting from scratch. Indeed, in a recent national survey, 65 percent of teachers reported that their principals develop "an atmosphere of caring and trust" in their schools (see Louis, Murphy, & Smylie, 2016). In addition, the Pew Research Center (2019) reports that 45 percent of U.S. adults say that K–12 public school principals care about others or "people like me" all or most of the time—more perceived caring than from police officers (37 percent) or local elected officials (14 percent). Our hope is that our discussion will help expand and strengthen caring school leadership and move it to even higher levels.

What Should Be Developed: A Review

We have written that the practice of caring school leadership is a function of three foundational elements: *aims, virtues and mindsets,* and *competencies.* It is also a function of how these elements are brought to life through actions and interactions, in small routines and in big events. We recall that developing the foundational elements of caring and translating them into practice will be influenced by interpersonal, organizational, and extraorganizational contexts. We also recall that these contexts can be shaped to help develop and enact caring school leadership. In all, caring leadership can be promoted as these foundational elements are developed.

The practice of caring school leadership derives from pursuing specific aims that include promoting the functioning, success, and general well-being of others; addressing their particular needs; and advancing their interests and projects. They include helping others grow and develop in their own right. Caring can aim to provide particular tangible and instrumental benefits, such as services and assistance. It can aim to provide experiential benefits, including social, psychological, and emotional ones. And caring can be pursued to beget more caring. Caring can be a response to many circumstances, including pain, suffering, and conflict. It can be an affirmative expression of appreciation, approval, or joy.

For principals and other school leaders, these aims should focus squarely on students. At the same time, they should focus on teachers and staff and families and communities. The aims of caring are consistent with promoting equity of educational opportunity. We argued that caring and caring school leadership can contribute much to equity work in schools, and we provided numerous examples of practices that make such contributions.

Caring and caring school leadership arise from a number of positive virtues and mindsets. These virtues include compassion, empathy, patience, sympathy, and kindness. They include fairness and justice, authenticity, humility, and vulnerability. And they include transparency, honesty, trustworthiness, prudence, and respect for others. Caring and caring school leadership also proceed from several mindsets that include attentiveness to others and a motivational orientation toward promoting others' success and well-being. Caring and caring school leadership are also related to personal, role, and professional identities that can enable caring. Finally, caring and caring school leadership can be supported through a mindset of playfulness, which enables creativity and flexibility in perceiving, thinking, and acting on behalf of others. Most people, when asked, believe that they already have many of these qualities. However, they may be more or less effective in putting them into practice. Thus, development should consider not only the strength of these foundational elements but also how well they translate into actions and interactions that can be experienced by others.

In this regard, caring and caring school leadership involve a number of competencies, that is, knowledge, skills, and attitudes that help bring the aims, virtues, and mindsets of caring to life. These competencies include the ability to develop authentic understanding of others and their needs, problems, joys, concerns, and situations. They include knowledge about human development and contemporary and historical issues and contexts affecting others, including race, socioeconomic status, language, culture, religion, gender, sexual orientation, ability and disability, and other relevant characteristics and conditions. Most principals possess some degree of this knowledge, although few would argue that they are as knowledgeable as they would like to be.

There is also a wide range of skills critical to caring, including the ability to ask, hear and listen, observe, assess, learn, and engage others in meaningful conversations. And there are the knowledge and skills of acting on behalf of others, including knowledge of potentially effective strategies and the skills to enact them well. We wrote of knowledge and skills for developing the capacity for caring among others and for developing school organization to form communities that are conducive to caring. Moreover, we identified knowledge and skills for fostering caring in families and communities.

Related to these competencies is social-emotional intelligence in forming relationships and interacting with others, intelligence that includes self-awareness, self-regulation, and self-management. Such intelligence concerns knowledge of one's self, including one's orientations and inclinations, strengths and limitations, predispositions and prejudices, joys and fears, and sense of one's own capacity for caring. Moreover, caring and caring school leadership are associated with the ability to wrestle positively with ethical and practical dilemmas posed by competing values, needs, and considerations.

We argued that caring can lead to a number of problems and negative, unintended consequences. There are potential negative consequences of actions and interactions born of caring intentions that go awry for lack of understanding, lack of competency, or weakness of motivational orientation toward others. We mentioned the prospects of under- and overattachment, embarrassment and vulnerability, inappropriate obligation and reciprocity, objectification, and reinforcement of asymmetries of power and control. We mentioned empathy traps, dependencies, codependencies, and transference. We also mentioned the prospects of unwarranted subjugation and infringement of privacy, autonomy, and rights and, in the worst instance, abuse and victimization. Finally, we recognized that for the ones caring, caring can be demanding and tiring. It can lead to stress and *compassion fatigue* which, without support, can lead to burnout. Caring is promoted when such problems are avoided or managed and learned from when they arise.

As we come to our discussion of developmental activities and experiences, recall that the practice of caring school leadership is framed and guided by the norms, expectations, personal and professional identities, and parameters of the profession of educational leadership. Caring in leadership involves being caring of individuals, groups, and the school as a whole. It involves caring for students, as well as for teachers, staff, and parents and caregivers. It involves caring for families and communities outside the school. It involves caring for the institution of schooling and the profession of school leadership. And it involves caring for oneself. We believe that caring school leadership is principled practice, guided by the principles and values of the profession and defined by principles of practice.

Development Activities and Experiences

There are many activities and experiences that can promote school leadership development generally and caring school leadership in particular. Looking across a variety of sources (e.g., Allen & Hartman, 2008; Conger, 1992; Day, Harrison, & Halpin, 2009), we compiled several categories of activities and experiences:

- *Programs focused on knowledge and skill training and development*, such as classes, workshops, and training programs; e-learning; and self-paced learning from books, workbooks, videos, and other media sources

- *Guided experiential learning*, including group reflection, service learning, mentoring and coaching programs, developmental "stretch" tasks and job assignments, team building, and simulations, role playing, and games

- *Individualized learning experiences*, including role models, self-guided reflective practice, sabbaticals, action learning (e.g., action research and inquiry), job crafting or job rotation to enlarge the range of experiences, feedback from assessment centers, self-administered instruments, in-depth 360-degree review systems, and networking with colleagues and senior leaders

Such activities and experiences can be part of initial preparation programs for school leaders, as well as programs for on-the-job professional development. A number of them are currently being used in preservice and in-service programs (Taylor, Cordeiro, & Chrispeels, 2009; Young, Crow, Murphy, & Ogawa, 2009). Many respond to the call that values and ethics should be integrated into programs of educational leadership preparation and development (Craig & Norris, 2008; Taylor et al., 2009).

Each development activity and experience has benefits and limitations, but generally, their effectiveness depends on several key considerations. First, no one type of activity or experience will do the whole job of leadership development. Rather leadership is best developed through "systems" or "webs" of mutually reinforcing activities and experiences (Dalakoura, 2010; Day, Harrison, & Halpin, 2009). Developing caring school leadership requires attention to different areas of learning and development (e.g., Allen & Hartman, 2008; Conger, 1992). It involves developing personal values, virtues, orientations, and mindsets related to caring. It involves developing knowledge and understanding about others and their situations, about the efficacy of different caring practices, and about how to implement those practices. It also involves developing knowledge and understanding of caring, how it functions, and its problems and benefits. Moreover, it involves developing particular skills concerning relationship and community building, communication, and helping, among others. Thus, developing caring school leadership would involve a number of mutually reinforcing activities and experiences.

It is important to align development activities and experiences with persons, contexts, and situations. As these change and as learning and development occur, realignment should also occur. The individual and situational nature of development means that there is no one "best practice" nor best system of activities and experiences. Indeed, strict adherence to one particular strategy is likely to limit development (Pearce, 2007).

Of course, the individual and situational nature of leadership development does not mean that everything will work equally well. To the contrary, development activities and experiences are more effective when they embody several key qualities and characteristics (Day et al., 2009; McCauley, 2008; Van Velsor & McCauley, 2004). These include authenticity to the leadership work to be done and relevance to leaders' learning and development needs (McCauley, 2008). Development activities and experiences are more effective when they incorporate (a) challenge and stretch, (b) instruction and reflection on new ways of thinking and acting, (c) opportunities for enactment and practice, (d) assessment and meaningful feedback, and (e) relevant technical and social-emotional support from others. The most powerful development activities embody all of these elements and are related to experience and future practice.

It may not be possible that every development activity and experience embody every one of these qualities and characteristics. Yet it is not unreasonable to think that a web of development activities could. One can imagine, for example, that classroom-based learning opportunities might help aspiring or practicing school leaders become aware of and understand methods of attentiveness, inquiry, communication, and help-giving, all important to caring. However, without related opportunities to apply and reflect on such knowledge in practice, perhaps under the watchful and encouraging eye of a colleague or a coach, classroom experience alone is not likely to promote much development.

We turn now to consider development activities and experiences that are associated with positive, ethical, and authentic leadership. We also examine activities and experiences related to developing positive human relations and social-emotional intelligence in leadership. Each provides guidance for developing caring school leadership.

Developing Positive Leadership

We have described positive leadership as emphasizing the moral and ethical dimensions of leadership and stressing character and virtues. It considers leadership a function of human relationships, enacted largely through interpersonal interaction. Positive leadership is focused on promoting the best interests of others and brings to the fore the importance of personalism, caring, trust, and respect. Moreover, positive leadership focuses on growth and building up people, groups, and community through learning and empowerment. It proceeds from optimistic and asset-based views of human nature and potential. Many of the qualities of positive leadership are reflected in caring leadership. Kim Cameron (2012), who shaped ideas of positive leadership as a response to hard-nosed business leadership, contends that "being positive is teachable. Positive leadership is not inherent and can be learned by anyone" (p. 122). Through a technique called the Personal Management Interview (PMI) Program, Cameron highlights several elements of a general developmental approach.

A first element involves clarification of norms and values, expectations, responsibilities, standards of evaluation, and reporting relationships. The objective is to establish definitive ideas about the direction of development, set goals, and form a foundation of positive support. A second element involves working with another person to assess aspects of current leadership practice—such as caring—and, based on that assessment, to generate action steps for developing knowledge and skills to move leadership practice in a more positive direction. Some principals may have a coach, mentor, or valued colleague who can help assess current leadership practice and identify areas for development. Principals might join a leadership network for assessment and support. Or they might pair up with a colleague to do reciprocal observation and discussion. It is difficult to reflect oneself in the middle of a busy day. Having another person who can ask questions about what they observe and hear can be very helpful.

Cameron (2012) provides a list of behaviors on which leaders might focus. These behaviors are consistent with the actions and interactions of caring.

We have taken some of these behaviors and embodied them in the form of several reflective questions:

- How does a particular action or interaction reflect my values and the values of the profession? The values of caring? Values of the school?

- How often do I notice and interact with others? Share information? Ask open questions to learn more about others?

- How do I express emotions and feelings, whether verbally or in gestures?

- To whom am I offering a positive purpose and personal support? Who may be acknowledged less often?

- How do I express forgiveness and gratitude? How am I serving others?

- How do I avoid having a negative focus, adopting a narrow point of view, passing blame, and failing to see the good in others?

Cameron stresses the importance of guided practice of new behaviors, perhaps with a coach or a confidant. A coach can demonstrate new behaviors, assess attempts to enact them, provide positive reinforcement, and redirect those enacted poorly.

Developing Ethical Leadership

Brown and Treviño (2006) define *ethical leadership* as "the demonstration of normatively appropriate conduct through personal actions and interpersonal relationships, and the promotion of such conduct to followers through two-way communication, reinforcement, and decision making" (pp. 595–596). Ethical leadership is like caring leadership in that both are grounded in a set of norms, are exercised through personal actions and interpersonal relationships, and involve similar norm-based conduct.

Brown and Treviño (2006) identify three qualities that are strongly associated with ethical leadership and relate to aspects of caring leadership. The first is agreeableness, which reflects a tendency to be trusting, altruistic, and cooperative. As a source of nurturance, agreeable leaders are more effective as models because they attract and keep observers' attention. A second characteristic is conscientiousness, which is associated with reliability and dependability. Both qualities help make leaders effective and credible, which enhances their influence as ethical models. A third quality is neuroticism, which is negatively related to ethical leadership because it is associated with negative emotions, such as anger, fear, and anxiety. Negative emotions, like positive emotions, are readily noticed by others and can undermine a school leader's ability to be an attractive, credible model.

In addition, Brown and Treviño (2006) point to the importance of a leader's power orientation. They argue that leaders who are oriented toward using their influence for others' benefit will be better ethical leaders, while those who are manipulative or viewed as self-serving in their use of power will be poor ethical leaders, which undermines their ability to be authentically caring. Brown and Treviño also identify the capacity for moral reasoning as important to ethical leadership. Moral reasoning allows leaders to make principled decisions, demonstrate concern for the rights of others, and value fairness, all foundational for building positive leader–follower relationships. Leaders with higher levels of moral reasoning are more likely to be seen as credible and effective.

Brown and Treviño (2006) also identify several sources of learning that may be effective for developing these qualities of ethical leadership. Training in group sessions with individual follow-up can be useful to develop specific relational skills, such as interpersonal communication skills. Training that employs vignettes, cases, role playing, simulations, and other such activities can increase leaders' moral awareness of ethical issues likely to arise in their work and in their particular settings. Job-embedded professional development can also be effective. Observing multiple positive role models is likely to be productive. The behaviors of the "top leader"—for example, a school district superintendent—are also critical. They set the ethical tone for the system. When principals are faced with a district office that does not reflect the highest levels of ethical norms and behaviors, they will need to look to other sources—for example, other principals, teachers, noneducation leaders, and personal confidants—for their own ethical development.

Developing Authentic Leadership

May, Chan, Hodges, and Avolio (2003) point to similar strategies for the development of *authentic leadership*, a form of leadership similar to ethical leadership. They describe authentic leadership as genuine, reliable, trustworthy, real, and veritable. Authentic leaders exhibit a high moral capacity to judge dilemmas from different perspectives and are able to consider different persons' needs. Three factors are important to authentic leadership. Moral capacity, the first factor, comprises how a leader constructs their leadership role, perspective-taking, and experience with moral dilemmas. Moral courage, the second, is the leader's fortitude to convert moral intentions into actions. Moral resiliency, the third, refers to the ability to adapt positively in the face of significant adversity or risk, to stay true to one's moral code.

May and his colleagues (2003) contend that moral capacity develops as leaders participate in discussion and self-reflection about their roles and the moral responsibilities associated with leadership actions. Perspective-taking can be enhanced through exposure to and, with role models, discussion of moral dilemmas. Leaders can be taught different methods of moral reasoning. Exposure to moral dilemmas that leaders typically face can develop the *thinking system* that recognizes moral issues (p. 257). Moral courage can be developed through role playing, performance models, coaching, and encouragement. Finally, moral resiliency can be developed through graduated mastery experiences and training in healthy coping techniques, among other strategies. May and his colleagues stress that a supportive, ethical climate is very important for these strategies to be effective and for authentic leadership to flourish.

Developing Human Relations in Leadership

Some of the most relevant insights from the field of educational leadership for developing caring school leadership come from ideas for preparing aspiring school leaders for the human relations dimension of their leadership work. The most promising sources of learning and development for human relations in leadership may come from direct and vicarious experiences (Taylor et al., 2009). These experiences can provide deep insight into the dynamics of social relationships, especially if they are personal and introduce opportunities for problem-based learning. Examples include guided observation, simulations and role playing, sensitivity experiences, group discussions, and working on field-based problems. Vicarious sources include film, video, and other media-based learning sources—narratives, autobiographies, profiles, case studies, memoirs, diaries, and journals. Field-based action research projects, internships, and other work experiences can create powerful direct developmental experiences. They can help aspiring and practicing leaders identify problems in the field and test new approaches to address them.

Coursework that develops understanding of the intersection of contemporary social problems with the work of schools may be important for helping school leaders understand contexts of human relationships. So too may knowledge and skills related to communication, problem solving, decision making, conflict resolution, managing dilemmas, and reflection. These foci may also be useful subjects for network-based professional development opportunities.

Developing Social-Emotional Intelligence

In earlier chapters, we explored the role of social-emotional intelligence in caring school leadership. We discussed how social-emotional intelligence relates helping and guiding others and promoting their development. In emotional intelligence we find virtues and mindsets of empathy, humility, transparency, integrity, respect, and helpfulness. The competencies of emotional intelligence align with key competencies of caring school leadership, notably the ability to read, listen to, and understand others and their needs and concerns. These competencies also align with those of helping, guiding, motivating, and developing others, as well as with self-awareness and self-management.

Goleman, Boyatzis, and McKee (2013) argue that foundational to leadership development is strengthening leaders' understanding of who they are and who they want to be. A central mechanism for developing this understanding is self-assessment. A leader needs to develop a strong image of an *ideal self*, as well as an accurate picture of a *real self*, or the self as it is now (p. 109). Learning and development come when a leader understands the ways in which they can move from the real to the ideal self. Goleman and his colleagues contend that learning and development are triggered by experiences of discontinuity, from "wake-up calls," "wows," or "shocks" that frighten or enlighten us into action. Each discontinuity can be a springboard for discovery steps of a dynamic developmental cycle. These steps are most likely to promote learning and development when leaders are involved in learning with others, such as peers and coworkers, teachers, coaches and mentors, or even with friends or partners.

The first important step is the discovery of the *ideal self*, a personal vision of who the leader wants to be, not someone else's ideal of what a leader should be. This ideal image can instill a passion and stir motivation for development, guide decision making, and become a benchmark for developmental progress. For leaders, as for other professionals, having an ideal vision of a personal self is not sufficient. Leaders must also have an ideal vision of a professional self, which should be related to an ideal vision of the organizations for which they are responsible (Goleman et al., 2013).

Discovery of the *real self* involves developing an inventory of talents and passions, as well as shortcomings, both personal and professional (Goleman et al., 2013). Leaders can create a *balance sheet* of what is going well and what it not. Focusing only on the negative can be demotivating and suppress courageous action. So it is important to build a realistic appraisal of strengths and weaknesses. This discovery requires a great deal of self-awareness to recognize presumptions and biases, confront defenses, and overcome *the inertia of inattention* that fosters taken-for-granted ways of thinking and doing (p. 129).

Goleman and his associates (2013) observe that "the reality of our lives often can be hard to grasp. It's like looking in a clouded mirror" (p. 130). To correct "distortions" in self-awareness, leaders can seek feedback from people around them. But here too lie potential problems. Those from whom leaders seek feedback must overcome the propensity to "be nice," to please, and to hold back negative information, especially when there are asymmetries in personal and professional status, power, and influence. These and other dynamics can create for school leaders, who can be more isolated in their work than leaders in other settings, what Goleman and his colleagues call an *information quarantine* that may constrain or distort leaders' learning and development. Moreover, school cultures that may be conflict averse, with a norm of pleasantness, can suppress useful negative feedback. Leaders can break through this quarantine by using empathy and self-awareness to monitor their own actions and how others react to them (Goleman et al., 2013). They can engage in transparent self-critique when appropriate. An occasional "I was wrong" can go a long way toward establishing an environment in which others feel that they are able to offer less-than-positive feedback. Leaders can actively cultivate the voice of a devil's advocate. And leaders can expand and improve the information they receive by seeking feedback from different people and from multiple perspectives, such as employing 360-degree assessment processes.

This takes Goleman and his colleagues (2013) to the discovery of a positive learning agenda. The best kind of learning agenda focuses on what leaders want to become—their ideal selves. It would include specific goals for development that are personally and professionally meaningful and motivating. Goals should build on one's strengths and should be the leader's own—not goals imposed externally without involvement of the leader. Plans should be flexible and allow leaders to learn and develop in different ways. They should also be feasible and manageable and fit the leader's learning style.

The next discovery step comes from experimenting with new thoughts, feelings, and behaviors that follow from the learning agenda. Experimentation will involve slowing down to reflect deliberately about alternatives and outcomes. Also important is to consider the possibilities for further learning and experimentation.

Part of acting effectively on new thoughts, feelings, and practices is mental rehearsal, that is, forming a mental image of what a new practice might look like and what would need to be done to work toward that image. This leads to forming a second mental picture of oneself successfully performing the new practice. New ways of thinking, feeling, and acting can seem unnatural at first, a sense that can be overcome with growing familiarity, practice, and developing competency. Goleman and his colleagues (2013) observe that accomplished athletes (we would add musicians, actors, and other performers) spend a great deal of time practicing and only a little time performing. On the other hand, most leaders spend almost no time practicing and all their time performing. Without practice, without turning something that feels unnatural into something that feels natural, leaders risk reinforcing current ways. Naturally occurring situations in the workplace can provide good opportunities for practice, especially if a leader is able to engage a colleague to act as a critical friend to observe and provide unvarnished, instructive feedback.

A last, overarching consideration centers on the role of others in a leader's learning and development, persons who can help leaders articulate their ideal selves, assess their real selves, compare the real to the ideal, and measure progress working toward the ideal. As already mentioned, leaders can join a peer group whose members are working to develop similar aspects of their leadership. They can cultivate relationships with confidants, critical friends, mentors, or coaches. They can involve their own organizations in their learning and development. While it may be bold and feel uncomfortable, leaders might benefit greatly from making assessments of their ideal and real selves a project of the whole. They might benefit from making their learning agendas public and asking others for support and feedback on their efforts to develop. According to Goleman and his colleagues (2013), involving one's organization in developing a leader's emotional intelligence can help the leader and create opportunities for others to learn and develop alongside the leader. It makes the organization a *learning laboratory* for all (p. 166).

Learning From Experience

All experiences hold the potential to influence, but not all experiences are equally developmental (Day et al., 2009). The developmental potential of experience is shaped not only by its nature but also by how the experience is observed, understood, and enacted. We contend that learning from experience should not be haphazard but involve deliberate intentional processes. In this section, we expand our earlier discussion of how school leaders can use reflective practice and vicarious learning to develop caring school leadership. Notice the qualities and characteristics that contribute to effective learning and development, particularly assessment, instructiveness, experimentation and practice, feedback, and support. Note also that although reflective practice and vicarious learning are often considered individual processes, both benefit significantly from involving others.

Reflective Practice

We begin our discussion of reflective practice with the writing of psychologist Donald Schön. Schön (1987) observed that when we have learned to do something, we usually can enact smooth sequences of activity, recognition, decision, and adjustment without having to "think about it" (p. 26). Most of this time, we are able to get by. However, sometimes, our regular activity, our routine practice, produces an unexpected result, a "surprise," pleasant or unpleasant, positive or negative. Something fails to meet our expectations. We can respond by brushing the incident aside or by selectively ignoring it. Or we might respond to it through reflection. We can reflect "on" action, thinking back on what we have done in order to discern how various factors, including ourselves, may have contributed to the unexpected outcome. We can also pause and reflect "in" the midst of action to what we might do.

Schön (1987) proposes a multistep deliberative process to promote our ability to reflect productively *on* and *in* action. The first step involves attending, that is, perceiving "surprises" and recognizing them as such. A surprise might be an overlooked opportunity for caring, an expression of caring that went unnoticed, or a reaction to caring that was unexpected. A second step involves trying to understand the surprise and the things that may have contributed to it. We might ask, "What is this, and why is it surprising?" and "How have I been thinking about this person/event that was just shown to be incorrect?" By asking such questions, we focus on the surprising phenomenon and, at the same time, on our own experience of it. We are able to question our assumptions, our thought processes, and our actions and how they relate to the phenomenon. We exercise self-awareness.

This leads to the next step of considering whether and how to restructure our understanding of the phenomenon, our ways of framing problems, and our strategies and actions. This reflection gives rise to experimentation, trying out new ways of thinking and acting. By attending to the results of experimentation, we can alter our course, which itself may produce new surprises that call for further reflection and experimentation. This process can be learned, practiced, and incorporated into routines of professional practice (Osterman & Kottkamp, 2004). Its steps can be integrated into ongoing action, as a tacit process that can result in continual reflection and adjustment. This process also can be pursued as a matter of conscious discipline, becoming an intentional element of professional practice. Both tacit and intentional aspects are important for reflection to contribute to learning and practice.

Following Schön's and others' thinking, Dianne Taylor and her colleagues (2009) present a general framework for reflective practice for school leadership development. The framework begins with careful observation and self-assessment of current practice, which can be done by identifying a problematic experience and discerning what might be the likely sources or causes of the problem. It is important to examine deliberately biases and assumptions that may shape one's thinking and actions. Following observation and self-assessment comes gathering and analyzing information relevant to the experience so that it can be interpreted and stimulate reflection. Next comes developing ideas and strategies related to the problem. The framework concludes with acting, experimenting, and practicing new strategies, reflecting all the while on their effects and on reasons for why they may or may not be achieving their objectives. This reflective process can be enhanced by working with trusted learning companions who can provide different perspectives and help school leaders shed blinders and overcome defenses.

Gordon Donaldson (2006) expands this basic framework and applies it to what school leaders can do to develop and improve the relational aspects of their work. These suggestions can be focused on caring. For Donaldson, reflective practice is grounded in how school leaders are able to "stay in touch with themselves" and "with the emotional effects of other people and events that . . . shape their thinking and actions" (p. 173). Also important is *perspective taking*. Donaldson writes, "Leaders gain perspective in part by 'getting on the balcony' and watching themselves in relationship with others. In routinely reflecting on how they typically behave in leadership situations, leaders quite literally learn about their part in the complex interactions that constitute leadership relationships" (p. 174).

The big idea here is that the more deeply and accurately leaders can understand themselves in relationship to others, the more likely it will be for them to understand and address problems, understand ways that they can contribute to the development of others, and understand the particular ways they cannot.

Such self-reflection can be problematic. It can be influenced and impeded by particular presumptions and perspectives and by psychological and emotional defenses (R. Evans, 1996; Fullan, 2007). Those who write about professional development through disciplined reflection reiterate our message that school leaders find "partners" to share thinking and concerns (Pellicer, 2008). Where colleagues in one's school can serve in this role, reflective practice can contribute to the overall "density" of leadership that might make the entire school function more effectively (Donaldson, 2006, p. 174).

Leonard Pellicer (2008) also focuses on reflective practice in his recommendations for developing caring in school leadership. Like Donaldson (2006), he writes of going "up to the balcony" from time to time to "observe the dance" (p. 167). Going a step farther, Pellicer recommends going "down in the basement" for a bottom-up perspective. His point is that to be caring, a leader needs to see the entire school from different perspectives and needs to ensure that caring is not filtered through the lens of personal interest for "your people, your piece of the organization" (p. 167). A school leader needs to be mindful and caring of all in the school, as well as of families and community members who have a stake in the school. Such an inclusive perspective includes the school leader themself. Pellicer argues that one cannot begin to care for and serve others without understanding who one is as a human being and as an educational leader.

As we have noted, self-reflection involves defining, assessing, and prioritizing one's personal and professional values. This creates benchmarks that are helpful in situations that are ambiguous and involve tradeoffs, such as those involving conflicts between the well-being of a student and a teacher or differences between expectations of a parent and a teacher's professional judgment. By clarifying one's values, Pellicer (2008) argues, a school leader sets a standard for considering the consistency between one's actions and one's beliefs, especially when confronted with "crucibles of character" (p. 165). Such a stance would move school leaders—and perhaps others—out of their comfort zones, prod them to think afresh about their motives, and challenge them in ways that spur growth.

Pellicer (2008) suggests a number of activities that can help school leaders reflect and learn to become more caring. The most obvious, he says, is to set aside a regular time to think about who you are, what you are doing, and where you want to go in your practice. Another is to write in a journal, "chronicling thoughts, decisions, and actions while comparing these to the results expected and the results achieved" (p. 167). Like Donaldson, Pellicer points to the value of including others in reflective learning and development. A leader can ask for feedback from those who are close, who will be honest and open, and whose opinions the leader respects. A principal can survey students, faculty and staff, and parents and caregivers, among others, about their relationships with her and about their perceptions of her caring and effectiveness. Finally, Pellicer suggests that school leaders can seek guidance from models and mentors who reflect the values and behaviors of caring. In addition to being useful sources of direct and vicarious learning, models and mentors can provide social and emotional support as school leaders confront uncomfortable realities about themselves and their actions. They can provide feedback and guidance for reflection on becoming more caring leaders.

Vicarious Learning From Others

While reflecting on one's own practice lies at that core of developing caring school leadership, school leaders can also learn vicariously through the experiences of others. In earlier chapters, we spoke about modeling as a school leadership practice for developing caring among students, teachers, and staff and for fostering caring in families and communities beyond the school. Here, we consider modeling as a source of learning and development for school leaders.

Observing models may be planned and part of a formal learning activity, or it can occur through self-initiated and self-directed efforts (Day et al., 2009). Learning by keeping one's eyes open and observing others can occur informally through routine encounters. Continual observation will result in accumulated experience and learning that may improve caring leadership, especially as observations are reflected upon systematically.

The things we identified in Chapter 4 that make school leaders effective models for others apply to effective models for school leaders. Effective models for developing caring school leadership would embody caring leadership in their personal and professional behavior. Good models for developing caring school leadership would be visible by their presence and recognizable by their actions. They would be able to gain the attention of school leaders by making their messages about caring known through explicit and clear communication. And good models for caring school leader development would encourage and reinforce the norms and behaviors that are modeled.

In addition to learning from directly observing others, modeling can occur through narrative accounts or stories of others' actions and experiences. Modeling narratives can be factual or fictional, positive or negative (Day et al., 2009; Kruse & Louis, 2009). They may describe past events or be future-oriented. They can illustrate problems or convey expectations. No matter their form, narratives can be powerfully instructive, especially as they provide insight into the persons, situations, and contexts that are presented. As multiple meanings can often be gleaned from a single story, narratives can help leaders learn to take the perspective of others and to foster empathy. By reflecting on narratives and discussing them with others, leaders may be able to see patterns in and perhaps limitations of their own views and actions, enhancing their self-awareness in the process. Narratives can convey messages about desirable behaviors and shape expectations for leader development. Narratives that convey ethical dilemmas can encourage the development of moral reasoning. (See the companion to this volume, *Stories of Caring School Leadership*.)

Avoiding the Problems and Pitfalls of Caring

Developing caring leadership requires particular attention to avoiding the problems and pitfalls of caring. Earlier in this chapter, we recalled a number of potential problems and negative consequences of caring. We argued that learning and development might help school leaders avoid these problems and pitfalls and, if not avoid them entirely, help leaders manage and mitigate negative effects and learn from them. Several areas of understanding are important to develop.

One area is a deep understanding of caring itself and how caring can be manifest in school leadership. This includes the nature and function of caring in general and caring in school leadership, especially the aims, virtues and mindsets, and competencies of caring. It includes how caring can be enacted in different areas of school leadership. This book is devoted to developing such understanding. A second area of understanding concerns the foci and parameters of school leaders' professional calling and responsibilities, including the content and limitations of school leaders' personal and professional identities. This understanding may have little to do with written job descriptions developed by school districts. Indeed, we do not see many principal job descriptions that include a call to caring. Exploring and understanding one's professional values and commitments is an essential part of developing caring leadership. Another area of understanding concerns the nature and sources of potential problems and unintended consequences of caring in general and of caring in leadership in particular.

Developing these areas of understanding can help school leaders avoid the problems and pitfalls of caring by establishing a sense of *ideal* and a view of its antithesis. With these understandings, school leaders are better able to direct their thinking and actions from the problematic toward the caring leadership that is valued and sought. In addition, such understanding may help when tensions and dilemmas arise.

Another way to avoid and manage the problems and pitfalls of caring leadership is through targeted development of particular elements of caring. For example, school leaders may be better able to avoid misses and missteps in caring if they have developed a capacity for attentiveness and inquiry required for understanding others, their situations, and their needs and concerns. School leaders may be better able to avoid problems of caring by developing competencies for acting effectively and in caring manner to address others' needs and concerns, such as rendering help and assistance.

Yet another way to avoid and manage problems and pitfalls of caring is by developing and enacting processes of reflective practice. These processes can help school leaders continually assess situations and their own thinking and behavior, including their own motivations, presumptions, and biases. These processes can help school leaders assess and engage others' responses to leaders' thinking and behavior, rather than judging them. They can activate school leaders' sense of self-awareness and mindfulness, sharpen their ability to self-monitor, and enhance their capacity for self-regulation. And thus, these processes can help school leaders anticipate and recognize problems and adapt their thinking and behavior to avoid or manage them.

We discussed the importance of involving others in efforts to develop caring school leadership. We pointed to the importance of resonant group learning and to the importance of involving colleagues, confidents, critical friends, and coaches. We observed that involving others often provides useful feedback, guidance, and accountability. Involved others can help school leaders anticipate, identify, and avoid potential and real-time problems and thus enhance leaders' ability to avoid and manage the pitfalls of caring. In addition, the opportunities to understand how and why caring decisions are made are expanded. Last but not least, school leaders can avoid pitfalls in caring and, indeed, enhance their ability to be caring of others by learning to be caring for themselves. It is to the subject of self-care that we turn our attention.

Caring for Oneself

In Chapter 1, we argued that for school leaders to be caring of others in their practice, they must also be caring of themselves. This point was made well by a hospice chaplain who spoke about her ministry as a service of care. She described herself and other human service providers and caregivers as water pitchers. She described her service and theirs' as pouring water to quench the thirst of others; to comfort and heal them physically, emotionally, and spiritually; and to promote their well-being. She argued that to serve others well, human service providers and caregivers need to regularly replenish the water they pour. Without replenishment, they will run dry and be of little use to anyone.

Who will be caring of the ones caring? Who will be caring of the caring school leader? Ideally, we would look to colleagues—other school leaders and teachers. We would look to students' parents and caregivers, perhaps sometimes to students themselves. And we would look to district central offices. In several chapters of this book, we recognized the prospect of mutuality in caring, that persons in caring relationships may be, at different times and in various ways, both ones caring and ones cared for. We recognized the real probability that despite the strong asymmetries between them, students can be sources of caring for principals.

The fact is that most principals work alone, albeit in crowds. They are presumed to be the ones caring—it is their work. There is often little recognition of their need for care and support. It is not uncommon that central offices provide little support for principals in their work, invest little in their professional learning and development, and often, inadvertently, make decisions and create conditions that make principals' work more complicated and difficult. Many districts do not lead with caring, operating under dehumanizing precepts associated with bureaucracy. Such situations leave principals alone to ignore their need for caring, to seek caring from others, or to look for effective means of self-care.

Caring for oneself—self-care—can mean many things. It can mean attending to one's own professional learning and development and to the quality and effectiveness of one's own practice. But self-care means more. It means taking care of oneself as a person and a professional. Self-care means caring for one's own physical, emotional, and spiritual health and one's overall well-being. There is inherent value in self-care. As the hospice chaplain explained, self-care may be necessary to be fully caring of others.

Donaldson (2006) is among the few in the field of educational leadership who writes about the importance of self-care to school leaders' active caring of others. His notion of self-care is for principals to "stay in touch with themselves," "with how they are feeling," and "with the emotional effects" of their actions on other people (p. 173). For him, principals' self-care is anchored in recognition that they are not alone in their work. Accordingly, principals are caring for themselves when they "[cling] doggedly to the conviction" (p. 174) that they are only part of the whole leadership necessary for a school to be successful, that the responsibility for the success and well-being of so many is shared with others, and that they can rely on others for support and assistance.

Other human service professions, especially medicine, nursing, and ministry, place substantial emphasis on the importance of self-care. In medicine, for example, physician Ronald Epstein (2017) writes how important, yet how difficult, it is to be caring of oneself, to "bestow kindness on yourself" (p. 135). It is easier, he writes, to direct kindness toward a patient or a friend. British psychologist Caroline Elton (2018), whose patients are mostly physicians, recognizes the demanding nature of the medical profession and the toll it can exact on its members. She argues that it is sometimes difficult for physicians to feel that they are also human and might at some point need support and caring themselves. Like Epstein, Elton stresses the importance of routines of self-care. In a point that we will raise at the end of this chapter, she also emphasizes how important it is for physicians to seek out the caring and support of others, even to help them be more self-caring.

In nursing, Jean Watson (2008) writes that "nurses often become pained and worn down by trying to always care, give, and be there for others without attending to the loving care needed for self" (p. 47). They need to be self-caring and to engage practices that assist in their own evolution of consciousness for "more fulfillment in their life and work" (p. 47). For Watson, self-caring is necessary to be effective in nursing. Nurses who engage in self-caring can also be models of self-caring to colleagues and patients, becoming living exemplars of balanced, healthy, effective personal and professional lives. Julia Riley (2017), a registered nurse and nursing scholar, argues that self-care is the foundation of nursing. "As you care for yourself," she writes, "so you care for your clients. As you care for yourself, so you care for your colleagues" (p. 349). Again, with regard to nursing, Marian Turkel and Marilyn Ray (2004) write, "To awaken the creative, caring spirit within each of us, it is essential to acknowledge the power of caring for self as being essential" (p. 251).

Julia Riley (2017) contends that when nurses are off duty physically, they need to find ways to maintain healthy boundaries, a healthy separation from their work. She writes that when we work hard, we also need to play hard: "We need time for respite and activities with no social value—time that is just *fun*" (p. 349). Riley sees creative expression as a valuable tool for self-care. She includes in creative expression art, creative writing and poetry writing, and music. With the stresses that nurses routinely face, with the work squarely focused on the health and well-being of patients, Riley counsels nurses to actively consider how to add energy, fun, and laughter to their lives. She recommends engaging in physical activity and exercise: "Dance, play tennis, walk, or run; the list is endless" (p. 356). She cites yoga, stretching, deep breathing, centering and mindfulness exercises, and meditation as ways to manage physical and psychological stress. Among other self-care strategies she recommends are journal writing, expressive art, and music therapy. The list of self-care activities is long—caring school leaders have plenty to consider.

Turkel and Ray (2004) suggest that self-care strategies can be integrated, in small ways, into the work setting. In high-stress professional work, including school leadership, there is a need to consciously monitor and set aside time for self-care and renewal. Turkel and Ray suggest starting the workday with a centering activity, seeking out "mini-relaxation" experiences during the day, taking *all* vacation days and personal leave days provided, and participating in retreats and social gatherings focused on personal and professional health and well-being. Finally, Turkel and Ray suggest that nurses can create self-motivation to be caring of oneself as they teach and encourage others to be self-caring.

Self-care also receives substantial attention in the ministry. According to seminary professors Bob Burns, Tasha Chapman, and Donald Guthrie (2013), self-care for clergy requires acknowledging that everyone has gifts and also limitations. From their research on the work lives of practicing ministers, they argue that it is important for clergy to acknowledge that they are "whole creatures" with physical, emotional, mental, social, and spiritual needs themselves. It is also important for them to recognize that their work requires them to "nurture and steward" their own capacities (p. 250). Furthermore, it is important for members of the clergy to help their congregations understand that they are more than their role and calling. They are "human beings; they have hobbies and interests; they are siblings, children of elderly adults, marriage partners and parents" (p. 250). Self-care in ministry often requires that clergy establish responsible but clear boundaries between themselves and their congregations, between their work and their personal lives. Burns and his colleagues encourage clergy to preserve time for reflection, study, and mental, physical, and spiritual rejuvenation. They recognize the role that colleagues may play in self-care, encouraging clergy to join peer groups, form peer friendships, and seek confidants and mentors.

To these suggestions for self-care, former pastor and seminary professor Kirk Jones (2001) adds a few others, designed not only for clergy but for other caregivers as well. He speaks about the importance of rest, of moving to the "back of the boat" to disengage, to literally and figuratively sleep. It is in the back of the boat that we can refresh our bodies, minds, and spirits and remember who we are and what our work calls us to do. Jones points to a number of formidable obstacles that stand in the way of moving from the front of the boat, where responsibility lies and where work is done, to the back, where rest and replenishment await. These include the myth of our own indispensability, the delusion of our own invincibility, and our denial of our own personhood. He argues that clergy and other caregivers—including school leaders—must recognize these obstacles and confront them head on.

According to Jones (2001), an important aspect of self-care is the art of slowing down, of pacing, and of imposing healthy limitations on work. He cites Bryan Robinson's (1993) guide to help practicing clergy and other caregivers know if they are doing too much and need to spend more time at the back of the boat. Indicators for the early stage of overdoing include rushing, general busyness, inability to say "no," constantly thinking about work, overvaluation of one's own ability, and no days off. Indicators for the middle stage of overdoing include regularly working excessive hours per week; feeling compelled to work all the time; the onset of other "addictions" involving food, alcohol, money, and relationships; chronic fatigue; and aborted attempts to slow down and do less. Indicators of the late stage of overdoing include physical pain, emotional deadness, and moral and spiritual bankruptcy. To these indicators, Jones adds not having a moment when my partner or children request my time, putting stringent limits on it when I do have time, and having our youngest child (or anyone else) ask, "Why do you look so sad?" When such indicators present themselves and as they accumulate, argues Jones, it is time to be much more deliberate about going to the back of the boat.

Our last look at self-care comes from Willimon (2002), who also addresses the importance of self-care in ministry. According to Willimon, the need for self-care arises from challenges in the work of the ministry itself, challenges that resemble closely those of school leadership. As you read the next two paragraphs about challenges in ministerial work, think about school leadership. Wherever you read the words *clergy* or *the ministry*, substitute *school leaders* or *school leadership*; wherever you read the word *church*, substitute *school*; and so forth.

Willimon (2002) begins with the observation that the work of ministry (school leadership) is never finished. There is little sense of closure. There is substantial ambiguity of expectations and tasks that are to be fulfilled. It is, in large part, ill-defined work, and the outcomes are often hard to detect. The church (school) is often a source of support for people in great need and, therefore, can be a place of great challenge for those who work to address those needs. The ministry functions through a "persona" of professional identity and conduct that may create a disjuncture between who clergy are as persons and the roles that they are expected to perform. The effort to maintain appropriate distance and separation in work and to maintain an appropriate professional persona that is different from authentic personhood can become a source of significant dissonance. Willimon observes that clergy may become exhausted and overwhelmed by failure that, in one manifestation or another, is endemic to the work. And problems can emerge from the fact that the ministry is often not valued highly in the broader culture.

Moreover, Willimon notes that many clergy serve in situations of institutional decline, as evidenced by shrinking membership, weakening engagement, financial troubles, leaky roofs, and inability to perform functions needed to serve a congregation and community well. Daily and weekly demands can be daunting, and time management can be challenging. Also daunting can be a lack of harmony between a local congregation and its superordinate body politic. Last but not least, Willimon identifies biases and prejudices, say with regard to women or gays and lesbians in the ministry, that create another layer of burden that must be confronted along with the work of ministry itself. All of these challenges have their analogs in schools and school leadership.

Such challenges can lead to stress and tension and to what Willimon (2002) calls *brownout* and *blackout*. He prefers these terms to *burnout*, which to him connotes primarily lack of energy. In contrast, brownout and blackout point to a larger problem—the "gradual dissipation of meaning in ministry, a blurring of vision, the inability to keep the theological rationale for ministry that is necessary to enliven our imagination" (pp. 325–326). "We wake up one day," he writes, "and no longer have a reason or purpose for doing the things that the church expects us to do" (p. 326). The problem and the need for self-care is rooted more in distress than in stress, more in a loss of meaning than in a lack of energy. Again, is this an analog to school leaders and leadership?

Willimon (2002) suggests several self-care actions like those discussed previously. Perhaps his most important contribution to our consideration of self-care is his challenge to recenter on the basics. The ministry, like school leadership, is more than a job. It is, according to Willimon, more than a path to personal advancement or private contentment. The ministry, like school leadership, is a calling, a summons to service. Remembering and refocusing on the call, the summons, on a daily basis can be an important source of rejuvenation. Their respective calls remind both ministers and school leaders that the ones who so often give are also enabled to receive, to replenish their pitchers of water.

At times, the ones who are caring may need the caring and help of others, even to engage in their own sustaining self-care. Jaco Hamman (2010) writes that you protect your call by practicing self-care and by seeking out a community that can be significant to you and to your own care. He describes the relationship between the individual and a community through his favorite African proverb: "My friends who love me grow on me like moss" (p. 109). Hamman observes that in Africa and other parts of the world, mosses and lichens are used for their medicinal qualities. The proverb suggests that a person is healthier, is better protected from the stresses and wounds of life, and heals faster if friends and a community are part of that person's life.

Hamman continues that the support, care, and comfort we receive from others are life affirming. He invites us to imagine ourselves covered in a blanket of soft, green, life-giving moss as supervisors, mentors, colleagues, family, and friends surround us with love and care. Sadly, Hamman observes, most of us live by another proverb: "A rolling stone gathers no moss." He tells us that we become rolling stones when we neglect our own self-care and isolate ourselves from a significant community. And he challenges us with the question, "By which proverb will you live?" (p. 110).

Questions for Reflection and Discussion

1. How would you describe your *ideal self* as a caring school leader? How would you describe your *real self*? Comparing the real and the ideal, what are the similarities and the gaps? How do you think your assessment of your *real self* would compare with how others in your school might assess you?

2. Given your assessment of similarities and gaps, can you begin to develop an agenda of learning and development that might build upon the similarities (your strengths) and close the gaps (your weaknesses)? What objectives might you set for yourself? Who might you involve in developing your agenda?

3. What types of development activities and experiences might be most effective for you to fulfill your agenda? Where might you find support to work on your agenda?

4. In what development activities and experiences might you engage to avoid the pitfalls of caring in your leadership? Who might accompany and support you?

5. By which proverb about moss do you now live, personally and professionally? Think of the ways in which you live by this proverb. In what ways can you encourage more moss to grow and thrive on you?

References

Abbott, A. (1988). *The system of professions: An essay on the division of expert labor.* Chicago, IL: University of Chicago Press.

Abbott, P., & Meerabeau, L. (1998). Professions, professionalization and the caring professions. In P. Abbott & L. Meerabeau (Eds.), *The sociology of the caring professions* (pp. 1–19). New York, NY: Routledge.

Achinstein, B. (2002). Conflict amid community: The micropolitics of teacher collaboration. *Teachers College Record, 104*(3), 421–455.

Allen, S. J., & Hartman, N. S. (2008). Leadership development: An exploration of sources of learning. *SAM Advanced Management Journal, 73*(1), 10–19, 62.

Allensworth, E. M., Farrington, C. A., Gordon, M. F., Johnson, D. W., Klein, K., McDaniel, B., & Nagaoka, J. (2018, October). *Supporting social, emotional, and academic development: Research implications for educators.* Chicago, IL: University of Chicago, Consortium on Chicago School Research.

Antrop-Gonzalez, R., & DeJesus, A. (2006). Toward a theory of critical care in urban small school reform: Examining structures and pedagogies of caring in two Latino community-based schools. *International Journal of Qualitative Studies in Education, 19*(4), 409–433.

Argyris, C., & Schön, D. A. (1974). *Theory in practice: Increasing professional effectiveness.* San Francisco, CA: Jossey-Bass.

Arnaud, A., & Schminke, M. (2012). The ethical climate and context of organizations: A comprehensive model. *Organizational Science, 23*(6), 1767–1780.

Aronson, B., & Laughter, J. (2016). The theory and practice of culturally relevant education: A synthesis of research across content areas. *Review of Educational Research, 86*(1), 163–206.

Auerbach, S. (2010). Beyond coffee with the principal: Toward leadership for authentic school–family partnerships. *Journal of School Leadership, 20*(6), 728–757.

Autry, J. A. (1991). *Love and profit: The art of caring leadership.* New York, NY: Morrow.

Bailey, R., Stickle, L., Brion-Meisels, G., & Jones, S. M. (2019, January). Re-imagining social-emotional learning: Findings from a strategy-based approach. *Phi Delta Kappan, 100*(5), 53–58.

Baquedano-López, P., Alexander, R. A., & Hernandez, S. J. (2013). Equity issues in parental and community involvement in schools: What teacher educators need to know. *Review of Research in Education, 37*, 149–182.

Barley, S. R. (1989). Careers, identities, and institutions: The legacy of the Chicago School of Sociology. In M. B. Arthur, D. T. Hall, & B. S. Lawrence (Eds.), *Handbook of career theory* (pp. 41–65). New York, NY: Cambridge University Press.

Bass, B. G. (2002). Cognitive, social, and emotional intelligence of transformational leaders. In R. E. Riggio, S. E. Murphy, & F. J. Prozzolo (Eds.), *Multiple intelligences and leadership, LEA's organization and management series* (pp. 105–118). Mahwah, NJ: Lawrence Erlbaum.

Beck, L., & Foster, W. (1999). Administration and community: Considering challenges, exploring possibilities. In J. Murphy & K. S. Louis (Eds.), *Handbook of research on educational administration* (2nd ed., pp. 337–358). San Francisco, CA: Jossey-Bass.

Beck, L. G., & Murphy, J. (1993). *Understanding the principalship: Metaphorical themes 1920s–1990s.* New York, NY: Teachers College Press.

Benner, P. (1994). Caring as a way of knowing and not knowing. In S. Phillips & P. Benner (Eds.), *The crisis of care: Affirming and restoring caring practices in the helping professions* (pp. 42–62). Washington, DC: Georgetown University Press.

Benner, P., & Gordon, S. (1996). Caring practice. In S. Gordon, P. Benner, & N. Noddings (Eds.), *Caregiving: Readings in knowledge, practice, ethics, and politics* (pp. 40–55). Philadelphia: University of Pennsylvania Press.

Benner, P., & Wrubel, J. (1989). *The primacy of caring: Stress and coping in health and illness.* Reading, MA: Addison Wesley Longman.

Benson, P. L. (2006). *All kids are our kids: What communities must do to raise caring and responsible children and adolescents* (2nd ed.). San Francisco, CA: Jossey-Bass.

Billig, S. H. (2000). Research in K–12 school-based service-learning: The evidence builds. *Phi Delta Kappan, 81*(9), 658–664.

Blase, J. J. (1991). *The politics of life in schools: Power, conflict, and cooperation.* Thousand Oaks, CA: Sage.

Block, P. (2018). *Community: The structure of belonging* (2nd ed.). Oakland, CA: Berrett-Koehler Publishers.

Bloom, P. (2018). *Against empathy: The case for rational compassion.* New York, NY: Ecco, HarperCollins.

Boyatzis, R. E., Smith, M. L., & Blaize, N. (2006). Developing sustainable leaders through coaching and compassion. *Academy of Management Learning and Education, 5*(1), 8–24.

Brady, S. R., & O'Connor, M. K. (2014). Understanding how community organizing leads to social change: The beginning development of formal practice theory. *Journal of Community Practice, 22*(1–2), 210–228.

Brechin, A. (1998a). Introduction. In A. Brechin, J. Walmsley, J. Katz, & S. Peace (Eds.), *Care matters: Concepts, practice, and research in health and social care* (pp. 1–12). Thousand Oaks, CA: Sage.

Brechin, A. (1998b). What makes for good care? In A. Brechin, J. Walmsley, J. Katz, & S. Peace (Eds.), *Care matters: Concepts, practice, and research in health and social care* (pp. 170–187). Thousand Oaks, CA: Sage.

Brooks, G. (1970). *Family pictures.* Detroit, MI: Broadside Press.

Brown, M. E., & Treviño, L. K. (2006). Ethical leadership: A review and future directions. *Leadership Quarterly, 17*(6), 595–616.

Brown, M. E., & Treviño, L. K. (2014). Do role models matter? An investigation of role modeling as an antecedent of perceived ethical leadership. *Journal of Business Ethics, 122*(4), 587–598.

Brown, M. E., Treviño, L. K., & Harrison, D. A. (2005). Ethical leadership: A social learning perspective for construct development and testing. *Organizational Behavior and Human Decision Processes, 97*(2), 117–134.

Bryk, A. S., Sebring, P. B., Allensworth, E., Luppescu, S., & Easton, J. (2010). *Organizing schools for improvement: Lessons from Chicago.* Chicago, IL: University of Chicago Press.

Burke, W. W. (2018). *Organization change: Theory and practice* (5th ed.). Thousand Oaks, CA: Sage.

Burrell, N. A., Zirbel, C. S., & Allen, M. (2003). Evaluation peer mediation outcomes in educational settings: A meta-analytic review. *Conflict Resolution Quarterly, 21*(1), 7–26.

Burns, B., Chapman, T. D., & Guthrie, D. C. (2013). *Resilient ministry: What pastors told us about surviving and thriving.* Downers Grove, IL: IVP Books.

Caldwell, C., & Dixon, R. D. (2010). Love, forgiveness, and trust: Critical values of the modern leader. *Journal of Business Ethics, 93*(1), 91–101.

Cameron, K. S. (2012). *Positive leadership: Strategies for extraordinary performance.* San Francisco, CA: Berrett-Koehler.

Carroll, J. W. (2006). *God's potters: Pastoral leadership and the shaping of congregations.* Grand Rapids, MI: Eerdmans.

Centers for Disease Control and Prevention. (2018). Preventing youth violence. Retrieved from https://cic.gov/violenceprevention/pdf/yv-factsheet508.pdf

Cherng, H. S. (2017). The ties that bind: Teacher relationships, academic expectations, and racial/ethnic and generational inequality. *American Journal of Education, 124*(1), 67–100.

Children's Defense Fund. (n.d.). Positive behavior supports. Retrieved from https://www.aasa.org/uploadedFiles/Childrens_Programs/PBIS%20factsheet.pdf

Christens, B. D., & Speer, P. W. (2015). Community organizing: Practice, research, and policy implications. *Social Issues and Policy Review, 9*(1), 193–222.

Clebsch, W. A., & Jaekle, C. R. (1994). *Pastoral care in historical perspective.* Lanham, MD: Rowman & Littlefield.

Collaborative for Academic, Social, and Emotional Learning. (2013). *Effective social and emotional learning programs: Preschool and elementary school edition.* Chicago, IL: Author.

Collaborative for Academic, Social, and Emotional Learning. (2015). *Effective social and emotional learning programs: Middle and high school edition.* Chicago, IL: Author.

Comer, J., Haynes, N. M., Joyner, E. T., & Ben-Avie, M. (Eds.). (1996). *Rallying the whole village: The Comer process for reforming education.* New York, NY: Teachers College Press.

Conger, J. A. (1992). *Learning to lead: The art of transforming managers into leaders.* San Francisco, CA: Jossey-Bass.

Consortium on Chicago School Research. (2012). Measures and item statistics in 2012 student surveys. Chicago, IL: University of Chicago, Author. Retrieved from https://ccsr.uchicago.edu/sites/default/files/uploads/survey/2012student surveymeasurestatistics.pdf

Couture, P. D. (2014). Social policy. In B. J. Miller-McLemore (Ed.), *The Wiley Blackwell companion to practical theology* (pp. 153–162). Malden, MA: Wiley Blackwell.

Cozolino, L. (2014). The neuroscience of human relationships: Attachment and the developing social brain (2nd ed.). New York, NY: W. W. Norton.

Craig, R. P., & Norris, C. J. (2008). Values perception and future educational leaders. *Journal of School Leadership, 18*(4), 383–395.

Crosnoe, R. (2011). *Fitting in, standing out: Navigating the social challenges of high school to get an education.* New York, NY: Cambridge University Press.

Curry, M. W. (2016). Will you stand for me? Authentic Cariño and transformative rites of passage in an urban high school. *American Educational Research Journal, 53*(4), 883–918.

Curry School of Education. (2015, September 25). 4RS + MPT: A teacher consultation model and social-emotional intervention with an "innovative twist." Charlottesville, VA: University of Virginia. Retrieved from https://curry.virginia.edu/news/4rsmtp-teacher-consultation-model-and-social-emotional-intervention-'innovative-twist'

Cyr, C., Euser, E. M., Bakermans-Kranenburg, M. J., & van Ijzendoorn, M. H. (2010). Attachment security and disorganization in maltreating and high-risk families: A series of meta-analyses. *Development and Psychopathology, 22*(1), 87–108.

Dalakoura, A. (2010). Differentiating leader and leadership development: A collective framework for leadership development. *Journal of Management Development, 29*(5), 432–441.

Daunic, A. O., Smith, S. W., Robinson, T. R., Miller, M. D., & Landry, K. L. (2000). School-wide conflict resolution and peer mediation programs: Experiences in three middle schools. *Intervention in School and Clinic, 36*(2), 94–100.

Day, D. V., Harrison, M. M., & Halpin, S. M. (2009). *An integrative approach to leader development: Connecting adult development, identity, and expertise.* New York, NY: Psychology Press.

de Royston, M. M., Vakil, S., Nasir, N. S., ross, k. m., Givens, J., & Holman, A. (2017). "He's more like a 'brother' than a teacher": Politicized caring in a program for African American males. *Teachers College Record, 119*(4), 1–40.

DeMarinis, V. M. (1993). *Critical caring: A feminist model for pastoral psychology.* Louisville, KY: Westminster/Knox Press.

Demi, M. A., Coleman-Jensen, A., & Snyder, A. R. (2010). The rural context and secondary school enrollment: An ecological systems approach. *Journal of Research in Rural Education, 25*(7), 1–26.

DePree, M. (2004). *Leadership is an art.* New York, NY: Crown.

Deshpande, S. P. (1996). Ethical climate and the link between success and ethical behavior: An empirical investigation of a non-profit organization. *Journal of Business Ethics, 15*(3), 315–320.

Deiro, J. A. (2003). Do your students know you care? *Educational Leadership, 60*(6), 60–63.

Donaldson, G. A., Jr. (2006). *Cultivating leadership in schools: Connecting people, purpose, and practice.* New York, NY: Teachers College Press.

Donlin, M. (2012). You mean we gotta teach *that,* too? In J. W. Patchin & S. Hinduja (Eds.), *Cyberbullying prevention and response: Expert perspectives* (pp. 110–127). New York, NY: Routledge.

Dryfoos, J. G., & Quinn, J. (2005). *Community schools in action: Lessons from a decade of practice.* New York, NY: Oxford University Press.

Dunne, J. (1986). Sense of community in l'Arche and in the writings of Jean Vanier. *Journal of Community Psychology, 14*(1), 41–54.

Durlak, J. A., Weissberg, R. P., Dymnicki, A. B., Taylor, R. D., & Schellinger, K. B. (2011). The impact of enhancing students' social and emotional learning: A meta-analysis of school-based universal interventions. *Child Development, 82*(1), 405–432.

Dutton, J. E., Worhne, M. C., Frost, P. J., & Lilius, J. (2006). Explaining compassion organizing. *Administrative Science Quarterly, 51*(1), 59–96.

Dykstra, R. C. (Ed.). (2005). *Images of pastoral care: Classic readings.* St. Louis, MO: Chalice.

Elias, M. J., Arnold, H., & Hussey, C. S. (2003). EQ, IQ, and effective learning and citizenship. In M. J. Elias, H. Arnold, & C. S. Hussey (Eds.), *EQ + IQ = Best leadership practices for caring and successful schools* (pp. 3–10). Thousand Oaks, CA: Corwin.

Ellinger, D. A., & Bostrom, R. P. (1999). Managerial coaching behaviors in learning organizations. *Journal of Management Development, 18*(9), 752–771.

Ellinger, D. A., Ellinger, A. E., & Keller, S. C. (2003). Supervisory coaching behavior, employee satisfaction, and warehouse employee performance: A dyadic perspective in the distribution industry. *Human Resource Development Quarterly, 14*(4), 435–458.

Elton, C. (2018). *Also human: The inner lives of doctors.* New York, NY: Basic Books.

Enomoto, E. K. (1997). Negotiating the ethics of care and justice. *Educational Administration Quarterly, 33*(3), 351–370.

Epstein, J. L., & Associates. (2019). *School, family, and community partnerships: Your handbook for action* (4th ed.). Thousand Oaks, CA: Corwin.

Epstein, R. J. (2017). *Attending: Medicine, mindfulness, and humanity.* New York, NY: Scribner.

Etzioni, A. (1996). *The new golden rule: Community and morality in a democratic society.* New York, NY: Basic Books.

Evans, C. B. R., Fraser, M. W., & Cotter, K. L. (2014). The effectiveness of school-based bullying prevention programs: A systematic review. *Aggression and Violent Behavior, 19*(5), 532–544.

Evans, R. (1996). *The human side of change: Reform, resistance, and the real-life problems of innovation.* San Francisco, CA: Jossey-Bass.

Farrington, C. A., Roderick, M., Allensworth, E., Nagaoka, J., Keyes, T. S., Johnson, D. W., & Beechum, N. O. (2012, June). *Teaching adolescents to become learners: The role of noncognitive factors in shaping school performance: A critical literature review.* Chicago, IL: Consortium on Chicago School Research.

Federal Commission on School Safety. (2018, December). *Final report.* Washington, DC: Author. Retrieved from https://www2.ed.gov/documents/school-safety/school-safety-report.pdf

Felitti, V. J., Anda, R. F., Nordenberg, D., Williamson, D. F., Spitz, A. M., Edwards, V., . . . & Marks, J. S. (1998). Relationship of childhood abuse and household dysfunction to many of the leading causes of death in adults. *American Journal of Preventive Medicine, 14*(4), 245–258.

Fenstermacher, G. D., & Amarel, M. (2013). The inherent tensions between interests in schooling. In W. C. Frick (Ed.), *Education management turned on its head: Exploring a professional ethic for educational leadership* (pp. 57–76). New York, NY: Peter Lang.

Finch, J. (1984). Community care: Developing non-sexist alternatives. *Critical Social Policy, 9*(4), 7–18.

Fisher, R., & Shragge, E. (2000). Challenging community organizing: Facing the 21st century. *Journal of Community Practice, 8*(3), 1–19.

Frost, P. J. (2003). *Toxic emotions at work: How compassionate managers handle pain and conflict.* Cambridge, MA: Harvard Business Press.

Frost, P. J., Dutton, J., Worline, M., & Wilson, A. (2000). Narratives of compassion in organizations. In S. Fineman (Ed.), *Emotions in organizations* (pp. 25–45). London, UK: Sage.

Fullan, M. (2007). *The new meaning of educational change* (4th ed.). New York, NY: Teachers College Press.

Fuqua, D. R., & Newman, J. L. (2002). Creating caring organizations. *Consulting Psychology Journal: Practice and Research, 54*(2), 131–140.

Furco, A., & Root, S. (2010). Research demonstrates the value of service learning. *Phi Delta Kappan, 91*(5), 16–20.

Gadow, S. A. (1985). Nurse and patient: The caring relationship. In A. H. Bishop & J. R. Scudder Jr. (Eds.), *Caring, curing, coping: Nurse, doctor, patient relationships* (pp. 31–43). Tuscaloosa, AL: University of Alabama Press.

Garet, M. S., Porter, A. C., Desimone, L., Birman, B. F., & Yoon, K. S. (2001). What makes professional development effective? Results from a national sample of teachers. *American Educational Research Journal, 38*(4), 915–945.

Gay, G. (2010). *Culturally responsive teaching: Theory, research, and practice* (2nd ed.). New York, NY: Teachers College Press.

George, J. M. (2000). Emotions and leadership: The role of emotional intelligence. *Human Relations*, *53*(8), 1027–1055.

Gerkin, C. V. (1997). *An introduction to pastoral care*. Nashville, TN: Abingdon.

Glidewell, J. C. (1970). *Choice points: Essays on the emotional problems of living with people*. Cambridge, MA: MIT Press.

Goess, D. E., & Smith, P. A. (2018). Crossing boundaries: Organizational citizenship behavior and protecting students from bullying. *Elementary School Journal*, *119*(1), 52–72.

Goleman, D., Boyatzis, R., & McKee, A. (2013). *Primal leadership: Unleashing the power of emotional intelligence*. Boston, MA: Harvard Business Review Press.

Gomez, B. J., & Eng, P. M. (2007). Promoting positive youth development in schools. *Theory Into Practice*, *46*(2), 97–104.

Gordon, M. (2018). Empathy as strategy for reconnecting to our common humanity. In N. Way, A. Ali, C. Gilligan, & P. Noguera (Eds.), *The crisis of connection: Roots, consequences, and solutions* (pp. 250–273). New York: New York University Press.

Gordon, S. (1996). Feminism and caring. In S. Gordon, P. Benner, & N. Noddings (Eds.), *Caregiving: Readings in knowledge, practice, ethics, and politics* (pp. 256–277). Philadelphia: University of Pennsylvania Press.

Gossling, T., & van Liedekerke, L. (2014). The caring organization. *Journal of Business Ethics*, *120*(4), 437–440.

Green, M. G. (2014). *Caring leadership in turbulent times: Tackling neoliberal education reform*. Charlotte, NC: Information Age Publishing.

Greenleaf, R. K. (2002). *Servant leadership: A journey into the nature of legitimate power and greatness*. Mahwah, NJ: Paulist.

Gronn, P. C. (1983). Talk as the work: The accomplishment of school administration. *Administrative Science Quarterly*, *28*(1), 1–21.

Hallinger, P., & Murphy, J. (1985). Assessing the instructional management behavior of principals. *Elementary School Journal*, *86*(2), 217–247.

Hamman, J. (2010). Self-care and community. In M. Floding (Ed.), *Welcome to theological field education* (pp. 101–113). Durham, NC: Alban Institute Press.

Hamman, J. (2014a). *Becoming a pastor: Forming self and soul for ministry* (Rev. ed.). Cleveland, OH: Pilgrim Press.

Hamman, J. J. (2014b). Playing. In B. J. Miler-McLemore (Ed.), *The Wiley Blackwell companion to practical theology* (pp. 42–50). Malden, MA: Wiley Blackwell.

Harms, P. D., & Credé, M. (2010). Emotional intelligence and transformational and transactional leadership: A meta-analysis. *Journal of Leadership & Organizational Studies*, *17*(1), 5–17.

Harper, S. R., & Associates. (2014). *Succeeding in the city: A report from the New York City Black and Latino male high school achievement study*. Philadelphia: University of Pennsylvania, Center for the Study of Race and Equity in Education.

Hawley, T. (2000). *Starting smart: How early experiences affect brain development* (With M. Gunner, 2nd ed.). Chicago, IL: Author.

Heller, T., & Van Til, J. (1983). Leadership and followership: Some summary propositions. *Journal of Applied Behavioral Science*, *18*(3), 405–414.

Hinduja, S., & Patchin, J. W. (2015). *Bullying beyond the schoolyard: Preventing and responding to cyberbullying* (2nd ed.). Thousand Oaks, CA: Corwin.

Hollander, E. P. (1992). The essential interdependence of leadership and followership. *Current Directions in Psychological Science*, *1*(2), 71–75.

Howard, T. C. (2001). Telling their side of the story: African-American students' perceptions of culturally relevant teaching. *Urban Review*, *33*(2), 131–149.

Hoy, W. K., & Miskel, C. G. (2012). *Educational administration: Theory, research, and practice* (9th ed.). New York, NY: McGraw-Hill.

Ishimaru, A. (2013). From heroes to organizers: Principals and education organizing in urban school reform. *Educational Administration Quarterly, 49*(1), 3–51.

Jeffrey, A. J., Auger, R. W., & Pepperell, J. L. (2013). "If we're ever in trouble they're always there": A qualitative study of teacher–student caring. *Elementary School Journal, 114*(1), 100–117.

Jennings, P. A., & Greenberg, M. T. (2009). The prosocial classroom: Teacher social and emotional competence in relation to student and classroom outcomes. *Review of Educational Research, 79*(1), 491–525.

Jinkins, M. (2014). Religious leadership. In B. J. Miller-McLemore (Ed.), *The Wiley Blackwell companion to practical theology* (pp. 308–317). Malden, MA: Wiley Blackwell.

Johnson, D. W., & Johnson, R. T. (1996). Conflict resolution and peer mediation programs in elementary and secondary schools: A review of the research. *Review of Educational Research, 66*(4), 459–506.

Jones, K. B. (2001). *Rest in the storm: Self-care strategies for clergy and other caregivers.* Valley Forge, PA: Judson Press.

Jones, S. M., Boffard, S. M., & Weissbourd, R. (2013). Educators' social and emotional skills vital to learning. *Phi Delta Kappan, 94*(8), 62–65.

Jones, S. M., Weissbourd, R., Boffard, S., Kahn, J., & Ross, T. (2014). *How to build empathy and strengthen your school community.* Cambridge, MA: Making Caring Common Project, Harvard Graduate School of Education.

Jordan, P. J., & Troth, A. (2011). Emotional intelligence and leader member exchange. *Leadership & Organization Development Journal, 32*(3), 260–280.

Kerr, R., Garvin, J., Heaton, N., & Boyle, E. (2006). Emotional intelligence and leadership effectiveness. *Leadership & Organization Development Journal, 27*(4), 265–279.

Khalifa, M. A. (2018). *Culturally responsive school leadership.* Cambridge, MA: Harvard Education Press.

Khalifa, M. A., Arnold, N. W., & Newcomb, W. (2015). Understand and advocate for communities first. *Phi Delta Kappan, 96*(7), 20–25.

Khalifa, M. A., Gooden, M. A., & Davis, J. E. (2016). Culturally responsive school leadership: A synthesis of the literature. *Review of Educational Research, 86*(4), 1272–1311.

Kinnick, K., Krugman, D. M., & Cameron, G. T. (1996). Compassion fatigue: Communication and burnout toward social problems. *Journalism and Mass Communication Quarterly, 73*(3), 687–707.

Knight, J. (2009). *Coaching: Approaches and perspectives.* Thousand Oaks, CA: Corwin.

Koppel, M. S. (2008). *Open-hearted ministry: Play as key to pastoral leadership.* Minneapolis, MN: Fortress.

Kotok, S., Ikoma, S., & Bodovski, K. (2016). School climate and dropping out of school in an era of accountability. *American Journal of Education, 122*(4), 569–599.

Kroth, M., & Keeler, C. (2009). Caring as a managerial strategy. *Human Resource Development Review, 8*(4), 506–531.

Kruse, S. D., & Louis, K. S. (2009). *Building strong school cultures: A guide to leading change.* Thousand Oaks, CA: Corwin.

Kruse, S. D., Louis, K. S., & Bryk, A. (1994). Building professional community in schools. *Issues in Restructuring Schools*, Issue Report No. 6, pp. 3–6. Madison: Wisconsin Center for Education Research, University of Wisconsin–Madison.

Ladson-Billings, G. (1995). Toward a theory of culturally relevant pedagogy. *American Educational Research Journal, 32*, 465–491. doi:10.3102/00028312032003465

Ladson-Billings, G. (2009). *The dream-keepers: Successful teachers of African-American children* (2nd ed.). San Francisco, CA: Jossey-Bass.

Ladson-Billings, G. (2014). Culturally relevant pedagogy 2.0: a.k.a. the remix. *Harvard Educational Review, 84*, 74–84.

Lancer, N., Clutterbuck, D., & Megginson, D. (2016). *Techniques for coaching and mentoring* (2nd ed.). New York, NY: Routledge.

Lee, V., & Smith, J. B. (1999). Social support and achievement for young adolescents in Chicago: The role of school academic press. *American Educational Research Journal, 36*(4), 907–945.

Levinas, E. (1969). *Totality and infinity: An essay on exteriority*. Pittsburgh, PA: Duquesne University Press.

Liedtka, J. M. (1996). Feminist morality and competitive reality: A role for an ethic of care? *Business Ethics Quarterly, 6*(2), 179–200.

Lilius, J. M., Worline, M. C., Maitlis, S., Kanov, J., Dutton, J. E., & Frost, P. (2008). The contours and consequences of compassion at work. *Journal of Organizational Behavior, 29*(2), 193–218.

Lindsay, P. (1998). Conflict resolution and peer mediation in public schools: What works? *Mediation Quarterly, 16*(1), 85–99.

Lopes, P. N., Salovey, P., Côté, S., & Beers, M. (2005). Emotion regulation abilities and the quality of social relationships. *Emotion, 5*(1), 113–118.

Lortie, D. C. (2009). *School principal: Managing in public*. Chicago, IL: University of Chicago Press.

Louis, K. S., Hord, S., & Von Frank, V. (2016). *Reach the highest standard in professional learning: Leadership*. Thousand Oaks, CA: Corwin.

Louis, K. S., & Kruse, S. D. (1995). *Professionalism and community: Perspectives on reforming urban schools*. Thousand Oaks, CA: Corwin.

Louis, K. S., Murphy, J., & Smylie, M. A. (2016). Exploring caring leadership in schools: Implications for teachers and students. *Educational Administration Quarterly, 52*(2), 310–348.

Louis, K. S., Toole, J., & Hargreaves, A. (1999). Rethinking school improvement. In J. Murphy & K. S. Louis (Eds.), *Handbook of research on educational administration* (2nd ed., pp. 251–276). San Francisco, CA: Jossey-Bass.

Luthans, F., & Youssef, C. M. (2007). Emerging positive organizational behavior. *Journal of Management, 33*(3), 321–349.

Luttrell, W. (2013). Children's counter-narratives of care: Towards educational justice. *Children and Society, 27*(4), 295–308.

Mansbridge, J. (1983). *Beyond adversarial democracy*. Chicago, IL: University of Chicago Press.

Marshall, K. (2017). The big picture: How many people influence a student's life? *Phi Delta Kappan, 99*(2), 42–45.

May, D. R., Chan, A. Y., Hodges, T., & Avolio, B. J. (2003). Developing the moral component of authentic leadership. *Organizational Dynamics, 32*(3), 247–260.

Mayer, D., Aquino, K., Greenbaum, R. L., & Kuenzl, M. (2012). Who displays ethical leadership, and why does it matter? An examination of antecedents and consequences of ethical leadership. *Academy of Management Journal, 55*(1), 151–171.

Mayeroff, M. (1971). *On caring*. New York, NY: Harper Perennial.

McCauley, C. D. (2008). *Leader development: A review of research*. Greensboro, NC: Center for Creative Leadership.

McClure, B. (2014). Pastoral care. In B. J. Miller-McLemore (Ed.), *The Wiley Blackwell companion to practical theology* (pp. 269–278). New York, NY: Wiley Blackwell.

McCollough, T. E. (1991). *The moral imagination and public life: Raising the ethical question*. Chatham, NJ: Chatham House Publishers.

McGrath, K. F., & Van Bergen, P. (2015). Who, when, why and to what end? Students at risk of negative student–teacher relationships and their outcomes. *Educational Research Review, 14*(1), 1–17.

McMillan, D. W. (1996). Sense of community. *Journal of Community Psychology, 24*(4), 315–325.

McMillan, D. W., & Chavis, D. M. (1986). Sense of community: A definition and theory. *Journal of Community Psychology, 14*(1), 6–23.

Mediratta, K., Shah, S., & McAlister, S. (2009). *Community organizing for stronger schools: Strategies and successes*. Cambridge, MA: Harvard Education Press.

Merrell, K. W., Gueldner, B. A., Ross, S. W., & Isava, D. M. (2008). How effective are school bullying intervention programs? A meta-analysis of intervention research. *School Psychology Quarterly, 23*(1), 26–42.

Morningside Center for Teaching and Social Responsibility. (n.d.). The 4Rs program. New York, NY: Author. Retrieved from https://www.morningsidecenter.org/4rs-program

Morris, J. (1993). *Community care or independent living?* York, UK: Joseph Rowntree.

Murphy, J. (2016a). Teacher as unit leader: Defining and examining the effects of care and support on children: A review of the research. *Journal of Human Resource and Sustainability Studies, 4*, 243–279.

Murphy, J. F. (2016b). *Understanding schooling through the eyes of students*. Thousand Oaks, CA: Corwin.

Murphy, J. (2017). *Professional standards for educational leaders: The empirical, moral, and experiential foundations*. Thousand Oaks, CA: Corwin.

Murphy, J. F., & Louis, K. S. (2018). *Positive school leadership: Building capacity and strengthening relationships*. New York, NY: Teachers College Press.

Murphy, J., & Torre, D. (2014). *Creating productive cultures in schools for students, teachers, and parents*. Thousand Oaks, CA: Corwin.

Nathanson, L., Rivers, S. E., Flynn, L. M., & Brackett, M. A. (2016). Creating emotionally intelligent schools with RULER. *Emotion Review, 8*(4), 305–310.

National Policy Board for Educational Administration. (2015). *Professional Standards for Educational Leaders 2015*. Reston, VA: Author. Retrieved from http://npbea.org/wp-content/uploads/2017/06/Professional-Standards-for-Educational-Leaders_2015.pdf

National Scientific Council on the Developing Child. (2014). *Excessive stress disrupts the architecture of the developing brain* (Working Paper No. 3, Updated Edition). Cambridge, MA: Author. (Original work published 2005)

Newman, L., Sivaratnam, C., & Komiti, A. (2015). Attachment and early brain development—neuroprotective interventions in infant–caregiver therapy. *Translational Developmental Psychiatry, 3*(1), 28647. doi:10.3402/tdp.v3.28647

Noaks, J., & Noaks, L. (2009). School-based peer mediation as a strategy for social inclusion. *Pastoral Care in Education, 27*(1), 53–61.

Noddings, N. (1996). The cared-for. In S. Gordon, P. Benner, & N. Noddings (Eds.), *Caregiving: Readings in knowledge, practice, ethics, and politics* (pp. 21–39). Philadelphia: University of Pennsylvania.

Noddings, N. (2005). *The challenge to care in schools: An alternative approach to education* (2nd ed.). New York, NY: Teachers College Press.

Noddings, N. (2013). *Caring: A relationship approach to ethics and moral education* (2nd ed.). Berkeley: University of California Press.

Ogunfowora, B. (2014). It's all a matter of consensus: Leader role modeling strength as a moderator of the links between ethical leadership and employee outcomes. *Human Relations, 67*(12), 1467–1490.

Osterman, K. F., & Kottkamp, R. B. (2004). *Reflective practice for educators: Improving schooling through professional development* (2nd ed.). Thousand Oaks, CA: Corwin.

Parris, D. L., & Peachy, J. W. (2013). A systematic literature review of servant leadership theory in organizational contexts. *Journal of Business Ethics, 113*(3), 377–393.

Payne, A. A., & Welsh, K. (2015). Restorative justice in schools: The influence of race on restorative discipline. *Youth & Society, 47*(4), 539–564.

Pearce, C. L. (2007). The future of leadership development: The importance of identity, multi-level approaches, self-leadership, physical fitness, shared leadership networking, creativity, emotions, spirituality and on-boarding processes. *Human Resource Management Review, 17*(4), 355–359.

Pekel, K., Roehlkepartain, E. C., Syvertsen, A. K., Scales, P. C., Sullivan, T. K., & Sethi, J. (2018). Finding the fluoride: Examining how and why developmental relationships are the active ingredient in interventions that work. *American Journal of Orthopsychiatry, 88*(5), 493–502.

Pellicer, L. O. (2008). *Caring enough to lead: How reflective practice leads to moral leadership* (3rd ed.). Thousand Oaks, CA: Corwin.

Perren, S., Corcoran, L., Cowie, H., Dehue, F., Garcia, D., McGucin, C., . . . Völlink, T. (2012). Tackling cyberbullying: Review of empirical evidence regarding successful responses by students, parents, and schools. *International Journal of Conflict and Violence, 6*(20), 283–293.

Perry, B. D. (2002). Childhood experience and the expression of genetic potential: What childhood neglect tells us about nature and nurture. *Brain and Mind, 3*(1), 79–100.

Peters, T., & Austin, N. (1985). *A passion for excellence: The leadership difference.* New York, NY: Random House.

Peterson, E. H. (1994). Teach us to care and not to care. In S. Phillips & P. Benner (Eds.), *The crisis of care: Affirming and restoring caring practices in the helping professions* (pp. 66–79). Washington, DC: Georgetown University Press.

Pew Research Center (2019). *Why Americans don't fully trust many who hold positions of power and responsibility.* Washington, DC: Author.

Phillips, S. (1994). Introduction. In S. Phillips & P. Benner (Eds.), *The crisis of care: Affirming and restoring caring practices in the helping professions* (pp. 1–16). Washington, DC: Georgetown University Press.

Polanin, J. R., Espelage, D. L., & Pigott, T. D. (2012). A meta-analysis of school-based bullying prevention programs' effects on bystander intervention behavior. *School Psychology Review, 41*(1), 47–65.

Poplin, M., & Weeres, J. (1992). *Voices from inside: A report on schooling from inside the classroom.* Claremont, CA: Claremont Graduate School of Education.

Powell, W., & Kusuma-Powell, O. (2010). *Becoming an emotionally intelligent teacher.* Thousand Oaks, CA: Corwin.

Putnam, R. (2000). *Bowling alone: The collapse and revival of American community.* New York, NY: Simon & Schuster.

Putnam, R. (2015). *Our kids: The American dream in crisis.* New York, NY: Simon & Schuster.

Putnam, R. D., & Feldstein, L. W. (2003). *Better together: Restoring the American community*. New York, NY: Simon & Schuster.

Rauner, D. M. (2000). *They still pick me up when I fall: The role of caring in youth development and community life*. New York, NY: Columbia University Press.

Reese, L., Jensen, B., & Ramirez, D. (2014). Emotionally supportive classroom contexts for young Latino children in rural California. *Elementary School Journal, 114*(4), 501–525.

Regan, H. B., & Brooks, G. H. (1995). *Out of women's experience: Creating relational leadership*. Thousand Oaks, CA: Corwin.

Reverby, S. (1987). *Ordered to care: The dilemma of American nursing, 1850–1945*. Cambridge, UK: Cambridge University Press.

Riehl, C. J. (2000). The principal's role in creating inclusive schools for diverse students: A review of normative, empirical, and critical literature on the practice of educational administration. *Review of Educational Research, 70*(1), 55–81.

Riggio, R., & Reichard, R. (2008). The emotion and social intelligence of effective leadership. *Journal of Managerial Psychology, 23*(2), 169–185.

Riley, J. B. (2017). *Communication in nursing* (8th ed.). St. Louis, MO: Elsevier.

Robinson, B. E. (1993). *Overdoing it: How to slow down and take care of yourself*. Deerfield Beach, FL: HCI.

Rooney, J. (2003). Principals who care: A personal reflection. *Educational Leadership, 60*(6), 76–79.

Roorda, D. L., Koomen, H. M. Y., Spilt, J. L., & Oort, F. J. (2011). The influence of affective teacher–student relationships on students' school engagement and achievement: A meta-analytic approach. *Review of Educational Research, 81*(4), 493–529.

Rosete, D., & Ciarrochi, J. (2005). Emotional intelligence and its relationship to workplace performance outcomes of leadership effectiveness. *Leadership & Organization Development Journal, 26*(5), 388–399.

Rubin, H. J., & Rubin, I. S. (2008). *Community organizing and development* (4th ed.). New York, NY: Pearson.

Rutledge, S. A., Cohen-Vogel, L., Osborne-Lampkin, L., & Roberts, R. L. (2015). Understanding effective high schools: Evidence for personalization for academic and social emotional learning. *American Educational Research Journal, 52*(6), 1060–1092.

Salovey, P., & Mayer, J. D. (1990). Emotional intelligence. *Imagination, Cognition, and Personality, 9*(3), 185–211.

Sanders, L. C. (Ed.). (2004). *The collected works of Langston Hughes: Volume 6 Gospel plays, operas, and later dramatic works*. Columbia: University of Missouri Press.

Sanders, M. G. (2001). The role of "community" in comprehensive school, family, and community partnership programs. *Elementary School Journal, 102*(1), 19–34.

Sanders, M. G. (2014). Principal leadership for school, family, and community partnerships: The role of a systems approach to reform implementation. *American Journal of Education, 120*(2), 233–255.

Sarason, S. (1974). *The psychological sense of community: Perspectives for community psychology*. San Francisco, CA: Jossey-Bass.

Sarason, S. (1985). *Caring and compassion in clinical practice*. San Francisco, CA: Jossey-Bass.

Savage, S., & Bailey, S. (2004). The impact of caring on caregivers' mental health: A review of the literature. *Australian Health Review, 27*(1), 111–117.

Schein, E. H. (2010). *Organizational culture and leadership* (4th ed.). San Francisco, CA: Jossey-Bass.

Schein, E. H. (2011). *Helping: How to offer, give, and receive help.* San Francisco, CA: Berrett-Koehler Publishers.

Schein, E. H. (2013). *Humble inquiry: The gentle art of asking instead of telling.* San Francisco, CA: Berrett-Koehler Publishers.

Schön, D. A. (1987). *Educating the reflective practitioner.* San Francisco, CA: Jossey-Bass.

Sergiovanni, T. J. (1992). *Moral leadership: Getting to the heart of school improvement.* San Francisco, CA: Jossey-Bass.

Sergiovanni, T. J. (1994a). *Building community in schools.* San Francisco, CA: Jossey-Bass.

Sergiovanni, T. J. (1994b). Organizations or communities? Changing the metaphor changes the theory. *Educational Administration Quarterly, 30*(2), 214–226.

Sergiovanni, T. J. (1996). *Leadership for the schoolhouse: How is it different? Why is it important?* San Francisco, CA: Jossey-Bass.

Sergiovanni, T. J. (2000). *The lifeworld of leadership: Creating culture, community, and personal meaning in our schools.* San Francisco, CA: Jossey-Bass.

Shapiro, J. P., & Stefkovich, J. A. (2010). *Ethical leadership and decision making in education: Applying theoretical perspectives to complex dilemmas* (3rd ed.). New York, NY: Routledge.

Shirley, D. (1997). *Community organizing for urban school reform.* Austin: University of Texas Press.

Shouse, R. (1996). Academic press and sense of community: Conflict, congruence, and implications for student achievement. *Social Psychology of Education, 1*(1), 47–68.

Showers, F. (2015). Building a professional identity: Boundary work and meaning making among West African immigrant nurses. In M. Duffy, A. Armenia, & C. L. Stacey (Eds.), *Caring on the clock: The complexities and contradictions of paid care work* (pp. 143–152). New Brunswick, NJ: Rutgers University Press.

Simha, A., & Cullen, J. B. (2012). Ethical climates and their effects on organizational outcomes: Implications from the past and prophecies for the future. *Academy of Management Perspectives, 26*(4), 20–34.

Singer, T., & Klimecki, O. M. (2014). Empathy and compassion. *Current Biology, 24*(18), R875–R878.

Slater, R. O., & Boyd, W. L. (1999). Schools as polities. In J. Murphy & K. S. Louis (Eds.), *Handbook of research on educational administration* (2nd ed., pp. 323–335). San Francisco, CA: Jossey-Bass.

Smith, M. L. (1991). Put to the test: The effects of external testing on teachers. *Educational Researcher, 20*(5), 8–11.

Smylie, M. A., Murphy, J., & Louis, K. S. (2016). Caring school leadership: A multi-disciplinary, cross-occupational model. *American Journal of Education, 123*(1), 1–35.

Speer, P., & Hughey, J. (1995). Community organizing: An ecological route to empowerment and power. *American Journal of Community Psychology, 23*(5), 729–748.

Spence, C. M. (2009). *Achieving, believing, and caring: Doing whatever it takes to create successful schools.* Markham, Ontario, Canada: Pembroke Publishers.

Spillane, J. P., & Hunt, B. R. (2010). Days of their lives: A mixed-methods, descriptive analysis of the men and women at work in the principal's office. *Journal of Curriculum Studies, 42*(3), 293–331.

Starratt, R. J. (2003). The challenging world of educational leadership. In *Centring educational administration: Cultivating meaning, community, responsibility* (pp. 3–26). London, UK: Lawrence Earlbaum Associates.

Stefkovich, J. A., & Begley, P. T. (2007). Ethical school leadership: Defining the best interests of students. *Educational Management Administration & Leadership, 35*(2), 205–224.

Stone, F. (2007). *Coaching, counseling, and mentoring: How to choose and use the right technique to boost employee performance* (2nd ed.). New York, NY: American Management Association.

Swain, J., & French, F. (1998). Normality and disabling care. In A. Brechin, J. Walmsley, J. Katz, & S. Peace (Eds.), *Care matters: Concepts, practice, and research in health and social care* (pp. 81–95). Thousand Oaks, CA: Sage.

Tarlow, B. (1996). Caring: A negotiated process that varies. In S. Gordon, P. Benner, & N. Noddings (Eds.), *Caregiving: Readings in knowledge, practice, ethics, and politics* (pp. 56–82). Philadelphia: University of Pennsylvania Press.

Tate, J. S., & Dunklee, D. R. (2005). *Strategic listening for school leaders*. Thousand Oaks, CA: Corwin.

Taylor, D. L., Cordeiro, P. A., & Chrispeels, J. H. (2009). Pedagogy. In M. D. Young, G. M. Crow, J. Murphy, & R. T. Ogawa (Eds.), *Handbook of research on the education of school leaders* (pp. 319–369). New York, NY: Routledge.

Teaching Tolerance. (2016). *Critical practices for anti-bias education*. Montgomery, AL: Southern Poverty Law Center, Teaching Tolerance. Retrieved from https://www.tolerance.org/sites/default/files/2017-06/PDA%20Critical%20Practices_0.pdf

Thompson, A. (1998). Not the color purple: Black feminist lessons for educational caring. *Harvard Education Review, 68*(4), 522–555.

Tjosvold, D. (1998). Cooperative and competitive goal approach to conflict: Accomplishments and challenges. *Applied Psychology, 47*(3), 285–342.

Tronto, J. C. (1993). *Moral boundaries: A political argument for an ethic of care*. New York, NY: Routledge.

Ttofi, M. M., & Farrington, D. P. (2011). Effectiveness of school-based programs to reduce bullying: A systematic and meta-analytic review. *Journal of Experimental Criminology, 7*(1), 27–56.

Turkel, M. C., & Ray, M. A. (2004). Creating a caring practice environment through self-renewal. *Nursing Administration Quarterly, 28*(4), 249–254.

van Dierendonck, D., & Patterson, K. (2015). Compassionate love as a cornerstone of servant leadership: An integration of previous theorizing and research. *Journal of Business Ethics, 128*(1), 119–131.

Vanier, J. (1998). *Being human*. New York, NY: Paulist.

Van Velsor, E., & McCauley, C. D. (2004). Our view of leadership development. In C. D. McCauley & E. Van Velsor (Eds.), *The Center for Creative Leadership handbook on leadership development* (pp. 1–22). San Francisco, CA: Jossey-Bass.

Walker, J. (2012). A "toolbox" of cyberbullying prevention initiatives and activities. In J. W. Patchin & S. Hinduja (Eds.), *Cyberbullying prevention and response: Expert perspectives* (pp. 128–148). New York, NY: Routledge.

Wallace, T. L., & Chhuon, V. (2014). Proximal processes in urban classrooms: Engagement and disaffection in urban youth of color. *American Educational Research Journal, 51*(5), 937–973.

Watson, J. (2008). *Nursing: The philosophy and science of caring* (Rev. ed.). Boulder: University of Colorado Press.

Way, N., Gilligan, C., Noguera, P., & Ali, A. (2018). Introduction. In N. Way, A. Ali, C. Gilligan, & P. Noguera (Eds.), *The crisis of connection: Roots, consequences, and solutions* (pp. 1–62). New York: New York University Press.

Way, N., & Nelson, J. D. (2018). The Listening Project. In N. Way, A. Ali, C. Gilligan, & P. Noguera (Eds.), *The crisis of connection: Roots, consequences, and solutions* (pp. 274–298). New York: New York University Press.

Wei, R. C., Darling-Hammond, L., Andree, A., Richardson, N., & Orphanos, S. (2009). *Professional learning in the learning profession: A status report on teacher development in the United States and abroad.* Dallas, TX: National Staff Development Council.

Weil, M. (2005). *Handbook of community practice.* Thousand Oaks, CA: Sage.

Weissbourd, R., & Jones, S. (2014a). *The children we mean to raise: The real messages adults are sending about values.* Cambridge, MA: Harvard University, Graduate School of Education, Making Caring Common Project.

Weissbourd, R., & Jones, S. M. (2014b). Circles of care. *Educational Leadership, 71*(5), 42–47.

Wellman, N. (2007). Teacher voices: The impact of high-stakes testing on teacher caring. *Teacher Education and Practice, 20*(2), 204–216.

Welsh, R. O., & Little, S. (2018). The school discipline dilemma: A comprehensive review of disparities and alternative approaches (and supplement). *Review of Educational Research, 88*(5), 752–794.

Wenger, E. (1998). *Communities of practice: Learning, meaning, and identity.* New York, NY: Cambridge University Press.

Wenger, E., McDermott, R., & Snyder, W. M. (2002). *Cultivating communities of practice: A guide to managing knowledge.* Boston, MA: Harvard Business School Press.

Wheatley, M. J. (n.d.). Writings. Retrieved from www.margaretwheatley.com/articles/whyIwrotethebook.html

Wheatley, M. (2002). *Turning to one another.* San Francisco, CA: Berrett-Kohler.

Wiesenfeld, E. (1996). The concept of "we": A community social psychology myth? *Journal of Community Psychology, 24*(4), 337–345.

Willetts, G., & Clarke, D. (2014). Constructing nurses' professional identity through social identity theory. *International Journal of Nursing Practice, 20*(2), 164–169.

Willimon, W. H. (2002). *Pastor: The theology and practice of ordained ministry.* Nashville, TN: Abingdon.

Yoon, K. S., Duncan, T., Lee, S. W.-Y., Scarloss, B., & Shapley, K. L. (2007, October). *Reviewing the evidence on how teacher professional development affects student achievement.* Washington, DC: U.S. Department of Education, Institute of Education Sciences, National Center for Education Evaluation and Regional Assistance, Regional Educational Laboratory Southwest.

Young, M. D., Crow, G. M., Murphy, J., & Ogawa, R. T. (Eds.). (2009). *Handbook of research on the education of school leaders.* New York, NY: Routledge.

Yukl, G. (2013). *Leadership in organizations* (8th ed.). Boston, MA: Pearson.

Index

Figures are indicated by f following the page number.

Fight-or-flight behavior, 12
Firewalks, 103
Fisher, Robert, 123
Formal practice theory, 124–125
Foster, W., 75, 80–81, 105, 106
4Rs Project, 95
Frost, Peter, 34

Gerkin, Charles, 114
Gilligan, Carol, 17
Givens, J., 15, 90
Glidewell, John, 70
Goleman, D., 23, 137–140
Gooden, M. A., 102, 110,
　　121–122
Gordon, S., 21
Governance, 28–29
Greenberg, M. T., 95
Gronn, P. C., 45
Guided experiential learning, 132
Guthrie, Donald, 147

Hallinger, P., 12
Hamman, J., 20, 149–150
Hard caring, 50
Hargreaves, A., 77
Harper, S. R., 52
Heartfelt care (authentic cariño), 103
Helping, practices of, 66–70
High-stakes testing, 15–16
Hinduja, S., 100
Hip-to-hip relationships, 49, 104
Hodges, T., 136–137
Holman, A., 15, 90
Howard, T. C., 89
Hoy, Wayne, 61–63
Hughes, Langston, 10
Hughey, J., 123–124
Humble inquiry, 59–60, 60–61f, 69
Humility, 59, 65–66
Hussey, Cynthia Steiger, 23

Ideal versus real selves, 138
Identities
　　cross-cutting, 105
　　personal, 20, 131–132, 144
　　professional, 20, 131–132,
　　　144, 148
Incentive systems, 106
Individuality, 75–76
Information quarantines, 138
Instrumental benefits, 25–26
Interests, discernment of, 64–65
Interpersonal communication
　　practices, 61–63, 62f
Ishimaru, Ann, 126

Jeffrey, A. J., 51–52
Jennings, P. A., 95
Jensen, B., 90–91
Jinkins, M., 114
Jones, Kirk, 147–148
Jones, Stephanie, 93, 94, 101

Keeler, C., 45–46, 48, 51
Keller, S. C., 84–85
Khalifa, Muhammad, 44, 102, 110,
　　121–122
Kinship groups, 105
Klimecki, Olga, 30–31
Knight, Jim, 85
Knowledge/skills, 21–22, 132
Kroth, M., 45–46, 48, 51
Kruse, S. D., 87–88, 88f, 103, 113

Ladson-Billings, G., 90
Lancer, N., 86
Landry, K. L., 97
L'Arche communities, 102–103, 105
Latinos, 15, 52, 90–91
Leadership
　　authentic leadership, 136–137
　　civic leadership, 113, 114–115
　　as cultivation, 76–77
　　ethical leadership, 83–84, 135–136
　　as hosts, 77–78
　　human relations in, 137
　　as interpersonal networks, 45
　　pedagogy of, 81
　　positive leadership, 134–135
　　social-emotional intelligence
　　　and, 22
　　transformational leadership, 23
　　See also Caring school leadership
Leading by example. See Modeling
Learning communities, 89–91
Learning Forward, 87
Levinas, Emmanuel, 10
Listening, strategic, 56–59, 57–58f
Listening skills and practices,
　　62–63, 62f
"Little things," 48
Logic model of caring, 25, 26
Looping, 105
Louis, K. S., 77, 87–88, 88f, 103,
　　113, 130
Luttrell, W., 52–53

Making Caring Common Project,
　　14, 94
Management by walking around
　　(MBWA), 53–54
Marshall, K., 26

May, D. R., 136–137
Mayeroff, Milton, 10
McAlister, Sara, 125–126
McCollough, Thomas, 70
McDermott, R., 107
McGrath, K. F., 13
McKee, A., 23, 137–140
McMillan, David, 74
Mediation by peers, 96–97
Medicine, self-care and, 146–147
Mediratta, Kavitha, 125–126
Meerabeau, Liz, 10
Megginson, D., 86
Mental rehearsals, 139
Miller, M. D., 97
Mindfulness, 95
Mindful presence, 54–55
Mindsets
    negative, 57
    positive, 19–20, 36, 42, 131
    productive, 78
Ministry, 39–41, 81, 114–115, 147–149
Miskel, Cecil, 61–63
Modeling, 12, 83–84, 84f, 116–117, 143
Model of caring school leadership,
    34–38, 35f, 52–53
Moral courage, 136–137
Moral reasoning, 136
Morals, 42
Moss proverbs, 149–150
Motivational orientation, 20
Murphy, J., 12, 15, 30, 50–51, 75, 110,
    113–114, 118–120, 130
Mutuality, 18, 145
MyTeachingPartner (MTP) Project, 95

Nasir, N. S., 15, 90
National Association of Elementary
    School Principals (NAESP), 47
National Association of Secondary
    School Principals (NASSP), 47
Needs, discernment of, 64–65
Negative mindsets, 57
Netiquette, 100
Newcomb, W., 110, 122
Noddings, Nel, 10, 20, 28, 48–49,
    55, 101
Noguera, Pedro, 17
Norms, 39–40, 102, 103
Noticing, 55
Nursing, self-care and, 146–147

Observing, 55
O'Connor, M. K., 123, 124–125
Ogunfowora, B., 84
Openness, 23, 57

Organizational citizenship behavior
    (OCB), 98–99
Organizational culture, 28–29, 101–103
Osborne-Lampkin, L., 83, 102, 103, 105

Parents and caregivers
    as arena of practice, 36–37
    education and support for, 117–118
    engagement of, 108–110
    fostering caring in, 116–120
    involvement and, 73–74
    networks of, 118
    overview, 112–113
    support groups, 118
    support service access for, 118–120
Pastoral care, 12, 39, 40–41, 114
Patchin, J. W., 100
PATH (Alternative Thinking Strategies)
    curriculum, 95
Payne, A. A., 96
PBIS (positive behavioral interventions
    and supports), 95–96
Pedagogy of leadership, 81
Peer mediation, 96–97
Peer support for principals, 139–140,
    142–143, 145
Pekel, Kent, 126, 127f
Pellicer, Leonard, 142–143
Pepperell, J. L., 51–52
Performance coaching, 85–86
Personal Management Interview (PMI)
    Program, 134–135
Peters, Tom, 53–54
Peterson, Eugene, 53
Pew Research Group, 130
Phillips, Susan, 16
Physical presence, 53–54
Playfulness, 20, 131
PMI (Personal Management Interview)
    Program, 134–135
Politics and power, 28–29, 106–108
Poplin, M., 14
Positive behavioral interventions and
    supports (PBIS), 95–96
Positive leadership, 134–135
Positive mindsets, 19–20, 36, 42, 131
Positive virtues, 19–20, 36, 42, 131
Power orientation, 136
Practices of helping, 66–70
Practice theory, 124–125
Presence, 53–55
Prevention of bullying, 99–100
Principled practices, 41–43
Problem solving, 106–107
Problem-solving orientation, 57
Professional communities, 87–88, 88f

CORWIN

A SAGE Publishing Company

Helping educators make the greatest impact

CORWIN HAS ONE MISSION: to enhance education through intentional professional learning.

We build long-term relationships with our authors, educators, clients, and associations who partner with us to develop and continuously improve the best evidence-based practices that establish and support lifelong learning.

Leadership That Makes an Impact

LYN SHARRATT
Explore 14 essential parameters to guide system and school leaders toward building powerful collaborative learning cultures.

MICHAEL FULLAN
How do you break the cycle of surface-level change to tackle complex challenges? *Nuance* is the answer.

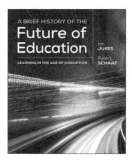

IAN JUKES & RYAN L. SCHAAF
The digital environment has radically changed how students need to learn. Get ready to be challenged to accommodate today's learners.

ERIC SHENINGER
Lead for efficacy in these disruptive times! Cultivating school culture focused on the achievement of students while anticipating change is imperative.

JOANNE MCEACHEN & MATTHEW KANE
Getting at the heart of what matters for students is key to deeper learning that connects with their lives.

LEE G. BOLMAN & TERRENCE E. DEAL
Sometimes all it takes to solve a problem is to reframe it by listening to wise advice from a trusted mentor.

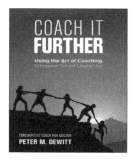

PETER M. DEWITT
This go-to guide is written for coaches, leaders looking to be coached, and leaders interested in coaching burgeoning leaders.

ANTHONY KIM & ALEXIS GONZALES-BLACK
Designed to foster flexibility and continuous innovation, this resource expands cutting-edge management and organizational techniques to empower schools with the agility and responsiveness vital to their new environment.

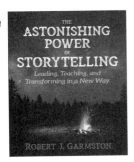

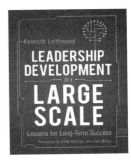
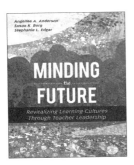

LDN19IJ1